Bryan

"The Bookshop"

15/1/1979

£1-35p

✓ = Read Once

✓ ((Jan 1979)).

VAGRANT ALCOHOLICS

VAGRANT ALCOHOLICS

TIM COOK

Routledge & Kegan Paul
London and Boston

First published in 1975
by Routledge & Kegan Paul Ltd
Broadway House, 68–74 Carter Lane
London EC4V 5EL and
9 Park Street
Boston, Mass. 02108, USA
Set in 10 on 12 point Plantin
and printed in Great Britain by
Ebenezer Baylis & Son Limited
The Trinity Press, Worcester and London
© Tim Cook 1975

ISBN 0 7100 8118 9

For Margaret, Miranda and Alastair

CONTENTS

TABLES

PREFACE

This book is an account of the birth and growth of the Alcoholics Recovery Project, a small voluntary organization concerned with the problems of vagrant alcoholics. The wider issues which impinge on these problems will be outlined, though in no way is the book a statement about the causes of vagrancy, still less of alcoholism. Rather it takes the problems experienced by vagrant alcoholics as accepted and relates one response to them. The terms used to describe the men involved, namely 'vagrant', 'homeless' or 'skid row', are in fact interchangeable.

My own work in this field has been almost entirely within the Alcoholics Recovery Project, so that inevitably my own development is linked closely with that of the Project. The work has provided opportunities and opened doors that initially seemed impenetrable. It is a constant amazement how much has been gained personally from the work; a constant humiliation on how relatively little can be put in.

The total effort of the Project owes a lot to many people and not all can be thanked by name. All those involved in the work of the Project throughout its history have made their own special contribution, and I hope that due appreciation has always been shown.

The committee members, all of whom have served loyally, some since 1966, have been a source of great support even when they disagreed with one another or with me. Tony Christopher has proved a model chairman throughout and kept us all going at all times. We are all indebted to Griffith Edwards, whose energy and late-night ideas so often provided the stimulus that was so essential.

The staff have always been asked to give more than I had any right to expect and somehow have maintained an enthusiasm and a loyalty that are still encouraging today. Frances Finney, Patricia Roberts, Joan Walley and Dougie Warke began the work in the shop fronts from which we have learnt so much. Sylvia Ghosh, Penny Newns and Sandra Vince have on the whole succeeded in keeping sanity in the office. Dennis Holland, David Whitehead and Peter Phillimore helped sustain the ethic of the houses. Benno Pollak and his colleagues have from the beginning given a fine medical service to the residents of the houses. Peter Archard showed us that research could be both relevant and exciting. The staff who have supported me in producing this book have every reason to be pleased that it was finally completed: Sally England, Brendan Flynn, Danny Levine and Greg Phillips can now have some of my time. Peter Foldes' work in Lewisham was greatly appreciated. We have all been glad of the psychiatric support and advice provided by Peter Rohde, Maurice Lipsedge and Paul Bowden.

But, above all, the men on the streets and in the houses should be thanked. They taught us more than they will ever know. Perhaps one man, Joe Kerr, who lived and died with us, should be particularly mentioned as an example of someone who pushed and probed at ideas far into the night. I know he would be questioning but none the less pleased to welcome the Project's new team of recovered alcoholics: Harry Bain, Ted Eagle, Tom Padden and Bob Westerman.

The funders, who have so generously supported us over the years, are to be most warmly thanked. The Carnegie Foundation effectively set up the houses. The City Parochial Foundation launched the larger Project. The Wates Foundation and Chase Charity have backed some of our experimental endeavours. The Home Office, the Department of Health and Social Security and the London Boroughs Association have provided official backing as our efforts became recognized. Our treasurer, Roy Witt, ensured that this money was honestly spent.

Finally, in the preparation of this book itself Celia Hensman and Guy Braithwaite, both loyal friends, deserve every praise for reading drafts and for commenting so wisely. Judy and Derek Beard typed heroically. My family, ever supportive, had to put up with even more than usual from me.

TC

1   INTRODUCTION

'Excuse me, guv, have you got the price of a cup of tea?' The bleary eyes, the drunken swaying, the dirty clothes and the slurred speech make it clear that the last thing this man wants is a cup of tea. He is refused and, shambling away cursing, stoops to pick up a cigarette end from the pavement.

The passer-by who was thus approached might be forgiven for wondering just what could be done for people like that. Why don't they get jobs? Doesn't anyone try to help them? Why not lock them up? We must ourselves ask just who 'they' are and what exactly is the problem they present. What has been done to save, control, reform, change or – as a policeman once said to me – resurrect them? 'They' are vagrant homeless alcoholics. This book is about them and the efforts of the Alcoholics Recovery Project (hereafter referred to as the Project) to understand and assist them. Vagrant alcoholics, as far as the Project is concerned, are male; there are of course female vagrants also, but we have dealt with so few of these that it would be misleading to discuss their particular difficulties. Their ground has been well reviewed by others (Garrett, 1973).

Probably the most certain single fact about vagrants in general and vagrant alcoholics in particular, is that they have evoked a depressingly pessimistic response from society throughout history. It is not appropriate here to undertake a full survey of vagrancy; such material is already well documented (Ribton-Turner, 1887; Vexliard, 1956, for instance). None the less, a few comments from a historical perspective may at least put the work of the Project into focus. Past accounts of ideas, attitudes, projects and legislation in this field do provide a wealth of clues and lessons for those still seeking to help the men and women officially described today as 'homeless single persons' (National Assistance Board, 1966). In reading official reports, individual societies' annual reports, autobiographies and the results of early research investigations, one is alternately encouraged by sensing some of the progress that has been made over the last two hundred years and discouraged by the similarity of this evidence to what is still being said and done in this field. There are of course moments when our delight at the increasing 'success rates' brought about presumably by the developing skills of casework and group work cause us to give thanks that we did not work in the nineteenth century! Even so, we should be cautious: in 1861 the London City Mission reported that it had 'reclaimed 1230 drunkards', a figure some of us would find hard to claim after twenty years in the field (Mayhew, 1967 edn, IV, p. xxii). But it may be said that in those days numbers were collected as an end in themselves with no meaning being attached to them. Is our behaviour today any different? Judge Harrison, giving evidence to a United States Senate Sub-Committee on Alcoholism (1969, p. 29) said, 'We have 65,000 signed names that have attended our court classes. We have them sign in so we have a record. We have 65,000 names on books now.'

Over the years a major part of society's response to the vagrant has been to classify him in numerable ways. Usually such classifications have been confidently neat and clear and no doubt they have provided rich evidence for today's advocates of 'labelling' theory. Classification is important since it indicates a response to the problem and, in particular, points the way to the kind of treatment or punishment that the author believes is needed. These varying classifications also reflect the mood of the time and the prevailing societal attitudes to the homeless man. One classic study made a basic division between the hobo, the tramp and the bum (Anderson, 1923). But in the 1950s the term 'uncontrollable alcoholism gained currency and to some extent replaced uncontrollable wanderlust and congenital laziness as the primary characteristic of the homeless man' (Bahr, 1973, p. 112). Much of the effort that past workers made to divide up their clientele was directed towards placing them in two broad categories, namely the 'deserving' and the 'undeserving' poor. Mary Higgs (1906) in her essay on vagrancy was preoccupied with who was or was not deserving, who was incapable of work and who in contrast would not work. She clearly felt unhappy about assisting those who had done little or nothing to deserve it. Turner (1971, p. 8) describes this attitude succinctly: 'It was implicit in the concept of the undeserving that they were feckless, irresponsible, idle people who preferred to beg and steal rather than to work for their living. They were, as someone described them, inoculated with indolence.' But as Owen (1965, p. 237) has pointed out, 'Was it not possible that the undeserving might be those most desperately in need of help?' We need to be surer and clearer about the descriptions we use. Is yesterday's loafer today's social inadequate? What will he be to-morrow? Have we advanced our understanding of him? To know you are an alcoholic for example, rather than a feckless drunkard, may well be helpful, but even in this instance scientific enquiry has not yet helped to remove the evaluative and moral tones. I would not wish to argue against the need for more specific diagnoses than existed previously. Yet the field of the homeless single person, because of the wide-ranging nature of its problems, tends to invite off-the-cuff divisions in an attempt to ease the difficulties of field workers. We should guard against this or we may too quickly find ourselves creating some vague form of priorities of deserving, even within a group that has been seen traditionally as itself the quintessence of the undeserving poor.

The remedies that past commentators went on to put forward further indicated the repressive quality of their thinking, with its lack of imagination and its insistence on legal, institutional and organizational solutions. In a sense, the seemingly primitive remedies put forward to deal with the various associated problems reflected a class division between reformers or legislators and vagrants. 'The vagrancy laws seemed to supersede the entire charter of an Englishman's liberties. They were used to put into prison any man or woman of the working class who seemed to the magistrate an inconvenient or disturbing character' (Hammond, 1949, p. 80).

Given such a deep-rooted and complex socio-economic problem, it is hardly surprising to find a host of well-meaning, energetic, enterprising, voluntary bodies manned by the wealthy and the middle class trying their hand at putting it all to rights. The state then, as now, viewed these voluntary bodies as playing a pioneering role experimenting in new ways to assist the homeless, the vagrants and the loafers. Valuable as this voluntary role may be, it can be one over-relied on by the state, leading the unknowing public into thinking more is being done than it really is, and serving in the end merely to paper over the deficiencies in the state service. Further, the adulation – 'what magnificent work you are doing' – leads the voluntary societies all too readily into an unreal view of how effective their contribution truly is.

For a length of time our philanthropic schemes have partaken too much of the character of mere surface appearances, directed to the amelioration of existing evils, but in no way likely to effect their expiration.We have been dealing with effects rather than first causes ... the latter have generally escaped detection (Tuckniss in Mayhew, 1967 edn, IV, p. xvii).

Voluntary bodies remain thick on the ground, and much has always been made of the desirability for such bodies to work more closely together. A vain desire this has often seemed to be. It was fine for the Royal Commission on the Poor Laws (1909, p. 518) to claim that 'the cure for overlapping is co-operation,' but such exhortations totally failed to allow for historical or religious differences, ideological conflict, the needs of the helpers themselves or, above all, the absence of hard evidence to show that co-operation would produce better results.

One of the few areas in which there has been little or no division of opinion for the past hundred years or more is the futility of sending men and women to prison for petty offences, including drunkenness, interrelated with the condition of vagrancy. 'No prison system yet devised has effected any improvement in the drunkard committed for the usual 7 days or 14 days imprisonment' (Gibbons, 1905, p. 8). The *Lancet* (1, p. 203) was sufficiently perspicacious to include a note in 1896:

At Salford Police Court, a woman made her 154th appearance for drunk and disorderly. There was, however, nothing dejected or miserable in her bearing, for she stepped jauntily into the dock with a polite curtsy, and wished Mr Markinson a 'happy New Year, your worship'. She was sent to jail for one month – an utterly useless proceeding.

In 1971 the Report of a Home Office working party on 'Habitual Drunken Offenders' was published (hereafter referred to as the report), which in essence stated once more that prisons were overcrowded and in any case totally inappropriate for drunks (Home Office, 1971). Clauses are contained in the Criminal Justice Acts of 1967 and 1972 designed to help implement some of the recommendations of this report but no concrete action has yet been taken. We surely should force ourselves to ask how views consistently expressed for so many years have not been acted upon to any measurable degree. Answers are less easy to provide. Part of the explanation for inactivity may lie in the ever-changing diagnosis of the problem, coupled with the failure of anyone today to accept full responsibility for resolving it. In 1972 drunkenness arrests figures for England and Wales totalled over 90,000, the highest for fifty years (Home Office, 1973). Were Mr. Markinson to return he would be in horrifyingly familiar territory, as would the lady with the curtsy before him.

Studies have clearly shown that among the vagrant population in London one-third to one-half of the men have a serious drinking problem (Edwards, 1968), and there is little reason to doubt that drink has always been a prominent feature in the life of the 'down-and-out'. Missions have always tended to 'home in' on the destitute drunkard and were a prominent feature of nineteenth-century provision. In some areas virtually no progress has been made and one city's alcoholism facilities have been reviewed and described as 'pre-stone age in quantity and conception' (Crousaz, 1972). Other cities may well feel they can improve on that description, though few could be satisfied that they have sufficient facilities either in quality or quantity adequately to help. In 1969 an alcoholic died on the steps of a Southwark church with aid seemingly nowhere to hand. Perhaps the most obvious advance which has been made as far as the drinking vagrant is concerned, is our new-found ability to draw some distinction between the drunkard and the person addicted to alcohol – that is the alcoholic. Though Trotter (1804, p. 178) so long ago was able to discern that repeated drunkenness was not simply a question of wantonness, but rather that 'the habit of drunkenness is a disease of the mind', he was still 'unable to describe the condition in terms which were free from moral overtones' (Harrison, 1971, p. 22). The concept of alcoholism as a disease took a long time to become established. Initially, however, alcoholism was seen as afflicting the middle and upper classes, while the vagrant was still termed a drunkard. That polarity has mercifully now been abandoned, albeit some men still describe themselves as 'drunkards' rather than alcoholics, which they not infrequently define as something that has nothing to do with their own particular condition. The distinction between 'alcoholic' and 'drunkard' was in its time important, since use of the first term distinguished the medical from the moral approach, and its adoption has led towards what is hopefully a better understanding of the problem.

However, the variety of differing analyses of the homeless alcoholic's situation led inevitably to a variety of proposals for solution of his problems. Religion, moral suasion, physical punishment, detention in reformatories, enforced work on the land, have been some of the less imaginative proposals of the past which have not entirely lost their appeal today – at least not in some quarters. More recently, suggestions intended to guide the chronic homeless drunk towards sobriety have centred on a range of provision aimed to meet the needs expressed at various moments in the alcoholic's career. Hospitals, job re-training centres, group therapy, vocational counselling, day centres, boarding houses, halfway houses are among the many proposals put forward by different proponents. Evidence for belief in their efficacy despite studies carried out is not always strong. There is clearly a need there-fore to keep trying with any number of systems of assistance if improve-ments are to be made on the rather markedly unsuccessful efforts of the past. Possibly the most popular of modern methods designed to assist the homeless alcoholic is the use of the halfway house or hostel. Rubington (1958) saw this as a new approach for the skid row alcoholic in America, offering a protective environment in a middle ground between therapeutic or punitive agencies and organized, respectable society. It is to an account of the establishment of such a house, as the first stage in the development of the Project, that I shall shortly turn.

In essence, then, neither the homeless alcoholic nor concern about him are new phenomena. The twin problems of homelessness and alcoholism do present a considerable challenge to anyone seeking to involve himself in recovery. Sadly, this is a challenge that seems rarely to have been taken up at all and, where it has, all too often this has been from an inappropriate perspective. Dealing with homelessness by provision of huge institutional lodging houses only serves to produce more problems and can be itself destructive to the men housed in them (Turner, 1960). Imprisonment for drunkenness, while clearing the street for a week or two, does little other than push the men concerned into the category of offenders. There have been three major government reports that have looked into the problem of public drunkenness and drunkenness offenders – in 1834, 1872 and 1971 – but to no present effect.

We believe that the Project has begun to edge some way towards an appropriate response to the problems posed by the vagrant alcoholic. Fundamentally we have sought to break through the mistrust that bedevils the whole field; mistrust by one agency of another, by agencies of alcoholics, by alcoholics of agencies, by men of other men. Such mistrust is the easiest response to make, but clearly one which carries with it distinctly unhelpful consequences. When mistrust is allied to the self-destructiveness that alcoholics so frequently demonstrate, we are indeed in for a hard time. The objective of the Project has been to try to discern more clearly the real nature of the problems faced by the vagrant alcoholic and to bear in mind the historical legacies we all share with him. It has been to try to penetrate the air of mistrust that at times envelops us all. The Project has sought to break down the stereotyped picture of the down-and-out alcoholic. Above all, we have come to see that controlling and reforming the man run perilously close together. To reduce such control enables the potential of the so-called 'hopeless alcoholic' to emerge. In some instances the analogy of a butterfly emerging from a chrysalis is not over-fanciful. In developing the work of the Project it has become increasingly obvious that we need to question ourselves as much as the alcoholics. When one sees the failure of government to act in any significant way on the recommendations of various reports of this or the last century, the ease with which second-hand stereotypes are used to put out of mind a whole group of people, then one is forced to ask once more – just what is the problem? 'The vagrant lacks motivation.' 'Society lacks interest.' These assertions are hardly the best start for any progress. Against the background that these two statements encapsulate, the Project's endeavours may however appear fairly encouraging.

2 THE BEGINNING*

How, where and why do new ideas evolve into schemes, emerge and see the light of day? This would seem to be a legitimate question for research; but it is alas a question which is rarely investigated. We tend too often to take it for granted that a hostel has been opened or a new project begun and then concentrate all our attention on how this hostel then functions rather than how it came into being in the first place. Yet if we truly believe in valuable experiments being replicated, then we surely must seek out the origins of the idea and the mounting of the plan of action which puts the particular idea into operation. It is with this in view that we wish to devote this chapter to a look at how Rathcoole House, one hostel for homeless alcoholics, came to be established in London in 1966; and how the growth of that hostel led on to the larger Project.

South London has for many years contained areas which are frequented by the down-and-outs. The borough of Southwark still has within it the largest Reception Centre in the country which houses a maximum of 900 men; as well as the only women's Reception Centre which has a capacity of eighty beds. A local newspaper (*Mercury*, 1 October 1965) described Southwark as 'one of the worst hit boroughs by "down-and-out" crude spirit drinkers'. During the 1960s, growing and increasingly organized concern was being expressed by a number of people engaged in various professions about the plight of the skid row alcoholic in Southwark. This concern was however being demonstrated in the wider context of concern for the alcoholic problem as a whole. For example, in 1962 the Camberwell Council on Alcoholism, the first of its kind in the country, had been set up, largely inspired by a recovered alcoholic, as an effort to educate the local community in South London about the problems associated with alcoholism. There was thus a coincidental emergence of a number of professionals who were becoming increasingly involved in the alcoholism problem. It then became apparent that one very local and visible area of need, namely that of the skid row alcoholic, was not receiving sufficient appropriate attention. It was not easy to have these alcoholics admitted to hospitals or to one of the handful of hostels that then existed. Hospitals which were sympathetic to alcoholics mainly admitted the better prognosis alcoholic and had little wish to have beds

* All quotations in this chapter, for which sources are not given, are taken from the minutes and reports of the Camberwell Council on Alcoholism, the Alcohol Impact Project and the Rathcoole Committee.

occupied by skid row alcoholics with nowhere to go on discharge. Social workers, albeit a few, were angered at this situation and challenged the local medical services to do something about it. Then in 1964 a local research unit was begun: the Alcohol Impact Project, which undertook an investigation into the clients of one skid row soup kitchen, and began work in 1965 with the Camberwell Council on Alcoholism in forming an 'Action on Skid Row' working party which was committed to bringing about some change in the existing situation. It is the work of this particular group that, in retrospect, seems to have been the key factor in changing what could so easily have become a series of well-meaning utterances of concern into an action-orientated programme that established a tangible service for at least some of the local skid row alcoholics.

Almost a year prior to the setting-up of that working group, a public meeting convened by the local borough council had been held in Southwark Town Hall (27 February 1964) 'to discuss the problem of crude spirit drinkers'. This meeting had principally resolved that 'despite all the good work being undertaken by various voluntary organizations the problem can only be dealt with by new legislation, including provisions for the compulsory treatment of addicts and the payment of grants for the establishment of hostels'. This and other resolutions were passed on to the sub-committee, of what was then the London County Council, on crude spirit drinking and on 16 June 1964 this sub-committee received a report on the problem in question. Among the fifteen recommendations of this report was one that a special hostel should be opened.

Very little appears to have resulted in practice as a consequence of either the Southwark Town Hall meeting or the London County Council report. Much more resulted from the voluntary efforts of the local meetings of the 'Action on Skid Row' group. Effort was now being directed at the least sympathetic group of the public drunkard, namely the derelict skid row drinker. The first major public meeting which led to the setting-up of the voluntary working party was held in Camberwell Town Hall (Camberwell then being a separate borough) on 4 February 1965. Over eighty representatives of slightly fewer organizations attended. The summing up stated clearly that the time for action had arrived and that we were looking

into the face of a scandal. It is a scandal that a man should spend over twenty years of his life in prison for stealing a few shillings to get the alcohol to which he is addicted. It is a scandal also that the means of addiction – surgical spirit – should be readily available at the cost of less than two shillings per bottle. It is a scandal that the alcoholic is made to circulate from one agency to another with no continuity of care.

What was needed was an experiment commensurate with the size of the problem, whereas what had been done to date had been no more than 'a puff in the face of a hurricane'. The meeting resolved to set up 'a small working party with representation from prison, probation, hospital and other services to draw up an immediate practical plan of action'.

The two meetings to which I have so far referred reflect two responses to the problem of the crude spirit drinker – local government response and voluntary agency response. While a few individuals were present at both meetings the two responses never seemed truly to merge, nor did one seem a response to the other. They read now as being remarkably independent of each other. That separation may well have had unfortunate consequences in terms of the role of other voluntary bodies coming into the area at a later stage.

In the next twelve months papers were prepared by the Camberwell Council on Alcoholism in a concerted attempt to document fully the problem of the chronic drunkenness offender. They were wide-ranging and imaginative, and indicate above all a thorough preparation of the ground before action was finally taken. These papers were sent to an official Committee examining the residential provision for homeless discharged offenders (Home Office, 1966). The result was that, when later the Carnegie Trust granted that committee funds for a Special After-Care Trust to pilot new projects, the hostel proposal for the skid row alcoholic was one of the four projects chosen (Rolph, 1971). The hostel, Rathcoole House, opened on 1 May 1966, less than eighteen months after the public meeting held by the Camberwell Council on Alcoholism.

We need to ask two major questions at this stage. How was it this voluntary *ad hoc* group succeeded where others had not? Was the achievement as complete as it might have been?

A number of factors seem to have influenced the successful course of events. Above all there was a high degree of commitment by the individuals involved. However, many ventures have been supported by enthusiastic individuals but none the less failed. Here the enthusiasm was planted on to a broad base of participation and interest so that no one person was felt to be imposing his idea or concern on an uninterested, or even hostile, community. Not only was there concern but also facts were available from the survey carried out by the Alcohol Impact Project in an East End soup kitchen (Edwards, 1966a). The authors' proffered diagnosis of the skid row alcoholic was threefold – 'a life-

long personality disorder, an acquired chemical disease, and a patho-
logical social adjustment'. The results of the investigation suggested
that 'many of the men on skid row would accept a place in a supportive
hostel without compulsion'. This survey is mentioned, as throughout
the book it is hoped to show how research and action have constantly
been linked; their close relationship is central to this whole account.
The availability of research findings meant that the subsequent action
had built into it both knowledge and feeling; too often in past endeavours feelings had run ahead of the knowledge. Another important
reason for the success of the voluntary group was that each member
had a real sense of being engaged on something new rather than merely
refining an old idea.

It should also be pointed out that the Camberwell Council on
Alcoholism had had previous experience in 1964 in establishing a hostel
for more socially stable alcoholics (Edwards, 1966b). But the founders
were still concerned about other groups of alcoholics: 'there is also the
problem of what is to be done to help alcoholics of the type who are not
suitable for this particular house'. This initial experience had led them
to see more clearly the different needs of different types of alcoholics,
one of which was the vagrant alcoholic. Above all, the group had a clear
sense of its overall plan, and had agreed upon the tactics to try to put
this into effect. It did not proceed therefore on an *ad hoc* basis but
within an agreed framework of action. The group's endeavour was
greatly strengthened by the 1965 political climate's being favourable to
the kind of scheme it eventually proposed. The Home Office, for
example, was anxious to relieve prisons of people who did not really
warrant the full rigours of imprisonment, and drunkenness offenders
definitely came into that category. Specialized hostels for alcoholics
were recommended by an official working party (Home Office 1966,
pp. 9–10, 28–30). Finally, local authorities in South London were
anxious and certainly not able to deny the existence of the problem, and
anxiety can often be turned to good effect if some kind of remedy for the
problem can be suggested. All these factors led to the Camberwell
Council on Alcoholism's working party obtaining very quick results:
the building for a hostel began to materialize by the end of 1965 with
the hostel committee formed by February 1966 and the first warden
appointed by March. Nothing succeeds like success.

Not being involved in all this endeavour and yet as a colleague subsequently of all those who were, I am in an advantageous position and
may be forgiven for venturing, in retrospect, certain criticisms. These
criticisms arise almost entirely because of the very high standards the
working group set itself. The group wanted to have 'a really significant

impact on the skid row problem' – the emphasis was on 'action which would take us beyond the pilot stage of a small scale voluntary activity'. The project was to provide 'adequate treatment for the hundreds of men in need'. A hostel of at least fifty beds was needed (a target finally modified to twenty). Yet when the hostel opened it was only for ten men; further it was a voluntary pilot experiment and it was in reality a 'puff in the face of a hurricane'. This transformation did not happen by conscious choice, in that the group was offered two hostels of fifty or ten beds, and chose the smaller. Rather the constraints of finance, the availability of houses, the obtaining of planning permission, the suitability of the neighbourhood and the need to start some scheme quickly – all combined to produce the end result of a much smaller and more limited venture than had originally been envisaged. The eventual size of the hostel was not chosen because it was an ideal figure but because it was the best house available in the time that was available. Subsequent debate has tended to say that ten to fifteen beds is the ideal number for an alcoholic hostel (Home Office, 1971, p. 96) though this may well be a rationalization in that the size of premises to be had is invariably ten or twelve beds. The fact remains however that the working group, though knowing that at least a fifty-bedded unit for vagrant alcoholics was necessary, was in the end compelled to start with ten if anything was to be started at all.

Looking back again, there appear to have been other elements that may have hindered the working of the group. For example, at no stage in the proceedings did anyone seem to wish to state who was in fact a 'crude spirit drinker' and what criteria were being used to define him. Local newspapers talked of 'methies', 'jake drinkers' and 'surgical spirit drinkers'; the London prisons reported on 'recurrent drunks'; research workers wrote about 'skid row alcoholics'. Yet all were agreed that a hostel for 'crude spirit drinkers' was needed. One document neatly illustrates the confusion: 'the task of this hostel would be strictly defined as that of helping the chronic drunkenness offender – in other words, the vagrant surgical spirit drinker.' Only now do we know just how varied is the drinking on skid row and how hard it is to define who is a crude spirit drinker – does the term mean a man who always drinks crude spirits even when money is available for whisky, a man who regularly drinks it or a man who once drank it? Linked to this issue was the fact that there still existed uncertainty as to how far habitual drunks were alcoholics. Subsequent research was to show they clearly were, to the extent that a man with six or more arrests for drunkenness 'had a 3 in 4 chance of being an alcohol addict' (Hensman, 1969). Yet prisons operated 'firm local distinctions between drunks and alcoholics, not according to need but according to conviction'. At other times hospital units were said only to be taking 'chronic alcoholics' and not by implication the habitual drunk. Yet another distinction was that between the sub-cultural derelict and the 'clinically recoverable alcoholic'. After some months the term 'vagrant alcoholic' gradually came to be accepted and by the time the hostel opened in May 1966 there seemed little dispute that, whatever the social manifestations, the down-and-out drunk was in the majority of cases an alcoholic too.

This natural confusion led on to even more uncertain debate as to how many skid row men there were who might need the help the proposed hostel would provide. One view was that there were 500 skid row alcoholics, another that there were 1,000 alcoholics in London prisons on any night but that only 100 of these were skid row men. Yet over a five-year period, 1961–5, the Royal London Prisoners' Aid Society had dealt with over 600 individual homeless alcoholics. Numbers, if anything, seem to have been rather under-estimated, not through any wish to underplay the problem, but rather because of a lack of clarity in definition. But as convictions for drunkenness are not centrally recorded and do not appear on a person's central criminal record there is always the problem of how, when and where to count habitual drunkenness offenders (Home Office, 1971, pp. 21–31). Subsequent work has tended to use a legal definition, namely that a habitual drunkenness offender is a person convicted of drunkenness three or more times in any one year. Such a definition is almost tautologous; worse, it stresses the offence rather than the condition. In so doing it does not include long-term prisoners who may have one or two drunkenness offences between longer sentences. Further, it does not take into account different police practices which can easily alter the rates of arrest for a group of homeless alcoholics in a given area.

Debate was also common at that time on whether the existing law, such as the Inebriates Act 1898 and the Mental Health Act 1959, could be used to compel offenders into some form of care and treatment. In the end no legal solution was felt to be realistic or practical. Preoccupation with this issue seems the plight of any group that looks at the problem of the habitual drunkard, but so far all the debate on the issue has proved singularly valueless.

The local working party quickly became alive to the thorniest problem of all, namely who was responsible for setting up any programme to assist the skid row alcoholic. It is a sad comment on official bodies that in the end a new voluntary charity, namely the Alcoholics Recovery Project, was formed to do the job. Yet another voluntary agency had appeared on the scene. As we shall show in chapter 9, there is still too much uncertainty about the various authorities' legitimate area of competence and responsibility and in 1965 the story was even worse. Some would say it has barely improved. One minute reads: 'A meeting should be convened to decide whether the responsibility lies with the Ministry of Health, Regional Hospital Boards, Greater London Council, Home Office or Prison Authorities'. Approaches were also to be made to the then Chancellor of the Duchy of Lancaster who was 'the man supposed to co-ordinate all the social service'. Governments have continued from time to time to make appointments of this co-ordinating nature but almost nothing has come from them. Nothing did on this occasion. It is therefore sad, but only to be expected, that following discussions, meetings and reports, a new body (i.e. the hostel committee) was created to take the action viewed as urgent and necessary by everyone. The belief of the group that 'the weapon of attack must measure up to the size of the problem' was not borne out in the cold light of day.

Finally it is of value to look closely at the group's recommendations for the hostel, which was aimed clearly to be a therapeutic alternative to repeated imprisonment. It was intended that the 'treatment' in the hostel would be 'the group pressures and group support brought to bear by the residents themselves'. To this 'milieu therapy' would be added 'more formal group therapy'. That the eventual hostel was initially some way from such proposals was due to several factors. The hostel had to be a small voluntary one, although a large statutory one had been urged, small groups having been declared to be 'too explosive' and 'better results' having been achieved in the USA with large groups (Myerson, 1956). Detailed knowledge of the skid row man in this country was still scanty and it was felt that, because the majority of skid row alcoholics drank in gangs, group pressure could be relatively easily applied. This failed to take into account that by no means all men drank in gangs or 'schools', as the men called them, and that even where they did, observations suggested that all the 'schools' agreed on was the terms of the drinking and little other group solidarity was shown (Rooney, 1961). Further, where any group cohesion did exist it was doubly hard to use when the men were sober as the loyalty was to the drinking group and no other. A gradual lessening of the therapeutic content of the hostel had to take place to take into account size, staffing and other constraints.

In essence then I have now looked at how a small voluntary working party of committed individuals fought through a scheme which tried to answer one of the problems of skid row. Some errors were made that led to a less than complete answer, but the errors only appear with a great degree of hindsight. At the time it was, and in a way still is, remarkable that from the public meeting to the first skid row man entering the hostel was a matter of only sixteen months.

The Prison Department had meanwhile in 1965 begun a scheme rather grandly titled 'The Springhill Experiment', which in essence took short-term drunkenness offenders from Pentonville Prison to the open prison at Springhill in Buckinghamshire (Kelly, 1966). At last drunks were not felt to need security conditions and their subsequent behaviour showed this to be correct. It was soon desperately apparent that, unless serious after-care could be provided then, the move to Springhill was a move to fresh air and green fields but little else, as on release men were returned to London by bus and deposited at the Elephant and Castle, one of London's major skid row areas. The desperate need for at least some new after-care provision was evident. Bartholomew (1968, p. 29) describes a similar scheme in Australia and criticizes the 'modest therapeutic effects of open air and sunshine'. It was with relief therefore that in January 1966 Rathcoole House was rented from the Greater London Council. It should be made clear that Rathcoole was not the first alcoholic hostel to open since the defunct inebriate reformatories of the turn of the century. St Luke's had been opened in 1960 and London House in 1965, both run by voluntary organizations.

The warden took up residence on 1 May 1966. As the reality of actually having a house for skid row alcoholics drew nearer, it should be noted that many of the concerns, wishes, hopes of the people demonstrated, in some instances at least, a revealing difference between the forecasts and the actual events. Concern had been expressed about neighbours and their children being upset by the possible dreadful goings on. 'Morning discipline' was another fear of the committee. Both proved to be totally unnecessary fears. This illustrates how the expectations of social work projects need to be challenged if any progress is to be made. The alternative is for gloomy prognosis to remain gloomy prognosis with no effort made to prove its aptness or otherwise. The history of the house has largely been one of the abandonment of almost all preconceptions. That is why it is relevant here to look at some of the features of the Rathcoole experiment as they developed over the years and how some of these features helped to give us the ideas and courage to develop the work into what now comprises the Alcoholics Recovery Project. The history of the hostel is an essential forerunner to the Project.

It is worth asking at this stage why a hostel was established as opposed to some other form of 'treatment'. Other methods of treatment were in fact not debated by the working party. The crucial element of homelessness led to the position that, unless a decent roof was provided, talk of recovery or sobriety held little or no meaning for the habitual drunken offender. Shandler (1972) was to write of a programme of rehabilitating public inebriates in Philadelphia:

It did not take too long or many follow-up reports to realize that the program's lack of emphasis on housing was in its own way creating a 'revolving door'. Placing a man in a specialized housing program was not a guarantee of successful rehabilitation and relocation. If the man was *not* in a good housing program it *was* a guarantee of failure.

However, people involved in the setting up of hostels are caught between two moods. The tension lies between realizing the innovations that can be brought about by halfway houses and at the same time the dangers that can come from being swept along in the excitement and not thinking clearly about the overall picture. 'Some criticism can be lodged, however, at those who have fostered their (hostels') unbridled growth for underestimating the extent of planning and professional resources needed for their successful operation and for overestimating their simplicity' (Apte, 1968, p. 112). It is to the credit of the Rathcoole working party that they did not fall into this trap. They were clear that what was required was a hostel in that there was not in existence a hostel specifically set up to meet the needs of the vagrant alcoholic. At the same time, the group did not overstate its case; it stressed that the men would be supported rather than cured; it built in an attempt to evaluate the work of the hostel; it set up a professional committee conversant with the general needs of the vagrant alcoholic. In these ways the group avoided the pitfalls that can come from blind adherence to a concept or an institution.

Rathcoole House and its operation

In looking generally at some important aspects of the life of the house the data on admissions are important. In Table 1 we give the statistical background to the admissions and departures in the house, 1966–73. It should be made clear that in the following account of the house we have looked at very broad issues and especially those relevant to the later work of the Project. Some detailed aspects of the work of the house have been looked at elsewhere (Cook, 1968; Pollak, 1970). Here I only wish to present a broader view, seeing the work of the house as a forerunner to other things rather than as an isolated event in itself.

The figures in Table 1 convey the sense of progress of the house. In the pages that follow it should become clearer as to how and why the

Table 1   Rathcoole, 1966–73

	1966-7 1st year	1967-8 2nd year	1968-9 3rd year	1969-70 4th year	1970-1 5th year	1971-2 6th year	1972-3 7th year	Totals
Residents at end of year		7	5	8	6	7	7	
New admissions	36	45	18	20	23	18	11	171
Re-admissions of former residents	18	15	1	2	2	4	5	47
Total	54	67	24	30	31	29	23	
Average bed occupancy	7·3	7·3	7·4	8·0	7·3	7·5	7·2	
Average period of residence in *weeks*	7·4	6·1	17·6	14·3	12·3	14·3	16·3	
Number of men staying for								
1 month or less	26	37	8	9	15	4	6	105
1 – 4 months	21	17	5	7	6	10	4	70
4 – 7 months	5	2	—	4	1	4	2	18
7 – 12 months	2	3	1	—	3	4	2	15
over 12 months	—	1	5	2	—	—	2	10
% staying over 4 months	12·9	10	31·6	27·2	16	36·3	37·5	

Total 218

differences in numbers of men admitted, for example, changed so strikingly after the end of the second year. At this stage, however, I would like to make a few general comments. The first two years show clearly the chaos and turmoil of a house unsure of what it was doing or where it was going. Of 218 admissions and re-admissions between 1966 and 1973, 121 (55 per cent) occurred in that first period 1966–8. Yet, despite the large number of men dealt with in that short period, only 10 per cent stayed for more than four months. Even that figure is reduced in significance when it is realized that the residents were not necessarily sober for that four months, whereas in subsequent years the period of residence is equal to the period of sobriety. High turnover in the first few months is generally accepted in hostels (Home Office, 1970), but the third year at Rathcoole shows this not to be a law of inevitability. The third year was clearly the breakthrough, and the low turnover and high rate of residence show this. Since that time, there has never been a return to the chaos of the earlier years. The community has consolidated itself and the steadier rates of admission and lengths of stay reflect this. The figure for the percentage of those staying for more than four months is given because we feel that a stay of less than that has little value, whereas after four months we feel we may have begun to influence a resident's thinking and outlook towards his problems, whatever his immediate future holds.

(i) *A resident profile*

Countless studies of skid row men have looked at their background and life-style in snap-shot statistical terms. They have tended to produce a sad and monotonously familiar portrait, which seems broadly to be true no matter where skid row exists, be it London, Toronto or Melbourne (Edwards, 1966a; Olin, 1966; Bartholomew, 1968). Within the broad generalizations there is of course diversity in individual histories and personalities. But our daily experience has led us to believe that the men in Rathcoole over a period of six years are similar to the men in other skid row populations. No average Rathcoole man exists, but over the six years outlined in Table 1 we have observed and recorded no important differences from year to year that leads us to believe we are no longer dealing with the group that would be recognized as skid row alcoholics. Reviewing our total residents' histories we find two-thirds are single, i.e. never married; two-thirds are Irish or Scots; half are Roman Catholic; three-quarters are unskilled workmen and have had no family contact for five years; half have at some stage been hospitalized for alcoholism; almost all have had at least ten or more convictions for drunkenness; two-thirds have been on skid row for at least three years; the average age is forty-five. What is far more difficult to do is to give an overall account of how well 'motivated' the residents were on arrival, their verbal skills, their record of past failure in treatment, their sense of humour or their anti-authority feelings, and a whole host of characteristics that still waited to be discovered.

(ii) *Drinking*

'What happens when a man goes drinking?' is invariably the first question asked of a unit concerned with alcoholics. It is in some ways a fair question but in others not. It presupposes that a clear and unequivocal answer can be given without fully taking into account the wider context of the life of the house and the skid row sub-culture of the area in which the house is situated. It is often used as a rough and ready litmus-paper test to see whether the house is kind, tolerant and understanding (i.e. relapses are tolerated) or harsh, selective and over-demanding (i.e. relapses are not tolerated). It is sometimes assumed for example that to be tolerant to drinking lapses is demonstrating an understanding of the problem, whereas to bear too heavily on the relapsed alcoholic is to deny him the very concern that is necessary for his recovery. It will be said that it is illogical to claim to help alcoholics in a house and yet at the moment when they show their alcoholism by drinking one asks them to leave the place of help. On the other hand it will be argued that to accept an alcoholic into a community on the hidden agreement that drinking incurs no serious sanction is to counter-mand the other message that drinking is killing him. Further, of course, the whole unit of which the man is a part needs to be considered when relapses are being reviewed. No one ever asks (or at least asks less often) 'what happens when a man stops drinking?' (Wiseman, 1972). None the less, 'what happens when a man goes drinking?' is a question that needs to be answered and, in so doing, it raises a myriad of subsidiary ques-tions. Initially Rathcoole was based on the premise that 'helping did not mean curing', and that relapses into drinking were likely to be frequent and were certainly to be expected and countenanced. Such a policy reflected the dilemma between containment and cure. It is unfortunate that too often this dilemma is polarized, for in practice it is not one thing or the other. We certainly believed that a return to social drinking was for skid row alcoholics not a realistic goal, so in that sense cure was not the aim. Others have tried a very tolerant attitude towards drinking – usually with disastrous consequences (Osterberg, 1972; McCourt, 1972).

Did this mean then that we were merely to contain men in some kind of cocoon keeping drink at bay? We were later to discover that 'cure' for gross lack of self-confidence, for example, was possible which reduced the need for alcohol and so to some extent contained the problem. But for the first twelve to eighteen months we struggled to cope with alcoholic relapses, unsure whether we were containing any-thing at all. Some days eight would sit down to breakfast but only one to supper – a stressful experience for staff and the remaining sober resident! Night visits by returning or wishing-to-return drunken men were common. No one was left in residence at all after the first Christ-mas holiday. Employers rang up to see whether Bill was coming in for work or not. Stomachs were pumped out at the local hospital when men drank on antabuse. It was to be expected; it was exhausting; it was even on occasions fun, but what on earth was it meant to be showing? We were able to show that, on average, the men in Rathcoole worked longer, went to prison less and slept rough less than in the year before coming into the hostel. But how long could this marginal improvement be seriously sustained, given the endeavour it required from staff even to advance that far? Moreover, it seemed that if this was what we expected we were not learning as much as we ought to be and, above all, nor were the residents. A report for the committee written after six months (December 1966) was bold enough to say: 'We have fully proved the correctness of our central contention – men who for anything up to eight years had scarcely drawn a sober breath outside prison or hospital, have been able to maintain periods of sobriety.' Some years later, residents would not regard that statement as satisfactory and would indeed be glad we had not stopped at that rather bold assertion. The high turnover, the relapse rate, the failure of 90 per cent to settle for more than four months and the wear and tear on staff led residents, staff and committee seriously to examine the drinking issue. If the rules of the house were made more rigid, would anybody stay at all? Were we being foolish to expect anyone not to drink at all? Were we doing a disservice to the residents in not helping to set expectations for them which did not conform to their self-image of 'I'm just an alcoholic dosser so don't ask anything of me'?

Eventually, a few residents with some previous experience of Alcoholics Anonymous began to feel that on entry to the house they were being given a double message. This was that drinking had ruined their lives and Rathcoole would help stop this, but if they drank it didn't matter. They therefore asked for a clearer statement as to where everyone stood on the drinking issue. After a number of house meetings it was resolved to give every man one 'chance' and then if he relapsed again he would be asked to leave. Very soon the residents realized they had merely produced a situation in which everyone, if offered licence to drink, took it as a matter of course. This meant there was always someone away on the drink or sitting about the house shaking and on edge, having just returned from his 'one chance bender'. It was therefore finally agreed on a unanimous vote that there was to be a no-drinking rule, which meant that if any resident drank he forfeited his right to a place in the house for at least several months. This has remained the rule ever since 1968. The first full year of the operation of the no-drinking rule, 1968–9, produced one of the most successful years in terms of both the house's stability and the long-term sobriety of the residents.

The no-drinking rule has been retained and has largely succeeded because it has operated within a context that made sense to the residents. The residents' decision to establish the rule overcomes the problem Tuominen (1968) put as, 'How can this place be called a home if a man is thrown out when he takes a drink?' Above all it was proposed and agreed to by the residents and is periodically reaffirmed by them at house meetings. It was not imposed by staff against the wishes of residents. There are no other rules the breach of which invites immediate departure. The 'boundary rope' of no-drinking is firm and visible but, within it, rules do not clutter the residents' daily lives. Further, since 1968 staff ceased to be resident in the house. This was made possible because of the increased stability of the house and was in a way a direct challenge to the residents to retain that stability. There was clearly a feeling that to come and go in freedom with one's own door key was for them a state more conducive to sobriety than to be watched over by resident staff. The responsibility for not drinking therefore became the resident's own, not someone else's; at the same time, panic and confusion were not caused at a weekend if a man drank and staff were not available, because all knew the ethic and the value of its enforcement. One difficulty of a strict no-drinking rule is that the community can too easily lapse into having abstinence as the only criterion of success (Bandt, 1970). There has to be strict awareness to guard against that. Finally, the departure of the drinking man, though always worrying, became less disturbing when the Project developed the shop fronts in 1970, which provided the opportunity for further help to be tried. This then was one way of coping with the essential issue in an alcoholic hostel of what happens when a man drinks. It is not the only way but it seems relevant for the context in which it is operated.

(iii) House meetings

It had been envisaged at the start that, if there was to be any therapeutic content at all in the life of the house, then there had to be some forum in which staff and residents could meet, discuss and share problems, and commit themselves to their resolution. A psychiatrist was to be present at these meetings, already having seen men individually on their admission to the house. As there was very little previous experience in holding groups with skid row alcoholics, the staff were unclear as to how best to run the group and indeed whether the concept of a regular group or house meeting would be acceptable to the residents themselves. During the first year from the house's opening it was obvious that psychoanalytic group psychotherapy was not appropriate, and that if any progress was to be made in creating interest in a house group it would need to concentrate on the here and now situations relevant to sobriety and the life of the house. Again, other houses have had very similar experiences (Osterberg, 1972). Even this step was, however, not as easy to achieve as we had anticipated. It was almost two years before staff and residents were in a position to say that the weekly meeting was an integral, valuable and welcome part of the house routine. The residents initially would resist efforts to become involved in any interaction between themselves or to become involved in accepting responsibility for aspects of the daily life of the house. There was a level of interest that the men had in each other that was always an extremely practical one – advice about where to find work, making sure a new resident had enough tobacco, or lending a man a clean shirt. Suggestions from staff that they should understand more about a man's problems, such as asking why he had given up a job, were greeted very sceptically. To mind one's own business has always been presented as the way to stay sober and get by. I say 'presented' because frequently residents would refer to late night discussions among themselves in which they grappled with their difficulties in understanding sobriety. In our efforts to persuade men to 'care' more for each other we perhaps failed to appreciate two factors. First, different social classes may demonstrate caring quite differently, some showing it more practically than others. Second, skid row itself militated against very close relationships: death and the police took men rapidly away. Men lived with a degree of 'here today, gone tomorrow', far greater than in other social groups. Such seeming indifference does not mean that there is no interest at all, for part of the life on skid row is to be constantly in receipt of information about many men. 'Jock's just got twelve months for begging; Tom's in Rathcoole; Harry's lost an eye in Wolverhampton.'

There were many examples of resident resistance, such as objections to the television being turned off, or, just as the discussion of house matters started, one man would flourish a new cigarette lighter, or introduce a skid row anecdote, so totally destroying the flow of events. Interpretation of this behaviour to the effect that it was transferring skid row behaviour to Rathcoole was generally viewed with incomprehension. One's past life was rarely discussed when on skid row, and so such discussion was generally regarded as a closed book when they were in Rathcoole. Further, all men had very ambivalent feelings about even trying to leave the skid row they knew for life in a house where all was quite strange. Little commitment was therefore made to the house and no man was willing to express himself too forcibly as he would soon be back on skid row. Men seeking to move off skid row do seem 'split by indecision' (Ross, 1970, p. 95). The interrelationship between men on and off skid row was something we had only guessed at prior to opening and we soon discovered that this was a complex and often destructive relationship. For example, within hours of entry into the house, a sober resident might be visited by drinking friends keen to see whether any money was yet at hand. For the men in the house to turn away such visitors was virtually impossible, as this would mean complete commitment to sobriety and a rejection by and of their friends on skid row with whom they 'knew' they would again be drinking after a fairly short spell of sobriety.

Finally, it is my belief that almost any new project that seeks to assist men on skid row is likely to be tested out quite strongly by the men. Some of the lore on skid row is that 'we cannot be helped, of course if we could, we would go along for the help'. Now if the help that is provided can be shown not to work – partly because of the pressure skid row alcoholics put on it – then there is no value in going off the drink to obtain the help. Comments such as 'he won't last long', 'he'll be back', 'Bill should break out soon' abounded in the drinking 'schools' from which Rathcoole drew the majority of its residents. As the drinking rule became clarified, as the need to test out Rathcoole decreased, as staff became more skilful and experienced, as the residents ceased to be drawn exclusively from one or two drinking 'schools' in the same part of London, so the meetings in the house took on an altogether different air and meaning. So much so that at one stage residents became chairman and secretary of the meeting, agendas and minutes were written, votes were taken on all house matters, including that of the admission of new residents, and eventually at the end of three years the psychiatrist felt able to withdraw from the meeting.

(iv) *Resident responsibility*

How was it that at one stage we were saying that a group of skid row alcoholics were 'impossible to do anything with', yet later the psychiatrist felt the group strong enough not to require his weekly presence? Two possible answers can be given to this question. First, that we were just lucky in that, as we were ourselves pressing for increasing involvement of the men in the house, we had by chance a group to whom this appealed. Certainly the group at the crucial stage was strengthened by the presence of men who had had previous favourable experience with Alcoholics Anonymous, but at the same time there were other men who had little interest in the house but who were willing to go along with the staff, this being less stressful than resisting the staff. What is clear is that, although there were one or two men who became strong 'culture carriers' (Jones, 1952, p. 51), none the less the majority were initially no more interested in long-term sobriety than any other residents who had been with us.

The second answer was that the staff became firmer in their resolve to create a therapeutic community, and more certain as to some of the ways of achieving this. Clearer leadership from the staff assisted the residents. While there was not instant consensus about the goal and the means of achieving it, at least there was an opportunity to debate the goal and from this conflict growth was truly possible. One resident (still sober many years later) once bitterly remarked, 'I came here for sobriety not all this responsibility!' In that outcry lay much of what went on at Rathcoole in its third year, the year when the real foundations of the house, as it is now, were laid. As we have seen in Table 1, the third year, 1968–9, marked the major breakthrough for the house. Turnover was low and stability was high. Valuable learning experiences had been laid by staff and residents and the whole community had benefited. The goal for the house became then one of giving the men as much responsibility as possible and increasing staff expectations of what the residents could do. It was not a question of debating this theoretically, but of discovering areas in which responsibility could truly be handed over. Occasionally efforts were made by the men to resist this with statements like, 'We're only alcoholics' or 'We're just a bunch of ex-dossers', the implication being that therefore nothing serious could be demanded of them. More important, they were forced to debate whether being 'sober' was merely 'not drinking' or whether it was entering a totally different way of life. Failure of the men to understand this could lead to a situation vividly described by one recovered alcoholic talking about another man: 'He hasn't had a drink for two years but hasn't taken one step towards sobriety.' To overcome therefore this lack of confidence and to challenge the men's perceptions of themselves, the staff raised issues where it was felt the residents could and should take over the responsibility. These ranged from the weekly parcelling and organizing of the laundry, the provision of front door keys, the paying of some of the bills, the cleaning of the house, cooking at weekends, the general management of the house as staff were no longer in residence and, above all, the selection of potential residents. The last two items were clearly crucial ones, but they could only be broached after the other issues had been resolved. It was not good tactics merely to withdraw resident staff until the residents had accepted the sense of undertaking lesser responsibilities.

The withdrawal of staff from the house and the involvement of the existing residents in selecting future residents required months of

3

heated discussion before it became possible for any change actually to occur. Both changes were helped by and linked to the establishment of the no-drinking rule, as without such a rule chaos could easily ensue in the absence of resident staff. Thus the non-residence of staff and selection by residents went naturally together: if the house was to be in any sense the responsibility of the men, the staff must not be available at all hours, neither must new residents arrive merely at the whim of the warden. 'This is your house' became the staff cry; men should not live in the house as if under some obligation to the staff, living by someone else's consent, but rather as invited and welcomed members of a community, each responsible for the whole. With staff no longer on the premises day and night it was easier for men to see the real need for their own involvement in selection of residents. The advantages that emerged were that the whole house was now involved in the decision to admit, thus avoiding the staff being 'scapegoated' for the awkward residents; the policies of the house on drinking were explained by the residents to the new man so that there was greater chance of their policies being believed, the culture was thus carried from resident to resident reducing the 'them and us' division: a vital learning experience was at hand. Above all, however, this was a process by which men could be seen to move away from the traditional skid row culture of non-involvement and passive acceptance of what others did to them. They were now participating and deciding. Involvement of residents in selection is often regarded suspiciously by visitors. It is in a way a challenge to the omnipotence of the helping professions. As has been remarked: 'It is surprising in view of the anti-authoritarian, anti-hierarchical emphasis on the half-way house movement, that the residents have so little part in the formal process of choosing a new member' (Raush, 1968, p. 114).

Considering selection means considering rejection. Some rejection was still done by the staff in that they conducted a preliminary interview in order to decide on the men to be put before the residents. Over the first two years of the house's life, for every man accepted (by whatever method of selection) there was one turned down by the staff. When the residents' selection meetings began, there were very few who were turned down at that stage. In the first twelve months of its operation only five men were rejected by the residents. In two of these instances the staff disagreed but accepted the decision. The fact that prospective residents are almost invariably selected by existing residents does not necessarily mean that the selection procedure is valueless. It still offers a decision-making opportunity. Further, it in some way ritualizes a man's re-entry into normal society from skid row. They go out by the ritual of the court. They can come back by the ritual of Rathcoole. Grounds for rejection by staff would obviously include the simple fact that there was no vacancy. Other reasons would include a mental history which we felt unable to help, a record of serious sexual offences, serious doubt in the man's own mind as to whether he was an alcoholic. Grounds for rejection by the men were usually doubt as to whether the man was an alcoholic or a strong feeling that the community could not help the particular individual at that particular time. The fact that so few men were rejected by the residents indicates that on the whole they felt willing to try to help most men.

There are both advantages and disadvantages in staff being non-resident yet responsible to and for a resident community. Naturally, living away from the job reduced some of the stress of constant twenty-four-hour availability, giving staff a degree of 'thinking space' in which to see the life of the community from a slightly more objective position. On the other hand, being away from the total life of the house on an irregular basis requires a heightened awareness of its dynamics. Most important, staff have to know when to intervene at the request of residents who ring up to seek advice and help. It is essential not so to overrate the residents' capacity that crises which need staff intervention are left to chance development; equally, matters which can and should be left to residents should not receive overmuch staff attention by their rapid intervention at every telephoned request. It is less easy to assess what is really needed in a house when all one has to go on is one resident ringing up. Even here, misjudging the moment of intervention is a fruitful and productive area for staff–residents discussion, enabling all to work out their separate and joint responsibilities.

Finally, two incidents must serve to illustrate the difference in house atmosphere and dependency on staff, when a staff-dominated house is in operation and when it is not. In 1967 I was woken early one morning by an irate resident wanting to know why there was no tea (though clearly residents using the tea should have foreseen the need for more as the current supply dwindled). But then that was not their job, it was the staff's! In 1969, while away on holiday, I was rung up to be told that everything was fine and that, as the roads were icy, would I please not come back for a few more days, there being no need for me!

(v) *Was Rathcoole a therapeutic community?*

Much mystery still seems to surround the concept of the therapeutic community. Perhaps the only thing anyone would agree on is that the term is over-used and seriously misused.

The notion of a therapeutic community has in its short life been so abused that it has become attenuated to little more than a popular psychiatric cliché. A change in ward décor, the institution of group therapy, giving patients a vote about television programmes – any of these can apparently warrant the title, a therapeutic community (Raush, 1968, p. 13).

Clark (1965, p. 73) has said that the therapeutic community 'is both an attitude and a method, a system of treatment and a battle cry, a charm and a password'. Redl (1959) has remarked on the ubiquitous use of the word therapeutic, which he says can mean anything from 'don't put poison in their soup' up to 're-education for life'. Given these warnings, it seems important to try to define more precisely the nature of a therapeutic community. Jones (1968, p. 85) has said that

what distinguishes a therapeutic community from other comparable treatment centres is the way in which the institutions' total resources, staff, patients and their relatives, are self-consciously pooled in furthering treatment. This implies, above all, a change in the usual status of patients. In collaboration with the staff they now become active participants in their own therapy and that of other patients and in many aspects of the unit's general activities.

'But the fact is, of course, that we have as yet no single model of a therapeutic community' (ibid., p. 115).

While there may be no single model, that does not mean there is licence to rush off in all directions under the general umbrella of the therapeutic community concept. A hostel like Rathcoóle, because it is physically non-institutional, small, more comfortable than a prison or lodging house, more caring than a court, can easily slip unthinkingly into the belief that all is good in it, forgetting that no milieu is good or bad in itself but depends on many factors (Redl, 1959). The fact that at Rathcoole the men were out at work all day and that no relatives were ever present meant that, if it was a therapeutic community at all, it was bound to be different from the hospital model. We would prefer to regard Rathcoole as having a general therapeutic community approach rather than being the therapeutic community proper, namely 'a small face to face intensive treatment facility with extensive social re-structuring' (Clark, 1965, p. 948). We eventually avoided what has been described as 'the under-estimation of the residents' capacity to take responsibility and of the corresponding need for staff to assume a parental role' (Jansen, 1970, p. 1499). With increased resident responsibility came their commitment to the culture of the house. This brought the much-needed stability.

I wish very much to avoid discrepancies between written accounts

and actual practices, but feel that the general development of Rathcoole as outlined shows its movement from a paternal to a therapeutic
community approach. Given the particular problems of middle-aged
homeless alcoholics, it seems to us that the Rathcoole experience is an
alternative model to the family model and in some important respects
at least approaches that of a therapeutic community model. The
limitations of houses like Rathcoole however should always be
recognized.

Halfway houses probably can never be more than narrow range
institutions with strict behaviour expectations, although within their
range they can provide an extremely valuable function. No type of
service can or should try to be all-encompassing and no community
should expect this (Cahn, 1969, p. 57).

That Rathcoole as it developed was not a strange quirk of good luck
and guesswork was shown when another house was opened in 1968 to be
run on the same lines as Rathcoole. The history of the second house is
less dramatic than Rathcoole, as there was not the need to work through
as many teething troubles. We 'seeded' the new house, Lynette
Avenue, with two men who had been successful in Rathcoole. Apart
from these two men, other residents in the future were not moved on
from one house to the other as a form of promotion. What we quickly
showed at Lynette Avenue was that we could replicate Rathcoole.
Weekly meetings were held, staff were not resident, a no-drink rule was
established, the turnover was low, resident responsibility was accepted
and welcomed. Such was the growth that by 1969 the two houses were
run by the one non-resident member of staff. This pattern has
continued.

(vi)   *Emergence of the Project*

Constant questioning of the activities at Rathcoole, from its inception,
had led us to realize that its residents had greater potential than we
anticipated. Yet too many still left us too soon and returned to drinking.
Referrals failed to arrive for interview. Many alcoholics never came into
contact with anyone even to have an interview arranged. Of those that
left drinking, some retained contact but others were simply never
heard of again. The isolation of the house became evident in many
ways; men rarely went out or knew anyone apart from their old drinking
friends. To many social work agencies the house was just somewhere to
which to send a man, and little if any interest was shown in the ethic the
house was trying to create. Referral agencies criticized the fact that
other residents voted on a man's admittance or that no drinking was

allowed. 'Surely if he had a few drinks at Sunday lunch the other men could put him to bed' was the comment of one probation officer. Staff and residents were isolated from the mainstream of social work. Monger (1969, p. 14) has commented on 'wardens struggling to achieve a sense of identity'.

Residential hostels too often become a type of emotional ghetto and residential social workers invariably complain of their professional isolation. However, the fact that Rathcoole was not too peculiar in these respects did not obviate the necessity to develop a scheme away from the house that would increase the opportunities for homeless alcoholics to consider entering a treatment system rather than a punishment circuit. The Rathcoole Committee therefore agreed in 1968 to put a proposal to the City Parochial Foundation which would develop further the work of Rathcoole and seek to overcome some of the weaknesses inherent in working solely in the residential setting. The homeless alcoholic was himself after all part of a much wider 'system' of agencies and services. Rubington (1967, p. 553) has stated how the homeless alcoholic is in essence the 'man between'. Official agents of social control always confront him in a state of transition. 'On the street sober he is frequently on his way from jail, hospital, mission, or clinic to a job, a "flop", a drinking group or a solitary bottle.' The proposal, which was accepted for funding by the City Parochial Foundation in 1969, stated that 'experience has convinced us that the most effective answer to the problem of the drunkenness offender will be found not in a hostel working in isolation, but in the setting up of an integrated service of which the hostel would be an important part'. Request for support was therefore made for 'an experimental integrated rehabilitation service for chronic drunkenness offenders, the experiment being centred on Rathcoole and serving a designated area of London'. As soon as the money was granted I was asked to direct the wider project, now commonly known as the Alcoholics Recovery Project, and the new duties commenced on 1 September 1969. The house remained under my overall control and I continued to provide support and guidance to both residential units. There had certainly been a gathering momentum since the public meeting in February 1965 and since the first resident moved into Rathcoole House in May of the following year.

3   THE FIRST PHASE

The establishment of the Project was planned as being in two phases, outlined in the original proposal to the City Parochial Foundation:

For the first phase (first year) we would require the services of a key social worker/organizer . . . whose job it would be to negotiate with all the agencies already operating in this field, and generally to lay the organization foundations for the second phase (second and third years), which would then involve the opening and staffing of our own shop-front centre. Phase two, with its special staff, would be built on the basis of and integrated with a rationalized consortium of voluntary and statutory action which would have been brought about in phase one.

There was thus to be a period of about one year during which I would obtain an overview of what was happening in the area in so far as it involved the homeless alcoholic. Some programme would need to be developed before social work action in the Project could commence. A programme was drawn up by me and approved by the committee in February 1971. This programme was intended as a public statement of what we were about, as well as a 'creed' by which we might be able to assess our progress at the end of three years, the period for which the initial grant was obtained:

The essential aims of the Project were threefold:

(1) To seek to establish a more integrated and co-ordinated system of treatment and care for the homeless alcoholic;

(2) To identify the gaps in existing services and to press for new developments where they are seen to be necessary;

(3) To mount a research project to investigate more closely the sub-culture of the homeless alcoholic so that we might have a better understanding of the problem, enabling us thereby to provide more effective means of help and treatment.

In order to implement the first two aims, a general overview of all the facilities was seen as essential. The whole skid row problem was clearly already confused enough, so that we could not proceed without at least some rudimentary map and compass. The planning of alcoholism programmes had been the subject of great interest in the USA (Plaut,

1966), but had received little attention over here. Edwards (1972) has since drawn attention to the need for such planning and programming. We were of course concerned to develop a system of help for the skid row alcoholic rather than for the whole alcoholic population in our particular geographical area of South London. However, some workers have said that a programme to deal with the skid row alcoholic could eventually be. the basis for a total community programme for all alcoholics (Shandler, 1969). The initial planning of any programme seems invariably and immediately to create some tension. This tension is usually between the immediate need for services to treat the individual alcoholic, and the wish to stand back from the fray, look more closely at the nature of it and assess whether indeed the services are appropriate anyway. Do we content ourselves with catching alcoholics coming off the conveyor belt or do we examine the nature of that conveyor belt? Some of this conflict was demonstrated when the Project began its work not by immediately interviewing alcoholics but by simply finding out more about the area, the various agencies in it and their interaction with homeless alcoholics. One hospital doctor hoped we were not 'another research project that came and went leaving others to do the work'. Others would make comments to the effect that, as we knew there were lots of homeless alcoholics, why didn't we just get on and help them? The necessity that we felt to stand back a little, for a time at least, was seen by some as a luxury.

A further difficulty in the attempt to work out a programme was that it might well assume a degree of order and reason that in practice did not exist. How far can rationality be a major part of any plan or programme concerned with services for people, especially a group of people as unpredictable as homeless alcoholics? Demone (1965) has argued cogently on the limits of rationality in planning, and the need to take into account 'unanticipated consequences'. Cross (1967) has enumerated reasons why alcoholism programmes present particular difficulties. Two reasons are especially relevant to the skid row problem. First, alcoholism is not strictly or exclusively a medical problem. Second, no simple preventive or therapeutic technique exists. The consequences of the first can mean that there is much criss-crossing of social work and medical boundaries, with resultant tensions and conflicts. It might even be argued that the skid row alcoholic is a socio-economic problem, not a health one. The consequences of the second reason are that anyone feels that his system of treatment is as good as anyone else's if only because no treatment is any good in terms of 'high success rates'. Hymn-singing and prayers in the mission may be on a par with group therapy in the hospital unit. To attempt to co-ordinate agencies operating in such diverse ways with the same target population is a considerable undertaking. It is relevant to bear these factors in mind as we relate the development of the Project's programme during its first year.

Area of operation

We decided to work primarily in the borough of Southwark in southeast London. It was, however, realized that, given the mobile nature of the men in whom we had an interest, we would not try to keep rigidly within borough boundaries. The residents and their elected representatives on the local borough council had every reason to ask why yet another voluntary organization should be working in Southwark. Comments were made to the effect that 'there are too many voluntary bodies in the area already' and such agencies 'only attract more vagrants into the area'. Such reactions were not hostile but rather those of frustrated, confused and pressurized people: pressurized because of the enormous demands made on services in a poor inner City area; confused because few voluntary bodies explain exactly what they are doing; frustrated because repeated requests to central government to deal with the vagrant alcoholic problem had, they felt, been unsatisfactorily answered, or scarcely answered at all (Home Office, 1971, pp. 44–51). The challenge that voluntary bodies only serve to attract a problem into a particular area is not an easy one to meet. The fact was, however, that for many years there had been vagrant alcoholics in Southwark. The agencies came in to relieve the problem rather than arriving and hoping clients would follow. Whether the presence of an agency attracts additional clients above the number already in the area is difficult to assess. Our experience of vagrants in London suggests that many keep to their favoured areas and do not move to another area merely because another social work agency has set up stall. None the less, feelings can still run high about voluntary agencies whatever the facts of the situation, and it is imperative for such agencies to explain their presence and their rationale to those in the area in which they have chosen to work. This we attempted to do.

Subject of study: the homeless alcoholic and skid row

We made it clear that the Project was only to be concerned with the homeless alcoholic, male and female. This meant that we undertook no commitment to assist alcoholics in settled conditions such as those living in flats, houses or lodgings. Primarily we only had funds and skills to work with the homeless alcoholic; additionally however the local authority social services have a responsibility to help the alcoholic of 'fixed abode'; and, perhaps most decisive, the potential caseload would be too high if we were to offer advice and assistance to the potential and actual alcoholic population of a borough of 200,000 adults. We made no attempt to define the term 'homeless'. In practice the term is well understood, although nowhere in the legislation does homelessness appear to be defined, which may indicate a reluctance to face up to the full implications of the problem (Greve, 1971, p. 123). Whatever else it is, homelessness is certainly more than the absence of a roof. Nor is to provide both bed and roof to remove the stigma of being homeless. Bahr (1968) sought to define homelessness in his study, but such attempts have been uncommon. We in fact aimed to work with alcoholics on the street as well as those in lodging houses, reception centres and hostels, even though they might have been resident in these for quite lengthy periods.

Reference to skid row is frequent in any discussion of homeless alcoholics. Yet in an English setting it can be misleading. One research team did feel able to produce a report entitled 'London's Skid Row' although the authors could not say what was meant by the term (Edwards, 1966a). Skid Row was originally an American term which described a distinct geographical area with its flop-houses, pawnshops, cheap restaurants, taverns and missions. As it was a physically separate area of the city, it is possible in America to talk in terms of urban renewal as a solution to the problem (Blumberg, 1971). In so far as it is appropriate to talk of a skid row in England, it is possibly true to say that the phrase represents an attitude of mind, an outlook on life, a resignation to the worst society can do, a lack of belief in self and a feeling of rootlessness. It is not getting the man off skid row that is the problem, but getting skid row out of the man. Skid row is 'as much a state of mind as it is a place' (Ross, 1970, p. 113). There is a need, in other words, to distinguish a moral from an ecological entity. This implies considering skid row as perhaps some kind of continuous psychological territory or as an institution without walls. In this deeper meaning of the term, skid row is a desperate phenomenon in most English cities of any size. The details may change but that essence remains. Whatever the difficulties involved in trying to focus on skid row in Southwark, there was no doubt that the problem of the homeless alcoholic in the area was a real and troubling one both for the social and medical services and for the local residents. The latter had complained of the 'daily occurrence . . . in full public view . . . of drunken orgies' (*South London Press*, 10 November 1972).

Assessment of existing resources

As part of the early work of the Project, it was decided to try to produce a base-line statement of the extent and coverage of the facilities that existed within the proposed area of operation. The term 'resources' was interpreted in a very wide sense, including any activity that sought to influence or was likely to be influenced by the homeless alcoholic. Some facilities had been set up specifically for the use of the homeless alcoholic; some facilities had been set up for the use of the general community and then had come to act as gathering places for homeless alcoholics. It was clearly essential in any case to understand the range and variety of services involved in some way or other in the life-style of the homeless alcoholic. Above all, we could scarcely plan facilities before we were sure as to what existed and, hence, what the gaps might be.

What we discovered surprised us, only serving to demonstrate that the complexity of the skid row problem cannot be underestimated. Within the boundaries of Southwark a great variety of 'facilities' could, at any one time in 1970, be in contact with homeless alcoholics. The residential facilities included seven registered lodging houses, six hospitals, three small boarding houses, two government reception centres, two specialist houses for alcoholics and one working man's hotel (Rowton House). The day-time non-residential facilities included twenty-six churches with some regular contact with the homeless alcoholic, four missions, four soup kitchens, four probation and after-care offices, two community centres, two courts, local authority social services, a special Social Security office for homeless men, the Inner London Probation Service and After-Care Registry and Resettlement Unit for homeless ex-prisoners, a church crypt and Alcoholics Anonymous. There were then some miscellaneous 'facilities' that included the police, numerous off-licences and stores selling alcohol and crude spirits and ten parks where the men frequently gathered, being a particular problem in three of them. All the above are actually sited within the borough of Southwark. The problem becomes more confusing if we extend the boundary slightly to include services adjacent to the borough and concerned with the homeless men and women regularly in the area. As the so-called vagrant has no roots, borough boundaries are after all of no consequence to him. The facilities named above could therefore have added to them eight further houses for alcoholics, seven churches in contact with the men, four hospitals, two missions, two prisons, two hospital alcoholic units, a women's hostel and a soup run.

With the help of an assistant I established contact with all of these facilities, ranging from shops selling crude spirits to general hospital departments. In some instances questionnaires were used as, for example, in the case of churches and hostels. The opinions among people interviewed ranged from 'all welfare rights should be abolished and the drunks put to sea in a boat and there sunk' to 'far more resources are needed to help these men'. In order to try to assess the efficacy of current resources we were anxious to examine certain aspects in particular, namely (a) the total numbers of homeless alcoholics dealt with, (b) the personnel available and (c) the financial and other resources available.

(a) *Numbers*

It is difficult to try to establish services for any problem group unless one has some notion of how many individuals constitute that group. The problem was one of discovering whether we were actually dealing with the needs and demands of fifty homeless and highly mobile alcoholics who appeared regularly and rapidly in every park, court and mission, or whether there were hordes of separate alcoholics known separately to each agency which, as it were, had its own unique clientele. Most probably the position was between these two extremes; but where? Seeking to establish numbers has other advantages apart from help with realistic service planning. One of these is to provide the community with a better idea of the reality of the size of the problem. Local residents can, for example, complain about their area being 'invaded by meths drinkers' (*South London Press*, 30 July 1971), giving the impression of the existence of hundreds of such men. It is more likely to be the case that a few men, because of the nature of their outward appearance and behaviour, create the impression of a total 'take-over' by vagrants. We would not wish, however, to discount the reality of local feelings but to keep them in perspective.

Any attempt to assess numbers of vagrants, be they alcoholic or not, creates its own problems. Figures must always remain rather uncertain and can consequently be in danger of seriously over-representing or under-representing the actual size of the problem. An example of this followed a statement by a social worker (Brandon, 1972a) that 'it is probable that on any one night of the year more than 4,000 people sleep rough in Britain'. Correspondence followed including one letter which ended with the sentence, 'A survey of rough sleepers can be made to show whatever the surveyor wants it to show' (*New Society*, 6 July 1972, p. 34). As a first step we therefore went to various agencies to learn of their views as to the numbers of homeless alcoholics in the area.

As a result of these visits and enquiries, we came to the conclusion that we were initially concerned with a group of homeless alcoholics which numbered no more than 500. When due allowance was made for the mobility of the group, seasonal fluctuation, counting men twice, and the difficulties of definition, we felt confident that within Southwark there were 250–300 people, at a conservative estimate, who were the hard core of the homeless alcoholics.

From the two local magistrates' courts we found that in a six-month period they dealt with 986 drunkenness offenders, of whom 106 appeared three or more times in that period. From the thirty-three churches approached we obtained a figure of about 150 regular callers who were homeless and probably alcoholics. Park-keepers estimated a total of 115. Lodging houses which offered a total of 1,000 beds probably had at least 200 alcoholics resident there, as most studies show 20 to 25 per cent alcoholics in a lodging-house population (Laidlaw, 1956). The Camberwell Reception Centre, which of course drew its population from all over London, had up to 40 per cent of its users classified as having serious drinking problems (Edwards, 1968). Its nightly population was about 700. Local crypts and missions said they had 500 callers each week of whom a 'significant proportion' were alcoholics. Evidence from the hospitals was the most difficult to assess. One local casualty department said it saw four drunks a day. A local alcoholic unit admitted about eighty homeless alcoholics a year. However, hospital studies of the hospitals in the area show the problem of the alcoholic is numerically not very high but is much more a problem of nuisance value (Watson, 1969; Anstee, 1972).

(b) *Personnel*

No doubt, like others before us, we tended to think when we began our investigation of the problem that, given the large numbers, what was most needed to tackle the problem effectively was a vast increase in caring personnel. This was an erroneous impression. Only five of the individual organizations felt that having more staff would help them deal with the problem more effectively. The one group of people who felt most strongly that more staff were desperately needed within their own organization was the clergy (of all denominations). This would seem to raise much wider questions as to the role of the Church in dealing with social problems in inner city areas.

With regard to the statutory services, there were generally no personnel engaged specifically on work with homeless alcoholics.

Certainly there were sound arguments put to us against the employment of specialist social work staff within a probation and after-care
office, for example. But when we looked at the complicated system
surrounding the homeless alcoholic it meant it was the latter who was
likely to be the specialist, leaving social workers to follow in his wake.
Some probation officers felt strongly the need for specialists, the
existence of whom would free their colleagues from what the latter
viewed as time-wasting efforts. There is a real danger that, in such a
situation, the problem of homeless alcoholics comes to be regarded as
some individual's 'hobby' rather than its being the concern of the whole
service, on which legitimate demands can surely be made.

(c)   *Financial and other resources*

We were not able to gain any accurate idea as to how much money was
being spent in this field; but it was significant that only four organizations complained that their work was hampered by lack of money. One
resource which seemed to be in abundant supply was food and, to a
slightly lesser extent, clothing: the number of organizations which
regularly and willingly handed out food and tea was remarkable. One
lodging-house resident remarked that 'it's a hard day's work getting
round all the hand-outs' and recommended that all should be located
in one place! Given the abundance of 'hand-outs', we were forced to
ask why this was such a popular form of assistance, both to give and
receive. It is undeniable that this represents an easy way to help,
direct, quick and with no committing relationship involved. Above all,
the hand-out is both practical and humane. Undeniably also, its
existence can block off any discussion of real needs. On one occasion
I saw a man knock at a mission door following which the head of a
helper appeared round the side of the door, a few words were uttered,
sandwiches were handed to the man and the door was closed. Human
contact was minimal. Maybe that was all the man in question wished
for; but how could anyone be sure?

Even when the homeless man is clothed, fed and has money in his
pocket, there remains the problem of his finding a bed for the night.
During the winter months almost all lodging houses regularly have to
turn away a number of men seeking accommodation. The Camberwell
Reception Centre had to open overflow units in 1971 when its own
nightly population averaged 900 men. In May 1970 the closure of the
Rowton House in Southwark at one stroke removed 800 beds from the
market. This closure highlighted for a number of agencies, including us,
the incredibly haphazard methods of providing basic accommodation

for homeless single persons. No organization, no single government department, was found to have any responsibility to plan the development of the accommodation that was so urgently required. The closure of this Rowton House in Southwark which was to be followed by the closure of another such hostel in West London in 1972 led to a widespread movement to draw attention to the overall problem of accommodation for the homeless (Brandon, 1972b; Camberwell Council on Alcoholism, 1972). This housing movement continues, yet provision has not dramatically increased.

Assessment of needs

We tried in our initial surveys to examine needs from three viewpoints, namely those of the agency, the community and of the homeless alcoholic.

(i)   *The agency's point of view*

Most agencies tended to agree that more facilities were urgently required, though not everyone stated it as emphatically as we had anticipated. There was, for instance, a strong minority opinion which considered that we should do a great deal more with what we had prior to making hasty additions to it. One agency asserted that there was a need for at least a further twenty specialist hostels for alcoholics. Another, on the other hand, felt that what was most needed was a 'system' of houses in some of which drinking would be allowed; suggesting that the existing gap between, for example, the reception centre, and the specialist alcoholic hostel, was too large and that what was glaringly lacking was something in between. The absence of a sheltered workshop was commented on by one agency, specialized rehabilitation centres by another, while the need for places of containment 'for meths drinkers' frequently seen as 'beyond help' was widely acknowledged. Would another twenty hostels necessarily fill the gaps however, or would the provision of these only widen them, obscuring issues by creating an impression that something effective had been done?

There were two aspects of the situation on which almost every agency commented: co-ordination and communication. These are no new concern, but are important because the demand was constantly made to us for 'a central agency to pool resources'. Medical services were most frequently regarded as failing in this respect. Linked in with the idea of co-ordination and pooling of resources was a universal plea for more information on individual alcoholics, more effective and less dishonest referrals between agencies, more rigorous follow-up and more adequate feed-back on clients' subsequent progress. Of the ten specialist alcoholic hostels questioned, seven were critical of the way referrals were usually made to them. Yet these same agencies were criticized by one another. The lack of information passed on in this respect seemed universally inadequate, and the problem was consequently seen as crucial.

We were left with this overall impression of enormous fragmentation, and it appeared necessary for all services to come to see themselves as part of one complex, each with an essential individual role to play, but capable of functioning to maximum effect only because of the co-operation of all the other agencies. We had the feeling that such co-operation would lead to improvement in referrals and that, eventually, an altogether new service might be created which would reduce the feelings of panic and isolation felt by many agencies. There may never be sufficient services to meet all requirements and we admitted the difficulty of translating hopes into realities. One telling comment was that 'we don't need services, we need friendship', which points to an all-important and elusive factor which can too easily be overlooked. Improved co-ordination should not imply a loss of human concern, but in 1970 the majority of agencies seemed to be involved in the operation of a system about which each knew frighteningly little. Misunderstanding between agencies was hardly unexpected when we looked at the varying objectives all had. These objectives fell into three categories. The first of these categories is embodied in such statements as 'we aim for complete rehabilitation into society', the provision of 'an alternative way of life', or 're-integration into society'. The second category is less comprehensive, expressed as an aim to 'put them on the road to recovery', 'give him his self-respect', 'keep them dry as long as possible', or 'provide the client with motivation to accept the help of experts'. The third category is much more limited, including such aims as 'to let them talk' or 'to keep them happy'.

(ii)   *The community point of view*

We felt it essential to have some understanding of how the community, the non-specialists, viewed the problem on their doorstep. Accordingly, we sought to learn the views of local residents, clergy and shopkeepers who were involved in selling alcohol to homeless alcoholics.

'Guard dogs sniff out addicts from GLC estates' (*South London*

Press, 10 April 1970). This type of local newspaper headline could serve to give even the guard dogs a bad name. It is sometimes difficult to gauge whether press accounts do reflect local opinion. Articles have claimed, for example, that 'social problems such as meths drinkers have been brought in from outside' (*South London Press*, 31 July 1970) or that 'kids have to play among meths drinkers' (*South London Press*, 11 August 1970). These statements may reflect the reality or they may merely illustrate one of the many problems experienced in an inner city area in the 1970s. There was, however, little doubt that one of the local problems was that of the vagrant alcoholics. What we needed to know was whether this was really viewed as a major problem and whether those angry letters published in the local press were typical of local feelings. We therefore undertook a brief survey of the attitudes of local residents which was not scientifically rigorous, but which involved interviews with a sample of fifty-three residents on one GLC estate and a sample of twenty-eight residents in a quiet residential street. The results showed at least that the stereotype of a local resident hostile and unsympathetic to the vagrant was largely a myth. In addition to the use of this questionnaire, I also attended a number of local tenants' associations' committee meetings in order to explain the work of the Project, and to hear the committees' views on the problem. Without exception, the committee members were concerned to show their sympathy and to offer help if it was appropriate. One association subsequently included in its newsletter a brief account of the Project and its intentions.

Vicarages always seem to have been viewed as the source of a good hand-out and yet the Church does not seem to have thought out fully its role in this regard. Attempts were therefore made by the Project to find out about the clergy's involvement in and attitude towards the problem of the homeless alcoholic. Each church of every known denomination was contacted by telephone to enquire whether its clergy had any dealings with homeless alcoholics. If so, they were visited and a brief questionnaire was then sent to them. Of thirty-three churches who were sent questionnaires, twenty-five completed and returned them. Varying forms of provision were made by the clergy; including counselling (the majority), accommodation, food and drink, money, vouchers for food and accommodation, clothing, and washing facilities.

We then asked whether the clergy felt that there were any further services needed for the homeless alcoholic in the area. At least half wished to see the development of more hostels, centres, shelters, and small community houses. A smaller group felt that there was a serious

4

need for co-ordination and co-operation among all the agencies. One telling but typical comment was:

There is very little co-ordination between the agencies statutory and voluntary. Nobody knows what anybody else is doing, everybody is spread too thinly all over the place. A body is needed to co-ordinate the activities of all the agencies, and most desperately for the man in the street and, say, the local parson, there is a need for some system of reference for people who approach them. I take hours of time and shillings-worth of 'phone bills to refer even the simplest case at times.

We asked the clergy to comment on their clients, the resources of their own organization, those of other organizations and the attitudes of the community at large. Over half felt that the vagrant callers were only interested in money and that they were not interested in solving their problems. In essence they felt that it was very difficult to discover which men were interested in any aspect of rehabilitation. With regard to their own organization, there was the general feeling that lack of time, money and personnel restricted any efforts they might wish to make. Comments on other organizations were generally favourable and most clergy seemed to have been helped when they contacted these. They accepted the overall existence of insufficient resources and the fact of the state provision being 'not adequately thought out'. For one clergyman at least, 'bingo was more of a problem'.

Finally, we discussed with about twelve off-licencees and the owners of hardware stores in the area whether they had any problem with homeless men coming into the shop to buy drink. The involvement of some of them in the problem was really quite extraordinary. Two off-licencees whom we visited, estimated that they had anything up to twenty men a day who were clearly vagrants coming in to purchase drink; another had about twenty-four a week. They had no complaints at all to make about the behaviour of the men, indeed they were at pains to point out that men frequently apologized for their dirtiness and untidiness. Most of the shopkeepers were sympathetic to the vagrant drinkers. It is doubtful if this was just because they were able to make money out of them, as it was equally arguable that the regular presence of a vagrant drinker in the shop could just as well drive away more respectable trade. It is worth referring to the views of one hardware store proprietor who sold methylated spirit to the alcoholics, so that the rationale behind the sympathy can be seen in clearer detail. The proprietor admitted openly that he was sympathetic to the meths drinkers and sold meths to them when they requested it. He felt that if they did not get their meths, the men would become sick and die. He thought that alcoholism was an incurable sickness and that all he could do was to keep the alcoholic happy. Clearly, whatever a local community feels about the problem of the homeless alcoholic, and whatever it wishes to do about it, it must at some stage involve the people who sell the liquor, be it wine, beer or methylated spirits.

(iii)   *The alcoholics' point of view*

It was not possible to carry out a formal investigation of what the homeless alcoholic perceives as his own needs. However, through a discussion group at Pentonville Prison, some picture emerged. For about four months, the then warden of Rathcoole House held a weekly group meeting with twelve or more short-term drunkenness offenders in Pentonville Prison. The aim was to seek out the drunkenness offender in prison and to discuss with him the possibilities of help, rather than wait for him to be referred in the normal way. With this particular offender in Pentonville, it was generally impossible for the welfare staff to see him unless very specific requests were made. The fundamental difficulty with the group was that at no time was it remotely stable because of the very short sentences being served: almost every week there was an entirely new set of faces. The men tended to see themselves as merely at a staging post between drinking bouts, for a seven- or fourteen-day sentence is certainly not long enough for any major reorientation in their thinking about alcoholism. At times it was almost as if a bottle-gang, albeit sober, had gathered together within the walls of Pentonville Prison. Almost all conversation was anecdotal and it frequently referred back to what were seen as the good old drinking days. The ethic of the skid row sub-culture was reinforced with almost every breath. After four months' effort in this direction only two or three men had come forward wishing to move into Rathcoole House. It seemed that for the very short-term offender, i.e. one month and under, there was a need for a continuous daily group discussion, rather than one a week. It is doubtful if the work done by these men in prison can have any significance economically, and there is a strong argument for spending all the available time, as well as resources, on breaking through and breaking down the sub-culture, which at present seems to inhibit progress.

The homeless alcoholic in prison understandably tends to see his needs as reflected in the relief of immediate physical distress. Ironically, it seems that in this area there are usually more short-term resources available than long-term treatment. There is certainly no shortage of people who are willing to give money, a suit of clothes or a meal. Where facilities fall short seems to be in the follow-up to the contact which has been made via the relief of immediate physical need. The homeless alcoholic is always going somewhere, having come from somewhere else. He is always, for example, between the gaol and the lodging house, or on his way from the Probation Office or the mission. Each of us deals only with a fragment of the problem and fails, therefore, to meet a man's real needs. In turn, the men fragment their own needs, stressing only those which are appropriate, either to the moment or to the agency with whom they are momentarily dealing. There may also be a moment at which the homeless alcoholic only expresses his needs in terms of what he knows is available, rather than what he would truly dare to hope for.

Goals and objectives

It was vital both for ourselves and for all other agencies that the Project tried to establish some reasonably clear idea of just what it was that we wished to achieve. To communicate this we divided our goals and objectives into three, namely, the ultimate ideal, the long-range goals and the short-term objectives.

(i)   *The ultimate ideal*

This must be the co-ordination and creation of a comprehensive treatment service for the homeless alcoholic which does not leave help to chance and in which all resources, both statutory and voluntary, are utilized effectively. It should be a service which both receives and reaches out to the homeless alcoholic and which at no point colludes with the despair of the men and women concerned.

(ii)   *Long-range goals*

Some of the goals that we set ourselves were clear from the outset, others emerged as we talked with other people in the area concerned with the homeless alcoholic.

(1)   *A service's commitment to social work and the work carried out by other concerned agencies in the area*   With this we had of course to avoid the danger of giving other agencies the illusion that they had tackled the problem by merely passing it on to us.

The establishment of a central refferal point containing information about services and clients

We anticipated that, as far as services were concerned this would not be difficult but that many problems would present themselves with regard to a central record of clients. Problems of mobility, confidentiality, absence of record-keeping in many agencies, and the use of aliases were some of the problems that immediately challenged the realistic possibility of such a central record system, however desirable it might be. It was daunting to realize that even the courts had no cross-referral system as far as the drunkenness offender was concerned.

(2) *The establishment of shop-front offices to reach out to the homeless alcoholic*   We wished to seek to introduce into the existing network of facilities an altogether new concept of the street-level, walk-in office. This was new in so far as the homeless alcoholic was concerned, though of course some hospitals have a twenty-four-hour walk-in emergency psychiatric service. Methods of reaching out to the homeless alcoholic, of being where he is, had been shown to be eminently workable by the Manhattan Bowery Project (1969). Similarly, in London, the soup-run used by organizations such as St Mungo Community was a means of contacting homeless people and eventually placing some of them in residential communities. The work of the shop fronts was to become a key feature of the Project and is described in detail in chapter four.

(3) *The creation of a wider public interest*   The Project workers were keen to see if there were any ways in which the unpopular issue of the homeless alcoholic could be made more understandable and less threatening to the general public. We did not feel that we could continue to complain about the public's hostility or its lack of interest unless we made use of opportunities to convey our views and experience to a wider public than the readers of learned journals.

The establishment of new facilities where in the light of the earlier part of the programme these were seen to be necessary

It was considered important that we should be prepared to develop new facilities ourselves and cajole others into so doing, if it became apparent that a new approach was needed. We were not anxious just to reproduce replicas of what we already had but to determine whether new styles and ideas could be developed.

(4) *The establishment of drying-out or detoxification facilities*   While both Europe and North America had by 1970 introduced a number of detoxification centres, England still had none. We believed that if the public drunk was eventually to be taken out of the penal system then drying-out centres would be needed. The establishment of such a centre in South London needed the combined support and commitment of a

wide range of statutory and voluntary agencies. The Project wished to assist in achieving that.

(iii)   *Short-term objectives*

These were stated as three:

(1) To examine the practicability of an on-going Register of all resources and the alcoholics using them. This was to be the basis for the central referral point, part of our long-term goals.

(2) To inform and involve all those concerned with the Project of its aims and methods of implementation.

We wished to ensure that everyone would be as fully informed as possible about the work of the Project. We did not wish to appear as it were in the dead of night, leaving other organizations involved with the same problem to find out about us by chance. Open communication with all was viewed as essential.

(3) To establish a forum where, a few times a year, opportunities would be provided for discussion and, hopefully, the emergence of new ideas.

Even within one borough there were differences in the way the homeless alcoholic operated and we envisaged that possibly the local shop-front office might become a centre for both formal and informal discussion of problems.

This then was the basis of the Project's programme. We had started work with the visiting of all the agencies. From this, several interesting features emerged.

The first thing that we discovered was that it was not only the local residents who were occasionally angered, resentful or mystified at the problem; local professionals engaged in law, medicine, the Church or social work had similar attitudes at times. The following exchange, for example, took place at one court we visited.

R.C. had pleaded guilty to begging. He was an alcoholic of no fixed abode and claimed that he had tried to get work but had no insurance cards.

Magistrate	You've got to have cards before he can employ you.
R.C.	I'm a casual worker.
Magistrate	I should think you were very casual. You're one of these people who lounge around doing nothing, living off honest people in this country.
R.C.	I. . . .
Magistrate	Shut up. You've had your say. Now it's my turn. If you keep pestering people, you'll land up in real trouble. Five pounds or fourteen days.

Such hostility, frustration and lack of understanding were shown in more covert ways by other agencies. It was not uncommon for social workers to ask whether the Project's work would make any difference to certain clients and then produce for discussion the most difficult alcoholics who had visited their agency. In the then state of knowledge and know-how, it seemed unlikely that any system would reach such individuals, yet they were produced as a form of instant test of the worthwhileness of the Project. At the same time, the agency concerned would be tending to use such extreme problems as their reason for avoiding contact with any homeless alcoholic clients. It was rare for an agency to admit that homeless alcoholics were low on their own list of priorities but nevertheless they would be interested in discussing ways in which they might make some contribution to the solution of their problems. Rather, they tended to claim this group was impossible to help, ruling out any immediate consideration of new ways of helping them.

Resistance to involvement was spelt out in other ways. The element of research in the Project was for instance sometimes singled out, especially as in Camberwell many felt there were already more research workers than social workers. It was made clear that we were not to be welcomed if all we did was to raise expectations and then pass on after three years to write up the research leaving others to pick up the pieces. A slightly different form of criticism emanated from the demand that something should be done immediately, the nature of the problem being obvious. The clergy in particular, when talked to in groups, demanded instant action. This to some extent arose from their own frustration as it was not always easy to see what they wanted to be done, nor was it always possible to dissuade them of the value of merely another one-off exercise which might only postpone a deeper examination of the whole problem. They seemed to want to work together and yet would say that co-ordination is only a 'more superior version of human chess'. It was not easy to discern when they were resistant to us as a secular agency and when rather they were uncertain about their own role and that of the Church in regard to the homeless.

That there was another voluntary body in existence was clearly for some people a problem in itself. One eminent psychiatrist expressed the view that voluntary bodies made themselves into amateur doctors and social workers and that a clearer stand was required by the professionals to prevent indiscriminate activities by voluntary bodies! This particular psychiatrist has always worked well with us as he saw that we were not 'amateur doctors', but this statement of his views showed that agencies which are eccentric, ill-thought out and poorly managed may well be independent but leave their backlash when others come on to the scene. Some local authority officials also were initially quite suspicious of us and asked whether we had any connection with certain groups, indicating that we needed to be reputable and professional if we were to gain acceptance in the borough.

A second factor which impressed itself upon us was that the people in the front line of contact with the problem felt themselves to be the least supported and were certainly the least trained, in any formal sense. An official at the Camberwell Reception Centre remarked, 'I would like to have my best staff handing out the blankets.' It never will be possible of course, but the perception which led to this remark is an interesting one. There are four groups of staff who have immediate and regular face-to-face contact with the homeless alcoholic, long before more highly 'trained' staff are ever seen; these are the counter clerks in Social Security offices; the porters in the Reception Centres, the park-keepers, and the staff of lodging houses. We spoke to several of the last two groups and to the managerial staff of the first two groups. All admitted that the workers in the front line contact need more help, advice, support and training than they presently receive. There was almost a situation in which it was admitted that dealing effectively with the homeless alcoholic was a specialized task and yet to become specialized in that task was to prevent promotion; nowhere was this officially stated, but it was several people's view.

Let me illustrate the point by an examination of the pressures and problems of the park-keeper. Numerous discussions were held with a number of local park-keepers and the majority of them were sympathetic to the plight of the alcoholic in their parks. They believed that something should be done about the problem, but they were not appointed as social workers but as park-keepers. Frequently they had to make judgments about whether to move on a group of drinkers at the request of the other park users, whether to call the police or ambulance service to a man lying drunk, whether to become involved with the individual drinker (at the risk of getting lousy), whether to offer advice to new men who appeared drinking in the parks. None of their training covered these issues. They complained that they had seen policemen and ambulance drivers arguing as to who should take away a drunk; neither did, and the park-keeper was left. They explained the daily problem of moving men out of the park at closing time. They showed some real understanding of the problem. Yet they were offered little in the way of guidance and support. Their daily demonstration of sympathetic attitudes could be an important part of the local community's relationship with homeless alcoholics.

A third feature which struck us was the sheer denial of the problem's existence: one clergyman near a local park frequented by drinkers claimed he never saw any vagrant alcoholics; lodging-house keepers said there were definitely no alcoholics in their lodging house. It was in the lodging houses that most denials occurred. Some of this denial may be due to the lodging-house staff's view that 'drunkards' were not viewed as alcoholics. We did not believe that simply a different definition of alcoholism accounted for the denial. To admit to having alcoholics in the lodging house was, it seemed, to give the house a bad name – the last thing to do was to admit to outsiders that 'undesirables' lived within. As considerable numbers of homeless alcoholics were housed in lodging houses that denied the very existence of the alcoholic resident, it was difficult to see how a system could be devised that might at least introduce the alcoholics to the notion that help was available for their problem.

The final aspect of concern to us was the total absence of attempts by the agencies to evaluate in any way what they were doing – and doing so intensely. This was itself a product of what we could term insular certainty. Some organizations, usually voluntary, seemed able to operate oblivious of all other services, yet with the conviction that they had an 80 per cent success rate. Others would not claim any success at all but rather felt that, as the men were virtually 'unhelpable and incurable', then kindness and tea were valuable in themselves, and who knows but that may indeed shed light into the dark night of the soul. Obtaining hard facts was therefore difficult; even record-keeping tended to be viewed by some as dehumanizing the activity of caring.

Towards the end of its first year of activity, the Project was ready to embark on the tasks that it had set for itself. The shop-front offices were to begin operation; a programme outlining the aims of the Project had been circulated to all agencies, visits had been made to all other agencies; the task of co-ordination had now to begin; research into the sub-culture of the homeless alcoholic had to be planned. The full staff complement of seven was by now appointed. Three years suddenly seemed a minute period of time in which to make any initial impact on the complex issues that were seen to surround the homeless alcoholic.

4 SHOP FRONTS

Assisted by Joan Walley

From its inception, the Project held as a fundamental tenet the desirability of trying to develop ways of 'reaching out' to the homeless alcoholic. Experience at Rathcoole had shown for example that men were often referred to the house more by luck than design. This 'reaching out' is now a familiar approach in many areas of social work as, for example, in local authority social services' area teams which are situated in the neighbourhood, not in the town hall. It was less easy to see how best a vagrant population could be reached. It was necessary to have some regard for the rights of the men to drink in peace and to be free from social work interference and control. At the same time an appropriate helping agency must be accessible to them and, above all, be perceived as such by the alcoholics themselves. However fine the service being provided, it remains as it were in its wrapping paper, unless it is actually 'delivered' (Ryan, 1969).

The idea that the Project decided to try to develop was the shop-front office, which was in essence an on-the-street service located in an area frequented by homeless alcoholics. The Project's first shop front was opened in Camberwell in May 1970 and antedated the report which was to recommend that 'a small shop front be established, as an experiment, in one of the main skid row areas of London' (Home Office, 1971, p. 120). The report went into some detail on the principles that would underpin shop-front work. It is instructive to examine those principles in the light of the Project's experience in its three shop fronts. We shall then give a fuller account of one of the Project's shop fronts, typical only of itself, but demonstrating the practical issues that occurred.

(i) 'The nature of the premises is not particularly important' (ibid.)

All the Project's shop fronts were opened in church premises, either crypt or vestry. This was primarily due to churches being in the key inner city areas with their physical plant being largely under-used. We have not found any resistance from the men to coming to the shop fronts because they see us as religious by association. Some of the premises have had a well-used air about them which, together with ease of access, has made them attractive: purpose-built premises could well have seemed too glossy and kept people away. We have found it important to have the use of at least two rooms so that individual interviewing can take place in private, which has meant that two workers are really essential in each shop front. In view of our having a separate administrative office it has been possible to keep the shop fronts free of files and documents: they must be action centres, not bureaucratic departments.

A key factor when the shop fronts are on other organizations' premises is that the landlords have to be fully in sympathy with the nature of the work being conducted. In one instance there was a conflict which eventually resulted in one shop front closing. The position in this case was that the premises were used also for evening theological lectures and other church events. Drunken men would from time to time interfere with these activities, unable to understand that the premises were not at that time a shop front. The fact that this conflict of interests resulted in the closure of this particular shop front may have been partly due to the behaviour of the men, but was also partly due to our failure to involve fully all the church authorities in knowledge of our activities. It had largely been the enthusiasm of one priest that had helped us obtain the use of these premises and, when he left, we lacked a friend at court. A secure base is necessary psychologically as well as physically.

(ii) 'An ever open door to immediate help *for their drinking problem*' (ibid., report's italics)

This statement of principle has in practice raised enormous problems. In no instance has the maintenance of an 'ever open door' proved possible; indeed this has not always been seen as desirable. In one sense, the doors are open in that there is no screening prior to entry, but it has been found necessary to ask some men to leave, although we had always hoped to avoid rejection, especially at this early stage. Drinking in the shop front was never allowed, as to do so seemed only to provide a dry shelter for drinking 'schools', which was not our aim; nor did the recovered alcoholics, working with us, regard that as helpful. An especially difficult group were those men who arrived very intoxicated, as in practice little could actually be achieved unless there were obvious medical problems for which hospital referral was necessary. It is sometimes worth hoping that much will be learned from a drunken client; experience suggests otherwise. Little time has therefore been spent with heavily intoxicated men, although they would not necessarily be asked to leave. But men who, for whatever reason, came in drunk and intent upon destroying the uneasy sobriety of the group in the shop front, were asked to leave. Fortunately such behaviour has been rare. It should be made clear that no blacklist existed; it would in any case be impossible to enforce. The key workers in all three shop fronts were female, which, while presenting anxiety both for them and for me, has at times, we believe, been the reason for there being so little serious trouble: more might have been predicted.

How far can and should 'immediate help' be available? In some instances immediate help must be obtained: men who are about to have acute withdrawal symptoms or who need assistance to negotiate a week's rent with the Social Security office. But to convey the expectation that help will always be immediate would be to frustrate client and worker alike, and might on occasion even be harmful in the long term. The area where the immediacy of action is particularly crucial is accommodation. To place a man in a lodging house or in the Reception Centre requires little skill and can be done immediately. To place a man in an alcoholic rehabilitation centre requires a degree of skill and an amount of time that almost certainly cannot be given immediately. It is however a place in such a centre that many men want and, understandably they cannot always appreciate the reasons for delay. 'You could get me into a house if you really wanted to' is a not uncommon retort when the need for patience is explained. But the fact remains that the shop-front social worker is constrained by the shortage of places in alcoholic centres and is indeed competing for available places with other agencies and even to some extent the other workers on the Project! In such a situation it is tempting to fall back solely on what can be achieved immediately, such as providing letters for clothing or money for food, but we have sought to resist that. The emphasis has been rather on the possibilities of recovery based on a good relationship begun in the shop front. Many places already offer immediate short-term assistance and shop fronts are not needed to provide that.

The final element in this section is that the report saw help as being 'for their drinking problem'. As is perhaps already clear, help for the drinking problem of the homeless alcoholic may well begin with the provision of reasonably supportive accommodation. The statement in the report indicates a clear medical model of input – treatment – output, while in the shop-front setting this is not often the case. Men come in to the shop fronts for many reasons, which tend to be 'mystical rather than concrete' as one client put it. The reason may be to find out whether he has a drinking problem, or to see how others are being helped, or even to seek help for a friend while declining it himself. Some men may require weeks of visiting before they will even discuss a problem at all; one man took three months even to reveal his surname. Yet, despite the open door nature of the shop front and the fact that very few men start off by saying, 'I've come for help with my drinking problem', it is extremely rare for anyone to call who does not indicate that he has a drinking problem. The non-alcoholic homeless man does not call, the grapevine seems to screen him out.

(iii) 'The nature of the help being offered should be properly understood . . . its acceptability should not depend on a reputation for handouts' (ibid.)

This statement would suggest that callers should understand the nature of the help on offer, whereas we often found that we ourselves had considerable confusion as to just what was being offered. As the shop fronts were envisaged as being experimental and as each area in which they were situated was different, it seemed unwise to state too categorically what was to be offered, as this could well not meet with the needs of any of the men in the actual area of operation. Certainly, we had no wish to offer hand-outs; a few early callers left when it was clear no soup or money was on hand.

More important however was the workers' own wish not to be 'just another referral agency', to avoid the appearance of yet another agency to be added to the already overcrowded referral network. In our efforts to avoid being simply hand-out and referral points, we found it easier to say what we were not than what we were. The idealism of all staff constantly compelled us to question what we were engaged upon in the shop fronts. It was difficult to reconcile the understandable wish of the staff to avoid acting only as a referral-on point with the fact that men did in fact need to be referred to doctors and hostels: the shop front could never be an end in itself. We hoped that the distinctive feature of the shop fronts would be enabling earlier referrals than had previously been possible and further that the social workers would follow up each man who was referred to any other agencies.

Continuity of care became a key principle; the avoidance of men feeling that they were merely parcels in an ever-growing parcel postal service. Resistance to mere referring-on sprang also from the fact that existing methods of treatment have proved remarkably unsuccessful and on occasions totally inappropriate for the homeless alcoholic. Why then should we engage in a ritual of referral that had little chance of success? In practice, however, this attitude was difficult to sustain. It was not possible to persuade every man that a hospital alcoholic unit was not the answer to all his problems: because from his very desperate and disadvantaged position it was not unreasonable for him to believe that it was. Working pressures meant that, as one staff member expressed it, 'The work became routinized in terms of channelling into the treatment system as we know it, and the original plans of avoiding the wellworn paths . . . were lost.' It was felt that an initially 'clearer rationale would have been useful'. Such early clarity of perception did not however seem possible, given the number of imponderables that existed at the time of actual opening of the shop fronts.

It soon became apparent that the exact type of help offered was less crucial than the time, place and manner in which it was offered. The worker at one shop front for example found that the Reception Centre was practically the only place to which men could initially be referred. For this course of action to be acceptable and at all pro-ductive, referral had to be made in a style rather different from, 'Well, there is only the Reception Centre and here is a bus ticket to get there!' The referral became personalized with a weekly follow-up visit to the Centre, so that negative aspects were to some degree mitigated. Throughout the history of the shop fronts, there has been a constant tussle between trying to be different and becoming just one more component in the whole ineffective system of skid row services. We believe that, in some way, we have been successful in avoiding slipping into the latter role.

(iv) 'The success as a motivational and pre-treatment agency is more likely to depend on its accessibility; its constant availability (a 24-hour service, for example, is desirable); the absence of an institutional atmosphere; and the approach and attitudes of the staff' (ibid.)

This statement immediately raises the question of whether the success of shop fronts should be judged merely in terms of their functioning as pre-treatment facilities; the corollary being that the more people who go on to other treatment facilities the more successful the agency. But this leads on to the further question of how well the men perform in the treatment facilities, and how is that performance to be measured. It is significant that staff almost always rationalized furiously if they were asked what our 'success rates' were or how many men were now sober. We did not wish to be caught too firmly on the hook of numbers, as we were not convinced that long-term sobriety was what we were always aiming at, though that was the easiest factor to measure. Further, nearly all other treatment facilities were out of our control, so that we had relatively little influence over subsequent events once men moved on from the shop front.

It should already be clear that men did not come to the shop front merely to seek treatment: some were too familiar with the treatment circuit, some had never been involved with it at all, others had different needs and were currently not interested in treatment. It was not possible therefore to assess the shop front purely in terms of its motivational function. There was a period when 'motivation' was a taboo word at staff meetings, and to some extent this is still so.

But how then do we see the aim of the shop front? 'To reduce the chaos of men's lives' was how one worker described it. It is hard to know if that has been achieved, even in an individual case, but using this latter criterion does enable the worker to move away from the position of trying to get an unwilling man into a treatment facility merely in order to raise the 'number count'. One member of staff described this dilemma in her field notes:

We acknowledged that many and possibly most men were not going to be able to cope with society's demands on a sober individual, and that for many it would be only a desirable and usually very necessary 'break' from a pretty ropy existence. We don't have many 'answers' and in the present methods of treatment the exceptional success seems to prove the rule. Much more acceptance and help is needed, possibly on a 'when it is needed' basis, otherwise the situation too frequently met is that hospitals and hostels count the attempts different men have had and then begin to reject after the third attempt. Do we not believe a man when he tries to convince us this time 'it's different' and do we accept that he still needs help, if only as a temporary measure? This is of course a very hard goal either to aim for or to accept, and it creates enormous difficulties in terms of satisfaction.

What then of those factors which the report saw as important in determining the shop fronts' success, however defined? Accessibility was stressed at all three shop fronts, and all were sited in key skid row areas. Church premises are generally conspicuous and proved so in these instances. Constant availability has, however, not so far been a feature of the shop fronts as we have run them. Initially a twenty-four-hour service would have been a practical impossibility, unless we had chosen to place all the workers together in one shop front. We decided against this because we did not wish to concentrate our efforts in one area only, and only have one model in action. No premises were available to us for twenty-four hours a day, whereas several could be used for a few hours each day. Finally, the longer a service is open the greater the expectations and the demands made on it and consequently the more back-up resources are needed, but the Project in no way controlled the availability of the latter.

All three shop fronts thus began operating only for two or three hours each weekday and have continued in this way. While we would now be interested in putting our experience into a twenty-four-hour service, we believe there are some advantages in a more limited service, a service limited, that is, in terms of availability; for serious emergencies twenty-four-hour services already exist in London – the hospital casualty departments, psychiatric emergency clinics, reception centres and the open line telephone services run by organizations like the Samaritans and St Martin-in-the-Fields. A shop front, even if always open, could never be able to provide these types of service: some of the skills of a shop-front worker involved in a hostel referral could not be used at 3 a.m. Careful thought needs to be given as to whether a round-the-clock service in a skid row shop-front office would not subtly collude with the men's part belief that they are so ill-equipped as to need a social worker to be available every hour of every day. What other problem groups have such a twenty-four-hour service, and is this really desirable? Further, we believed that the problems inherent in setting up and sustaining a good twenty-four-hour service were such that we felt an institutional atmosphere was more rather than less likely to result. Another decided advantage for staff in only being in the shop front a few hours each day was that they were able to follow up the men who moved into other agencies. One result of a total involvement in one spot can be to institutionalize staff so that they are less aware of what is on the outside than are the clients they see.

'The approach and attitudes of staff' are probably the most vital elements of all. It is of little value devising a fine scheme if the staff selected still believe that skid row alcoholics should really 'pull themselves together'. The staff selected were chosen primarily for their enthusiasm and commitment to trying new ideas. We have only once had a member of staff with a professional social work qualification – this was chance, not policy. One shop front had, as one of its two workers, a recovered skid row alcoholic, whose experience and approach proved invaluable. From the start informality was stressed and formal interviews only undertaken when it was strictly necessary, never as part of a routine. No man who came in had to give his name and state that he wanted to stop drinking: if games were to be played they were not to be the old familiar ones. As numbers increased and as the result of other pressures, it was found necessary to increase the amount of more formal interviewing, though not in the man's initial stages when he was merely seeking entry to the shop front. It is worth noting that one recovered alcoholic on the staff disagreed with these informal methods, feeling strongly that the men 'thought you meant business if you sat down in front of them with pencil and paper and conducted a formal interview'. Further, other agencies required comprehensive social work reports, and our own evaluation requirements necessitated an increasingly more careful information-taking system.

While it was naturally assumed that the staff would have empathy and acceptance, there were certain features which seemed to us essential for those working in the shop front. Wiseman (1970, p. 48) has referred to every agency having 'a prescription for the type of defining encounter that takes place between the alcoholic and agent of social control at least initially'. We stressed that the man should define that encounter and that he should 'pace the contract'. Staff needed then to accept intermediate goals as signs of success for 'there is no real sense of failure when a Row man does not succeed' (ibid., p. 186). Where failure at any level did seem to occur, we knew we should not re-define the situation to cope with the low success rate or become resigned to the man's recidivism (ibid., p. 154). Rather we needed to re-examine our own roles and approaches, to learn rather than to re-define and avoid learning.

In all this, it was important to learn from alcoholics, whether employees or clients. To use and to encourage to be used the potential and actual skills of the men were essential. This could often be developed in an informal group so that there was no waiting-room atmosphere, which is often negative and anti-therapeutic. The efforts made to avoid the waiting-room phenomenon were necessary and important. Bessell (1971, p. 75) has said that the waiting-room 'proclaims unmistakably to the client, and to the rest of the world, that this is what the agency thinks of its clients'. So why not see care and concern beginning in the waiting room itself? Curiously enough Bessell thought waiting rooms should have televisions! In the shop front men were not allowed just to sit around the walls but were encouraged rather to develop some clearer identification with the shop front. We knew that we were seen as part of a whole skid row network, and we had to use that fact and see our work in relation to it, not as apart from it. Finally, as staff dealt with only alcoholics, we were able to avoid judgmental feelings about drunken men who had kept us from dealing with more deserving clients. Any client at any time could be drunk – a sobering thought for staff.

(v) 'The first link is a long chain extending from Skid Row . . . it is however a tenuous chain . . . therefore . . . reach out with a helping hand again and again' (Home Office, 1971, p. 120)

5

It would be more accurate to say that the shop front is the first specialist link, in that some men for example are referred from hospitals where they may have been admitted for bronchitis, discovered to be homeless alcoholics and referred to us. In these instances the shop front is not itself the point of departure from skid row, but is rather exercising a support function while long-term arrangements are being discussed. Staff prefer self-referrals, which form about one-third of the total. For the self-referral in particular the notion of the 'first link' is an accurate one. How far the staff are able constantly to reach out with a helping hand is determined less by their own resilience than by what other agencies will offer the tenth time round. Considerable discernment is required to determine whether it is realistic to ask a centre to reconsider an ex-resident or to consider a man who has already left six other alcoholic centres. Always magnanimously offering to help can only produce disenchantment if practical action cannot follow. If on the other hand a relationship with the man has been built up over months or even years, then it may be possible to help that man to obtain sobriety in lodgings – when a hostel is out of the question and when therefore the relationship itself is the helping hand.

(vi) 'Links with hostels, hospitals and other facilities will be crucial. There would indeed be advantage in the centre being managed in conjunction with some facility or facilities' (ibid.)

The Project has always upheld the necessity for the shop fronts to be focal points of co-ordination within their own area. Without effective links with all other agencies in the area the shop front could not function at all. All workers in the shop fronts spent their first few months contacting all relevant local facilities. Few facilities however have yet come to see the shop front as equally crucial to their own effective performance with homeless alcoholics. It is one thing to establish links, to maintain them is much more difficult. With some facilities there is a need to re-visit every few months as staff change so often, for example registrars in hospitals. Potential referring agents also just forget if there is not consistent practical involvement with individual alcoholics. Above all, however, is the difficulty involved in making the links institutional rather than personal. One staff member wrote in her notes:

These (the links) worked very well on a functional basis whilst the shop front was in operation, especially as the link was on a personal level i.e. contacts established with the staff of the organizations and not just the 'man in charge'. I feel it a pity that when I left these contacts more or less ceased. There are no established links with those agencies which we had originally hoped would transcend the personal level.

The fact that the Project had under its direction two hostels, later to be increased to three, greatly enhanced the possibilities for the shop-front workers. Although there was not an automatic right of placement in these hostels invariably the practice developed whereby shop-front referrals were given preference and indeed became the main referral source. It also meant that neither type of facility could remain too isolated.

(vii) 'A great deal will depend on close liaison being established with the police' (ibid.)

The shop fronts in practice have never had any exceptional liaison with the police. They have been regarded like any other agency and involved where appropriate. On no occasion have the police referred anyone to us nor, possibly, would this be appropriate in any case. Only the drunken man would be the concern of the police, and if he was ill or acutely intoxicated then hospital services would be required rather than those of the shop front. There may be isolated cases where referral to the shop fronts would be desirable, but such referrals might seem to be needed at hours when we are not available. It would seem to us that the role of the police will be much more crucial with regard to the proposed detoxification centres referred to in the 1972 Criminal Justice Act.

(viii) 'A great deal will depend on . . . gaining the co-operation – understanding of the ordinary residents of the neighbourhood in which it is situated' (ibid.)

In no instance has this been a problem of the Project. In two areas in which we established shop fronts there were few if any facilities for the man on the street so that even our limited operation was welcomed both by the local authority and by residents in the area itself. We could not be seen as attracting alcoholics into the area as we only set up there because of the lack of resources for the homeless alcoholics who were already there. So far little specific comment has been made to us by local residents about the work of the shop fronts, which may seem much less threatening than residential units with their greater notion of permanence.

Shop-front offices now seem to us to be a valuable part of the skid row complex. If they are not to become too sucked into that complex they need to be constantly re-examined. The above account is of some of the general issues viewed in the light of the previously untested statements in the report. What follows is an account of the practical working of one of the shop fronts in the Project. It is worth noting that a government circular (Department of Health and Social Security, 1973) has drawn attention to the shop-front work at least indicating that some of the work we describe should be developed elsewhere.

One voluntary body, the Alcoholics Recovery Project, has been providing skilled social work help in walk-in 'shop front' offices in parts of Lambeth and Southwark where vagrant alcoholics congregate; this work is still being evaluated but seems to offer a way of reaching alcoholics who would shun other approaches (paragraph 7).

The Kennington shop front

The shop-front office at Kennington was one of the three offices that the Project established. It had as its area of operation the triangle stretching between Camberwell, Waterloo and the Elephant and Castle, thereby including parts of the boroughs of Southwark and Lambeth. Before the shop front opened its door for the first time, preliminary work had been done in the area. Key agencies, statutory and voluntary, had been contacted by the Project; clergymen and other interested individuals in the area had been approached. It was clear there was an indigent vagrant alcoholic population. Kennington and surrounding areas were full of resources for the vagrant alcoholic, and well suited to be the setting for a shop-front office. Yet, with the exception of St Luke's Centre run by the West London Mission, there were few long-term rehabilitation facilities. This may have influenced the local view of the problem, for the homeless alcoholic was seen only to frequent the parks, and other public areas. Local residents and helping agencies were thus concerned about and frustrated by repeated attempts to tackle the 'problem'. There was one Salvation Army lodging house in the area, and several other lodging houses in close proximity. Park-keepers and local residents were concerned about the number of 'horizontal meffers' in the parks. Local hospitals had not yet made any clear statement defining their responsibility for the homeless alcoholics in the area.

In summary, there was apparently no clear way in which the vagrant could be linked up to effective help and rehabilitation; meanwhile local frustration was increasing. For example, shortly before the office opened, a pavement seat intended for the benefit of the community had been removed on the grounds that it was attracting too many vagrant alcoholics into the area. We were fortunate however to have the co-operation of the vicar of St Anselm's church at Kennington Cross. He and his wife had been concerned by the high incidence of vagrant alcoholics in the area and in particular by the demands which the men had made on them. They gladly offered us the use of the parish office as a shop front for two hours each day. We had no guidelines to follow; we could only remain flexible and hope that we could learn rapidly from experience. During the first three months of the at times chaotic office, a pattern emerged which has provided the basis for the office's eventual structure. In order to outline the development of the shop front, we need now to look at some of the key areas of operation.

(i) *Setting-up the office*

The very first day of opening (1 September 1970) was not quite as memorable as some of the days that were to come. It was exciting and yet depressing to be sitting alone (initially the office was staffed by only one worker) in the parish office at the back of the church, on hard church chairs, surrounded by the hymn books and the surplices still scattered around after the previous evening's choir practice. After about an hour, without even the interruption of the telephone, the heavy oak door opened and in walked an elderly man, cider bottle in hand! The very first customer! He proved to be already a regular visitor at the church and was one of the original reasons for the concern expressed by the vicar and his wife. On calling at the vicarage that day, he had been referred to us – probably to his astonishment. Years later this particular man was still visiting the office. During this time he has never once stopped drinking in order to 'indulge' in sobriety. Nevertheless, there have been occasions when we have been able to assist him beyond the welcome cups of tea. What was important initially was that he was well known to all the drinking men in the Kennington area. On that first day, we explained our hopes of encouraging men to come to the office, and in following weeks, he was an invaluable contact. He spread the word on the grapevine about the shop front so that more and more men heard about its existence.

From the outset, we wished to be seen as a place where alcoholics on the street could spend two hours each day. The men were so used to being kept out of lodging houses during the day, and often were only acceptable to other agencies provided they offered a legitimate reason for attending, for example by claiming social security benefit or requesting medical care. We felt, therefore, that it would be useful to explore ways of making contact with the men on the street without establishing any criteria for eligibility. What we did offer to the alcoholics was an unlimited supply of tea, warmth, and specialized assistance. We were not just looking for alcoholics whom we felt to be already motivated towards wanting help. There was no onus on the men to commit themselves to long-term sobriety in order to be accepted at the office. No formal admission procedure to the shop front existed. Men were free to come and go, to ask for or to refuse a confidential interview with the Project worker. Material hand-outs were not available. We did not wish to deter clients from seeking help for their long-term needs by implying that material short-term help was our only resource. We had no wish to appear as if we were 'bribing' men to the shop front.

Although there were no formal controls on behaviour, no written rules of 'no drinking' pinned up on the walls, we did ask men not to drink while inside the office on the occasions when this activity arose. As time went on, we found that the sober men attending the office would themselves make it clear that, although it was all right to drink outside, drinking inside was showing disrespect for the office and its workers. The same applied when a man's behaviour, such as threatening violence, was perceived by the sober group as destructive to the effective running of the shop front.

While the grapevine was absorbing the news that a new place had opened, we were meanwhile inviting statutory and voluntary agencies to refer alcoholics to the shop front. It was suggested that they refer clients to the shop front whenever they felt that a man might benefit from the type of support and help the office was able to give. Agencies with little knowledge of the rehabilitation hostels and their selection procedure; agencies unable to deal effectively with the alcoholic because of work pressure and a statutory obligation to give other groups more priority; agencies who required a 'second opinion', all were involved in close discussion with us. Once a man had been referred, it was important that we kept close contact with the referring agency; this we hoped would increase the latter's understanding of the facilities available. So through our own groundwork and the men's grapevine we believed that the men on the streets would hear about us. Curiosity, unfounded hopes of receiving material hand-outs, a commitment to sobriety, all led men to the office. An important service, operating at the grass roots, began.

(ii) *The shop fronts in operation*

We shall look at three main areas of operation:

(a) *The daily routine*

(b) *The range of customers and their needs*

(c) *Response to customers' needs*

(a) *The daily routine* The office was opened for two hours each weekday. The first task was to make the tea. This was usually done by the men who also saw that everything was cleared away at the end of each session. An automatic kettle replaced its burnt-out predecessor; plastic beakers were used on the grounds that they were more hygienic and less dangerous than the original china mugs! Those customers familiar with the shop-front routine might in this opening period request an individual interview with the worker in the adjacent room. Also, as they walked into the shop front the worker made a mental note of those individuals she wished to see. New customers too had to be welcomed and helped to feel at ease. Worker and customers together then made tentative arrangements to cover the remainder of the session.

Following additional staff appointments in 1972 the availability of two extra workers for the two-hour daily session made a vast difference to the type and quality of service offered. Rapport between worker and customer had been encouraged from the outset. The presence of additional staff, especially staff who had themselves been on skid row for a number of years and had first-hand experience of many of the problems that were raised, meant that rapport was easier to establish.

The immediate advantages of this additional staffing were threefold. First, while one worker was conducting interviews, two workers were now structuring a positive strategy in the waiting-room. Although men had usually formed a cohesive group in there, the presence of additional staff meant that there was much more opportunity to relate to each other and discuss mutual problems. Customers had never been encouraged to remain isolated while in the shop front. Conversations among themselves and with the worker, when available, had always been developed rather than staff allowing a man to retreat behind a newspaper. But the dangers of men feeling anxious about entering what appeared from the outside to be a well-established group were now much better tackled by the presence of the additional workers. The latter's presence helped remove the negative culture that could easily occur in the waiting-room. It became therefore increasingly difficult for customers to perceive the shop front in the same way that they viewed the more (for them) traditional and familiar crypts where they were expected to queue to be admitted, to queue for any hand-outs such as soup or tea, to queue for interviews with crypt helpers (if help was provided) and then afterwards to sit alone waiting to be told it was time to leave. Bahr (1973, p. 151) has commented on 'the general sense of perpetual waiting imposed on the homeless man'. Some of the habits from the traditional approach were inevitably brought by the men to the shop front. The removal of these habits, or barriers, was seen by the worker as demanding high priority, and the possibility of this change was enhanced by the presence of the additional staff.

Second, customer expectation from the office could now be determined prior to the individual interview with the social worker. Lazare (1972) suggests that patient requests are closely related to the concept of patient expectations. Expectations differ, in that they represent the anticipation of roles, techniques, duration of treatment and outcome. Although Lazare's experience was in the American hospital setting, we would suggest that there is an equal need to determine the full range of patients' expectations of the shop front. On skid row, there was little doubt that stories from friends and previous relationships with helping agencies tended to shape men's expectations of what the shop front could offer. Discussion about the various helping agencies was a major ingredient of the skid row sub-culture. Men arriving at the shop front could easily make unrealistic requests from us, or alternatively, their prejudices tended to prevent other requests from being articulated. The presence of two workers in the waiting-room meant that customers had an opportunity to discuss why they had visited the office; why on that particular day rather than last week or last month, and what they hoped the service would provide for them. Often, previous experience with other agencies, where they perceived material hand-outs, however limited, to be the only assistance given, caused the alcoholic to be rather reluctant to acknowledge what he felt to be his real needs. By talking among themselves, and with the workers (especially the recovered alcoholics) and perhaps by drawing on the experience of sober men already in hostels but still visiting the shop front, it became easier to make specific requests to the social workers in the shop front.

One man compared his reception at the shop front with that at a more traditional, voluntary agency:

'I would wait there and then be told that I would get to see a social worker – someone I knew to be good. I'd be given a cup of tea if I was lucky, asked how things were going, tell him I was skippering. He [the social worker] would get out the case sheets – study them – and ask me whether I had ever really tried to stop drinking. I'd reply that I would like to, but didn't know how to. Then he'd tell me that they couldn't do anything. Maybe if I was lucky they would give me a bus ticket to a lodging house, a voucher for one night's kip, two shillings for tobacco, all of which was a passport to social security the following day. This was where it ended – it never went any further . . . they had done their duty . . . given all the help they could offer.'

It was therefore crucial that customers at the shop-front office were given every opportunity to talk over in an informal manner these feelings so that they themselves were able to identify what it was they were seeking; then to be reassured by the social workers that any decision taken about stopping drinking would be taken seriously by the staff and acted upon accordingly. Wherever possible it would certainly not end with a bus ticket to a lodging house. For the alcoholic, knowing that there existed a place where he would be accepted and where the other people there, be they customers or workers, demonstrated their concern for him as a person, was important. It might take many visits for him to be reassured that constructive help was available, that people there would encourage him to work out for himself why he was there and what, if anything, he was looking for. In this way he was then able to make appropriate requests in a confidential interview with the social worker.

Especially significant was that a sense of belonging often accompanied the alcoholic when he was away from the shop front, which suggested the value of the way we operated.

'My last appearance at court . . . the Probation Officer, she stood up in the court, and said that I was under the Alcoholics Recovery Project and trying very hard. The magistrate gave me and a mate of mine 'a day'. Coming out of court, we begged 60p in the waiting room for a drink. We were absolutely desperate . . . from the hangover and the sickness. I'd been told to go straight to the shop front by the Probation Officer . . . my mate went off and bought the wine. . . . I never touched it but went straight over to Kennington. I was sick, sick of drink. And I didn't want a drink. I had to go to Kennington, although I didn't want to go. I could have cried for a bottle of wine an hour before . . . when it was there I didn't want it. That was almost two years ago and I haven't had a drink since.'

A third advantage of the additional staffing was that the presence of the recovered alcoholic provided a positive support for those men thinking about sobriety. 'If he can do it, why can't I?' was a frequent reflection. When hostel referrals were particularly slow and temporary accommodation in common lodging houses was a necessary, although unwelcome, part of the programme, the recovered alcoholic was able to identify with the problem at hand, giving encouragement in a way the other staff could not. The alcoholic might also begin to feel acutely dissatisfied with his own circumstances, resolving to make certain changes in his own life. This in itself was anxiety-producing and needed to be skilfully handled by the worker. The presence of recovered alcoholics as workers was again invaluable. The men still drinking saw the recovered alcoholic as one of the few people he could genuinely trust; this was especially true for those men who had been drinking over a long period of time, who had often said they felt a barrier between themselves and orthodox social workers. Employing a recovered alcoholic in this capacity required that he be given as much support as possible and constant opportunity to discuss the different issues arising in the course of a day's work. It was easy for the recovered alcoholic on the staff to find himself less and less contented as he continually found himself face to face with the kind of situations which did not appear to have any immediate solution. We shall look at these issues in more detail in the next chapter.

(b) *The range of customers and their needs*   Numbers attending daily at the shop front vary from three to twenty-three. The perception of the vagrant alcoholic at the shop front as 'customer' rather than 'client' was deliberate. We did not wish a service, operating at a grass roots level, to be perceived by the target population as yet another agency where goods would be handed out to the deserving alcoholic, thereby placing him in a begging, dependent or supplicant position. The ideal, we felt, would be to involve the alcoholic in a discussion about his present position and need. As the providers of the service, we had no wish to dictate the future course of action for the alcoholic; we preferred him to be in a position where he had some element of choice. We felt choice to be crucial.

Although choice is invariably restricted by outside constraints such as high occupancy rates in both hospitals and rehabilitation hostels, we nevertheless felt that the means of establishing choice could in practice be as important as the end itself. Coleman (1968) has argued in another context that the American hospital emergency service should develop into a primary clinic treating patients with illnesses associated with poverty. He believes that persons who live in a 'culture of poverty' have suffered from a 'persistent erosion of their sense of self esteem, and self respect, which drastically interferes with their ability to assert a claim to rights and privileges which for most of us seem a matter of course'. We recognized this comment as being valid outside its particular medical context. We therefore sought to recognize clients as customers whose requests are usually legitimate. It would clearly seem preferable that the vagrant alcoholic should play as active a part as possible in the planning of any programme which will hopefully lead to sobriety, rather than be termed unmotivated if our directions are not accepted.

We have already made reference to the importance we place on the waiting-room situation. It is here worth noting what Coleman (ibid.) again has to say of the hospital setting. He suggests that the fact that staff and patient keep each other at a distance emotionally, socially and communicatively, accounts for the patient's inability to organize his expectations of care in such a way as to call forth the desired response in others, or even constructive responses in himself. This is further reinforced by the transiency of an emergency situation. At the shop front, however, distance of any kind, be it social, emotional or communicative is discouraged; ultimately it is the customers who are making the demands on us and not vice versa. Alcoholics come to us for a whole range of different reasons. When one particular man was asked his reason for seeking help, his reply was fairly representative of many alcoholics seen at the shop front.

'I'd go in the first place to try and con them . . . to get money for a bottle of wine . . . yet many times, I'd go along there even with a bottle of wine on me. . . . I would go to talk with someone . . . yet I wanted a drink again afterwards . . . yet I did want to stop drinking, even though I was carrying wine on me. I felt my life was ruined . . . upside down. . . . I wanted reassurance, looking back on it . . . to be told that I would do something with my life . . . wanting to talk . . . wanting to get away from the drinking team . . . to talk to a human being for a change, and not to the boys who couldn't understand . . . to talk to someone not leading the same life as I was leading.'

These comments reflect the ambivalence felt at different times by the man on the street. Wanting and yet not wanting sobriety; wanting to be out of the skid row sub-culture, but unsure of how this can be done; making token gestures to stop drinking, but back-pedalling when help is or is not forthcoming; always feeling that the help available is inadequate in that it stops short by not providing entry into the rehabilitation facilities.

The mix of customer needs produces an atmosphere conducive to customers talking freely about whatever they like. In this context social distance is reduced; problems, hopes, and anxieties are brought forward rather than suppressed, enabling the customer to participate more fully in making realistic demands on the staff, and being better able to identify his own needs.

Customers may be self-referred or agency-referred. They may be drinking, sober or in need of detoxification. They may be already well known to us or arriving for the very first time. They may already have crystal-clear expectations of what the office can do for them or they may be very unsure and initially anxious to explore various possibilities either with the social worker or with each other. Others may be sober, already placed in alcoholic hostels, but not yet in employment. The latter's sobriety and gradually changing attitudes can be invaluable to the learning experience present in the shop front.

There seems to us a marked difference between the men who are self-referred and those who are agency-referred. We have found that very often referrals from other agencies arrive with the impression that we will give them immediate help, or as one of us described it, 'expecting us to wave some magic wand to get them into hospital or accommodation straight away'. This occurs despite our efforts to educate agencies by informing them that immediate gratification of short-term needs is unlikely at the shop front. We have always stressed that customers should not arrive with fixed expectations. Self-referrals tend to be better prepared by the other men on the street and are rather more likely, in our experience, to want to replace their incessant drinking with sobriety, which often requires referral on to an alcoholic hostel. It is easier for the man in these circumstances to state that he is willing to work within whatever plans are finally but jointly decided upon, however long the waiting period, and as long as he feels that there is an end in sight.

What are some of the customer needs? The vagrant alcoholic attending the Kennington shop-front office has produced all manner of crisis situations in which homelessness, withdrawal from alcohol, indiscriminate pill-taking, medical complications, despair, threats of suicide, aggression, and merely the need for human contact, regularly appear. The crises of the vagrant alcoholic are sometimes medical, but more often they take non-medical forms.

If we consider change to be a central notion to the concept of crisis, and if alcoholic and worker together perceive a state of affairs to be dangerous, threatening and anxiety-producing, then the emphasis is on using that crisis as a learning experience. For example, a crisis situation for one alcoholic may revolve around the fact that he has no place to go, not even temporary accommodation which is acceptable to him, though it has been said by one recovered alcoholic that 'there is no such thing as an emergency in the life of a vagrant alcoholic; his life is one long chain of emergency situations, so regular that they are taken for granted.' Yet the man himself may suddenly feel that an everyday feature of his life (no place to go) has now reached the stage of a serious problem for which he is ready to look for help.

We would not like to suggest that all men perceive their first visit to the shop front as arising out of a crisis situation. Much depends upon the expectations the men have of the office before they even reach it, and also the prevailing atmosphere once they arrive. As one alcoholic put it, some men are

'happy to be there, even though they have little money. They need to have a place to go to, which they can identify with. They could beg more money in a day than they have in a week, but they are happier this way, sitting there joking. They have a full tin of tobacco, as for the other men, those still drinking, it makes them realize that what they think is impossible for themselves, is possible.'

There are men still drinking who ask for nothing more than a place where they can sit at ease. Some of these men may at a future date ask for help to get sober; a few never make any demands.

It is crucial that we tell customers what we offer. This amounts to telling some men on some occasions that there is very little we can do. We would not however attempt to change a man's life-style without his first asking, but if he is shattered by his life-style and can see no way out, we may be able to demonstrate that there is an alternative. Then there are the men whose life-style is unlikely to change: men who may be older and thoroughly used to the lodging-house environment. They do not come asking for sobriety.

Talking of one man in this last category, one of the other men commented:

'For him, it's a place to have to turn to . . . his dependence if something goes wrong. The shop front is his next of kin . . . there are times when the shop-front staff can do nothing for the men and when the men are asking for nothing. They come here to have a chat; it lets them know they have friends. They know there's no financial gain . . . they're just looking for friendship. . . .'

Finally, we hope that by recognizing the range of customers' needs and by involving the man himself, with others, in looking at those needs, we thereby increase the possibilities of a successful referral on to other services.

(c) *Response to customers' needs* There have emerged two basic responses to crises at the shop front. First, there is the remedial response which seeks to alleviate suffering, and is largely based on the medical model. This occurs when the alcoholic is experiencing acute withdrawal, and medical care and attention is the appropriate help to obtain. In such a case the alcoholic is rarely learning from the experience; he simply requires medical attention which will relieve suffering. Second, we respond in less tangible ways to men looking for some rather ill-defined help for a state of affairs which has produced in them anxiety and concern, though not necessarily as yet a crisis. A man may not easily state why it is he needs to seek out support or comfort, but whatever his unhappiness or despair, he is more likely to express his feelings to a shop-front worker with whom, throughout his drinking, he has already developed a relationship. But it is the crises resulting from, for example, lack of accommodation, or maybe a sudden unaccountable desire to stop drinking, which best illustrates the contradictions inherent in the shop-front policy. We say we offer help; yet help is rarely *immediately* forthcoming. Our aim can only be to facilitate the alcoholic's understanding of what is happening to him, then for both the alcoholic and the social worker to sit down together to consider future action.

What are the factors which determine what kind of care and treatment the alcoholic receives? The problem of the skid row alcoholic is fundamentally different from the problem of the alcoholic in other sections of society. The emphasis is on making available the basic services that are provided as of right to most other persons. Severe drinking problems are only one category of difficulties afflicting the homeless alcoholic. One study (Chafetz, 1970, p. 59) gives reasons which in the author's opinion militate against homeless alcoholics receiving appropriate care from an American hospital emergency service. They suggest that such people are too frequently labelled unmotivated, unreachable and untreatable. This view does have some relevance for hospital services in England. Hospital walk-in settings, such as psychiatric emergency clinics, deal with a wide range of psychiatric problems. Inevitably such clinics can only view the alcoholic as one of the many categories of patient vying with each other for attention and beds. Ideally emergency services would exist for and be accessible to all persons who feel they need to make use of such a service. In practice, they cannot serve all who would use it, and hospital staff in consultation with us have expressed their anxieties about insufficient hospital resources for the vagrant alcoholic, and the frequent inappropriateness of the hospital setting to deal with crises which are often socially rather than medically based, but which nevertheless appear at the hospital clinic.

The role of the shop front, dealing with crises at a pre-hospital stage, has emerged in some circumstances as that of acting as spokesman for the vagrant alcoholic by building inroads into some present facilities which would otherwise be almost inaccessible to the vagrant alcoholic. Appropriate action for emergency situations is dependent on our being able to do this. There is also the fact that the shop front must whenever and wherever possible establish channels of communication with the providers of the services so that gaps in the existing treatment network can be reduced, leading ultimately to an effective and comprehensive treatment service network. For customers who arrive at the shop front in need of detoxification the immediate response of the shop-front staff is to attempt to link the alcoholic to a hospital or other appropriate medical facility as soon as possible. We have indicated that this is not an easy task and this situation is likely to continue until a detoxification facility is added to the range of community resources. Meanwhile the alcoholic will in all probability also appreciate the difficult nature of obtaining hospital admission (he knows the 'score' as well as the workers). But if he can be made aware of the effort and concern expended by the worker to obtain a hospital admission – he hears the telephone conversations made on his behalf – a relationship with the Project worker conducive to after-care follow-up is a likely outcome.

It is worth quoting a particular instance of how one alcoholic was encouraged by the staff and, above all, the customers in the waiting-room to consider hospital admission. On this occasion the shop-front workers and approximately five customers were sitting round the table in the waiting-room. All individual interviews were over, and thirty minutes were left before the office closed. Through the door walked an alcoholic, well known to all present, who had obviously been drinking heavily and sleeping rough over the last few days. To quote one man: 'He was bad, I knew he was – over the week he had been getting worse. I thought he was finished.' This particular man had never retained contact with the shop front long enough for us to be able to assist with any permanent arrangements, always disappearing after a few days and then returning drunk. On the occasions when he had secured hospital admission for himself (a difficult task) he never informed us of his whereabouts, and was inevitably discharged without adequate after-care arrangements being made.

The men in the office encouraged the man to join them at the table, despite his adamant refusal of tea, and his statement that he fully intended to leave immediately in order to 'find' another bottle, to cure the 'horrors' which seemed imminent. The men conveyed their concern to the alcoholic about his present condition and suggested that he should consider letting the shop-front staff assist with hospital admission, rather than depart to look for more drink. An hour later, long after the official closing time of the office, the man had decided he would benefit from hospital admission and the staff contacted the local psychiatric hospital. The duty doctor was given relevant details of the alcoholic's condition and agreed to see him at the hospital with a view to admission once it had been ascertained that the Project would provide after-care arrangements on discharge from the hospital. The following day, the same men attended the shop front. They had in fact accompanied the alcoholic to the hospital on the previous day, and had encouraged him to return to the shop front once it had been made clear by the duty doctor that, although hospital admission was thought to be urgent on medical grounds, no beds were in fact available. The doctor had suggested that the staff should contact a second hospital the next day. Consequently, the men made sure they were at the shop front to give the alcoholic all the encouragement he needed. It was one of them who accompanied him on the fourteen-mile journey to hospital once new arrangements had been made. He was visited regularly by staff and customers while in hospital and, a year later, he was still sober in an alcoholic hostel to which he had been referred on leaving the hospital. He remained in contact with the shop front.

This incident highlights the difficulties for the shop front in making referrals to medical facilities, but shows that due to the shop front's accessibility to the man on the street, and due to rapport between customers and workers, medical facilities can be made available.

If a man wishes to be referred to an alcoholic hostel, it is then the task of the worker to discuss whether this decision is appropriate and which hostel is to be considered. These discussions may take place either in the hospital setting, or more commonly at the shop front for those men who have not needed admission to hospital. The selection procedures of most hostels make it difficult for anyone to refer himself, and often require a future resident to wait anything from two to six weeks before finally being admitted. The shop front serves several purposes in such a waiting period. First, it is the task of the social worker to gather together the social history that is needed as a basis for referral to the alcoholic hostel which seems most appropriate to meet the man's needs. It is difficult to generalize about the criteria used, but such things as size of hostel, average age of residents, programme offered, and locality are all taken into consideration. Second, once the long-term goal of referral has been decided upon, short-term problems relating to temporary accommodation, financial assistance, and social security appointments need to be resolved. These can be attended to on a daily basis, for the customer is expected to attend the office each day until the referral procedure is completed. This waiting period prior to hostel admission has its advantages and disadvantages; on the one hand it offers the opportunity for the customer to adjust to the idea of a different way of living, but on the other hand it is usual for customers to express despondency if the waiting period is excessively long.

Daily attendance at the shop front is likely to throw up a number of the man's problems, and these can be tackled. Apprehensions about expectations the receiving hostel may place on him, anxiety about the need to look for work once in the hostel, fears about how successfully he will adapt to the hostel – all are frequently expressed, and can be taken up by the worker. This is then an ideal setting in which to help prepare the alcoholic for his future in the hostel. Additionally, his regular contact with the office provides a firm basis for the relationship between customer and worker which will extend through to the hostel stage, and hopefully beyond that. Very often men awaiting hostel admission also gain immense support, advice and information from men already in a hostel but still visiting the shop front on an occasional basis. It is worth noting that the latter's presence gives support to the staff, by helping us to realize that out of numerous visits made to the shop front, some men do happily progress to a state of sustained sobriety!

The difficulties created by the waiting period must be seen in the context of the alcoholic's relationship to his own environment. He is expected to stay sober while simultaneously remaining in the drinking culture from which he is trying to escape. Temporary accommodation in lodging houses, lack of money, no place to go during the day, all illustrate the stress of surviving the initial stages of sobriety without having yet moved away from the culture which reinforces heavy drinking. The shop front, with its restricted opening times, can only go some way in meeting the need of men in this position, but for those two hours at least it can offer a more positive environment than for example the parks or lodging houses where the drinking culture is dominant.

As has been stated, the staff at the shop front retain contact with the alcoholic once he has been successfully referred on. In retaining contact and providing further support it is essential to be aware that the social worker may well be perceived by both residents and hostel

6

staff of both our own and other organizations, as a 'middle-man – a general peace-maker' between themselves. Outwardly, a man may appear to be very strong, self-supporting, but even so, may be hiding problems. It is fair to say that men in hostels look forward to a visit from the social worker. But because of the nature of residential work, it is easy for the men to perceive the hostel staff as 'them', as 'the people who put you out, back on the streets, if you do something wrong'. By comparison, they tend to regard the shop-front worker in a different light: 'someone who does not reject', 'a personal friend who has done something for you', remembering that in the very early stages of sobriety, the shop-front worker may well have been their major source of support and friendship.

Regardless of whether these feelings are right or wrong, the shop-front worker needs to be very skilled in his dealings with hostels. Both he and hostel staff need to have confidence in each other if tensions are to be avoided. The length and quality of the relationship between customer and worker is sometimes no more important than that between worker and hostel staff. Ideally the relationship between alcoholic and social worker will survive beyond the hostel and will continue once the man moves out into his own flat or bedsitter. Experience has shown that this final stage of complete 're-entry' into the community demands very regular contact and support from social workers. For example, it is important that the man securing his own flat should feel able to contact the worker if, and when, difficulties arise. He will welcome visits and the opportunity to entertain guests in his 'very own place'.

The shop front does of course receive visits from those men now back on the streets after a period in one of the various rehabilitation hostels. Although the rehabilitation hostels offer a wide variety of approaches, almost all apply the rule of 'no drinking'. A man is asked to leave if he commences drinking, regardless of his length of stay in the house. Re-admission may be considered in the next few weeks, but this depends on individual circumstances. But for the time being at least, the man is asked to leave. Similarly, the man in his own accommodation is unlikely to be able to keep up his rent payments if he returns to drinking. Should the alcoholic at any stage return to drinking, he is quickly caught up once more in the vicious circle of homelessness and imprisonment. He is rejected from the hostel, but he is not barred from the shop front. The fact that the shop front in the past has been a permanent feature of his drinking and of his sobriety makes it easier for him once again to seek contact, despite his feeling that he is 'back to square one'. The continuity of care which we seek to offer means that, if requested, the referral procedure can start again. The shop-front worker may find it easier to make future referrals based on a review with the man of his past progress and the difficulties encountered.

There are, however, inherent problems in this. Alcoholics wishing to renegotiate the alcoholic rehabilitation network for a second, third or even fourth time may well find themselves regarded as 'unhelpable' by many of the hostels. Agencies can take the view that, if a man has not achieved sobriety on his first or second attempt, then the hostel is unlikely to be able to offer a man the means to achieving sobriety at the third attempt. Thus the man who is very well known to the alcoholic hostels may find himself refused even before a selection interview takes place. This places the shop-front worker in a difficult position, since it is the latter who must relay the information to a man who may very well have had high expectations of being readmitted to the hostel of his choice. To avoid unwelcome consequences of his rejection, it is essential that the customer is constantly kept informed of the position he is in and can discuss with the social worker the reason for his possible rejection.

The implications of this are that lack of resources often makes it difficult to help those men who are ex-residents of several alcoholic hostels. This does not mean to say that everything is not done to link these men to a hostel once they are sober again. Men who fall into this category are, however, aware of their past record of failure and consequently do not seem always to seek out help quite so readily. They start to see themselves as total failures, realizing that even chances of hospital admission for drying out, often the very first essential step, become more and more remote. Over the years, we have concentrated as much effort as possible into discussing this problem with all hostels and persuading them very often that a man we feel has made good progress deserves yet another chance. We have no way of knowing when the time is 'right' for a man to stop drinking, but we should be concerned enough to begin working towards providing sufficient hostel beds rather than simply expressing despondency about the situation.

By no means all the customers request constructive help for a drinking problem. As was pointed out earlier, many men call and do not ask for anything, other than to sit, chat, drink tea, maybe have a wash and shave and enquire how their mates are faring. A few come with the intention of begging money from someone at the office, sometimes showing aggressive tendencies towards other customers, workers, or both. These have all been dealt with reasonably success-

fully and, on occasions, outbursts of violence have been put to constructive use by serving as a useful learning experience, later to be
examined by customers and worker together. For other men it is
enough merely to make doctors' appointments, dental appointments,
opticians' appointments, phone calls about their work. We seek to
respond to all customers' needs without ever exerting pressure on
them to express a commitment to sobriety.

It should be abundantly clear from the above that how effective
we are in responding to customers' needs is determined partly by
our own skills and sensitivity and partly by our relationship with
other agencies. Yet over-reliance on other facilities can easily reduce
the shop front to a 'people-processing' agency (Hasenfield, 1972)
and not allow it any role as a 'people-changing' agency (Ventner,
1963). Our efforts to respond adequately to the men at the shop front
and to liaise effectively with other agencies need to be viewed in the
context of seeing ourselves in both the processing business and the
changing business.

If a long-term relationship does develop with an individual, then
there may well be opportunities to assist in his move away from skid
row. The absence of such a relationship does not mean, however,
that the worker would have no part to play in any change that might
occur in the man. As already stated, referrals-on are a key element
of the work of the shop front and can often be a time of stress and
uncertainty for the man. Chafetz (1970, pp. 211–12) cites inter-
agency referral procedures as a major problem in motivating people
to help when they are in stress. Ryan (1969, p. 51) goes further in
stating that most referral practices in social and medical agencies
(in America) 'do not work and they involve many distressed persons
in a process that does not provide them with help and that doubt-
less leads to increased frustration and unhappiness on their part'.
In the shop fronts we have sought to avoid these dangers. Referral
is a lot more than pointing the man hopefully in the 'right' direction.
It requires a great deal of discussion with the alcoholic involved and
a detailed, up-to-date knowledge of the facility to which he might
be referred. This may read as obvious. We wish it were. It is not
uncommon for the Project to receive telephone referrals when the
man concerned has not even been asked how he sees his drinking
problem. 'Does he actually want to stop drinking?' 'I will go and
ask him.'

There is finally then the problem for the staff of navigating entry
into the facility that seems most appropriate for the particular alcoholic
being helped. Selection procedures for example differ from hostel

to hostel, as do the prevailing values hostels adhere to. Some hostels request only that we phone them, tell them the customer's name we wish them to see, and then send him along to meet the warden. He may be admitted immediately. On the other hand some hostels ask for a full social enquiry report, request the man to wait a few weeks before his interview and possibly ask him to visit them for a period of anything up to a week before they finally accept or reject him. We need to have at our finger-tips the details of each different selection procedure.

Conclusions

So far in this chapter we have examined the general principles which were embodied in the original concept of the shop front. We then examined in detail the problems of one such office. In this final section we present statistical data concerning the first two complete years of operation of all the shop fronts of the Project. We hope to show in hard outline how the shop fronts were in fact used and what was their immediate effect.

Table 2 Sources of referral to the shop fronts, 1970–2

	Number of individuals	% of total referrals
Social Security offices, Reception Centres	97	14·9
All hospitals	45	6·9
Prison	69	10·7
Probation and after-care service	123	18·9
Self-referral	212	32·6
Clergy	34	5·2
Others, e.g. park-keepers, AA	70	10·8
Total	650	100

The figures in Table 2 cover two full years for two shop fronts and eighteen months for the third shop front. When we compared the second with the first year there were no major differences in the sources of referral. The actual number of individuals seen did drop by almost 50 per cent in the second year; this is partly explained by one shop front, running down to closure in January 1972. We did in any case expect a drop in numbers for two reasons. First, some men initially call in at any new venture to 'sus it out' and may not really be interested in what it has to offer. Second, and much more important, the social workers themselves were less willing to take on too many new men after they had already built up a large number of contacts during the first year. Some men continued to visit one or other of the shop fronts throughout the first two years; and others who were now sober enjoyed being visited in hostel or lodgings. There was therefore a physical limit to the number of new men who could honourably be taken on.

The sources of referral show two clear factors. First there is the considerable use made of the shop fronts by the statutory services – half of all referrals coming from the statutory agencies. This serves as a useful illustration of how much these agencies do use voluntary bodies. Local authority social service departments, however, made so few referrals that they have not been included as a separate category. That situation arises because homeless alcoholics do not yet see such social service departments as an appropriate source of help. Second, there is the proportion of self-referrals, one-third, which would seem to indicate that we have been strategically placed to 'reach out' to the homeless alcoholic. (In the Kennington shop front the self-referral rate was as high as 42 per cent, showing that in an area having few other rehabilitation facilities men will themselves begin to explore the possibilities of help.)

Table 3   Outcome of referrals from the shop fronts, 1970–2

Outcome	No. of placements	%
Residence in Reception Centre	303	34·8
Admission to hospital	148	17·0
Admission to alcoholic hostel	179	20·6
Lodgings	80	9·1
Lodging house	48	5·5
Back to families	20	2·3
No action	93	10·7
Total	871	100

In Table 3 we examine the initial outcome of the referrals to the shop fronts. The first comment to be made is that the total number of placements exceeds the total numbers of individuals in Table 2, since some men had several immediate placements as a result of their visits to the shop fronts. For example, one man might be admitted to hospital for a few days and then move to an alcoholic hostel.

Second, the numbers placed initially in the Reception Centre came almost entirely from the shop-front office in Camberwell, which reflects the willingness of homeless men in Camberwell to use positively the Reception Centre as well as the skill of the particular social worker in assisting men into residence who might otherwise have avoided help altogether.

Third, it should be noted that nearly one-fifth of the placements were in hospitals, which reflects the fairly high level of medical need among the men, either related specifically to alcoholism or to more general health matters.

Fourth, we would comment that, allowing for those men who broke off contact after only one or two visits, there was only a small group with whom no action was possible or desired. Some initial steps were almost always possible with most of the men.

Table 4   Number of visits made to the shop fronts, 1970–2

No. of visits	No. of men involved	%
1–3	196	30·2
4–10	222	34·1
11–20	104	16·1
21 or more	99	15·2
No record	29	4·4
Total	650	100

In Table 4 we show the rate of visits made by the men to the shop fronts. To lose contact with one-third of the men after three visits or less would seem at best careless; at worst it would show how ill-equipped we still were to meet the needs of the homeless alcoholic in general. However, no agency hits the jackpot every time, and there is some limited comparative evidence available to suggest some do rather worse. Studies of three probation offices dealing with homeless ex-offenders showed that between a half and three-quarters of the clients only made one to three visits (Home Office, 1970, p. 29).

The trends that we have referred to in Tables 2 to 4 continued in 1973 when only two shop fronts were in operation. There were no major changes in the source of referral; self-referrals continued at about a third. Numbers of new referrals dropped to 120 – fortunately for us. The outcome of the visits to the shop fronts was similar, though admissions to alcoholic rehabilitation hostels rose to 36·1 per cent compared with 20·6 per cent in 1970–2. Apart from new referrals, there was also a total of 187 old referrals with whom active involvement continued in 1973. For example, of this 187, forty-nine were admitted into alcoholic hostels and twenty-one into hospitals. Unfortunately, what we never really know is how many men referred to us never arrived. All we can say is that, of these men who actually walk in through the doors, the degree of contact maintained is higher than might be expected.

The number of visits made to us does not of course take account of the number of visits made to the men when they are resident in hospitals or hostels. Even more important, it does not show the length of contact, which can also be an indication of the strength and value of the relationship. We felt it crucial to examine this aspect more closely. We therefore took one sample of 100 men and found that, twelve months later, 47 per cent were still in contact by letter, telephone or personal visit. On another sample of 102 it was found that, after eighteen months, 27 per cent were still in contact. In neither sample, of course, can continuity of contact automatically be equated with sobriety. Finally, the frequency of contact given in Table 4 for all the shop fronts conceals some remarkable achievements. In the second year at Kennington, for example, 26 per cent of the men called on twenty-one or more occasions: called, it should be remembered, at a church vestry offering no hand-outs, but housing social workers willing to explore openly the possibilities of help. It is here the concept of an agency fitting the 'client' becomes a reality, not just an impossible ideal. Shop-front offices might well have as their sub-title 'What price motivation now?'

5 OTHER WORK OF THE PROJECT

In the previous two chapters I have looked at the early stages of the Project and the work of the shop fronts. This chapter tries to draw together some other activities of the Project. I intend to look at five such themes: specific studies, the hostels, an information service, co-ordination and the alcoholic as helper.

Specific studies

From time to time various services with whom we are in contact have expressed concern at their own involvement with the homeless alcoholic, be he presented as an offender or patient. In response to these statements the staff has felt it important to try to look more closely at this concern and to see in what way the agency and we ourselves can better understand and deal with the problem. We have therefore on occasions conducted specific enquiries of an action-research nature. These have been intended to focus the concern of the particular agency on the alcoholic problem; to inform us better of the true nature and extent of the problem; to provide data as a base from which a more effective service might be provided; and to demonstrate the value of a flexible combination of social work and research. To dignify our studies with the term research is probably to give them a status they barely warrant. None the less, they were an attempt to head in that direction. Failure to look at the general picture in an agency can lead to hasty generalizations of an anecdotal nature which do little to illuminate the problem. The constant round of dealing with one apparently awkward alcoholic after another can produce an angry but unrealistic view of the total problem, which might not, for example, take into account the alcoholics who are not awkward and who do not come for help. With our enquiries, we wished to get much closer to the problem with all its subtleties and contradictions. At various times we carried out small action-research projects in two courts, a prison, a lodging house and a hospital.

(i) The Courts

We knew that the local magistrates' courts were dealing annually with hundreds of drunkenness offenders. It seemed essential therefore to see if there was any way in which we could understand more about the homeless alcoholic in court and intervene to assist him or her where appropriate. Some attention certainly had to be given to this area when we considered that in the last six months of 1970 one local magistrates' court heard 1,508 drunkenness charges. Further, in one year, the borough of Southwark had approximately 4,000 arrests for drunkenness. There have been previous local studies of the drunkenness offender before the courts (Gath, 1968). Also some American studies have reported court work with drunkenness offenders, though these have been programmes of rehabilitation directly linked to the court, such as attending a judge's evening class on alcoholism, or placing men on probation with a condition of attending a fixed rehabilitation programme (Brunner-Orne, 1951; Grosz, 1972). We have so far not been in a position to develop such schemes, nor are the results of these other programmes sufficiently encouraging to make us try. Initially we decided to work at Tower Bridge magistrates' court seeing drunkenness offenders on one morning a week after the case had been heard. This was done with a view to referring them either to our shop-front office a few hundred yards from the court, or to arrange hospital admission if men were felt to need this. Over ten weeks only twenty-five men were seen at the court and few of these took up subsequent appointments. One man was dealt with by the court, though in a state of delirium tremens, and was then admitted to hospital through the Project's worker.

Given the number of drunkenness offenders passing through the court on any one morning, we wondered why we had seen so few. Frequently we noticed that a man's craving for drink was such that he literally ran from the court once free. One man who ran past us, stopped, turned back and asked what we wanted. He was told this was an experimental exercise to . . . there was no chance to say any more. The man retorted with 'I don't want to be part of any experiment' and rushed away. On other occasions the court officers did not direct the offenders to the social worker, partly we felt because they saw the clients as too hopeless or our efforts as too inadequate. We came to the conclusion that a worker was needed at court every morning to see the drunkenness offenders before they appeared in court. Two years later we were to have the chance to do part of that. In 1971 a new court was opened at Camberwell Green, serving an area of south-east London well known for the vagrant alcoholic problem. Soon there was a monthly average of 200 drunkenness offenders. Section thirty-four of the Criminal Justice Act 1972 gave authorization to the police to take drunkenness 'offenders' to medical centres rather than the courts, when the former had been set up and approved by the Secretary of State for Health and Social Services. We were very interested to find out whether the drunkenness offenders currently going through the courts saw themselves as needing medical attention; and further what problem, if any, they presented that could be met by existing provision. Accordingly at the request of the chief stipendary magistrate and with the co-operation of the jailers and the probation service, we undertook in 1972 an investigation of the drunkenness offenders appearing at the court (Hershon, 1974).

On a series of Thursday and Saturday mornings we saw all the drunkenness offenders who had not been bailed and before they went into court. In all, over eighteen mornings, 132 offenders were inter-viewed and adequate information obtained. Only seven women were seen. Much of the basic data confirmed what we knew, that the habitual drunkenness offender is frequently homeless, out of work, single and middle-aged. There were more men in current employment (one-third) than we had anticipated. Over half the total sample had eleven or more previous convictions for drunkenness; a half had two or more previous convictions for other offences. We were particularly interested in how they saw their problems, what, if anything, had been done in the past about these and whether we could do anything now. Almost half felt they had no problems, while in contrast about 5 per cent presented a multiplicity of problems. Most saw their difficulties as social not medical, only a third were positive that they were alcoholics, though even then they did not see that the medical services were the relevant services for their problem. The men's previous contact with other social-medical agencies, as declared by the men, was minimal. Only forty-four admitted any previous contact with a relevant agency, including Alcoholics Anonymous. For forty-three cases, social work action was now recom-mended, for ten cases psychiatric help and for one, general medical help. Only fourteen men took the matter further, including two admitted to hospital and four into alcoholic hostels. There was a low take-up rate of the help that we were able to offer.

The interviews and work that were done at the court led us to conclude that in the court setting there are too many factors militating against effective help of the drunkenness offender. The limitations reflect not so much the motivation of the individual offender but the process of which he is inescapably a part.

First, although the psychiatrist and social workers were experienced with alcoholics, the fact is that for some men sitting in the court cells and who may well have been through the court process forty or fifty times, the sudden arrival of well-meaning officials was probably too much for them; certainly they were suspicious and guarded. Why should they suddenly respond to the offer of help? What was in it for them and for us? To some extent they may have even felt compelled to be interviewed. We found for example on one occasion, when the jailers did not call the men out to see us but left us to go alone into the various cells, that we had the highest refusal rate for any one visit. This would suggest that when the jailer asked the man to come and be seen, the interviewee felt he had no option.

Second, there is a danger in a superabundance of help being offered and of the system subtly replacing 'you have to be punished' with 'you have to be helped'. Men who are resistant and suspicious do not want to be cajoled either into help or punishment but really given an option, with time to think about it.

Third, the court setting is institutional and men tend to answer the questions just because they believe it may help us rather than them as 'no one can really help me in any case'. They seem to have a general belief that alcoholism (if they accept it as a problem) cannot be cured. Their passive, rather accepting characters made it difficult to tackle the problem seriously in the time available.

Fourth, the men by no means define themselves as having a problem. To some of them a court appearance, another drunkenness charge, is merely part of their life-style and not something too serious or important; certainly not something requiring the intervention of a psychiatrist or social worker. A hostel resident has described to me his 'social drinking' as getting very drunk, being barred from pubs, having blackouts, and waking up in the front garden in the early hours of the morning! When this social drinking took place it was not, in his terms, a problem.

Fifth, there is a general principle that the occasion of a man's need is not necessarily the best point of contact; a man probably responds to help when he really needs it, rather than when the situation dictates it. One man, for example, whom we contacted via the court and was still sober two years later, was desperate for help and would possibly have gone for it irrespective of whether he had appeared in court that morning or not.

Sixth, it is difficult to know what it means when the man himself says 'I want help.' He may well have thought that we had greater opportunities to intervene in the court process than we had, or he may have had fantasies about the extent and scope of the help we could ultimately offer. In a situation where men have received very little help in the past, or never sought it, it is difficult to estimate the degree of help that they require when they do say, 'Yes, I want help.'

Finally, it is probably advisable to have a social worker at the court on a regular basis rather than merely on one day every week. It is important to have some degree of continuity to try to build up relationships, to give the men an opportunity to 'sus out' the social worker rather than be suddenly subjected to an interview with a total stranger. It would probably be valuable for the probation service to have someone at the court dealing solely with the drunkenness offenders on a regular daily basis. One of us thought that a jailer should specifically be given the task to discover the drunks who are seeking help. We also wondered whether the response to us might have been totally different if we had used only recovered alcoholics to make the first contact.

In thinking about the court and the drunkenness offenders, we were forced to consider the implications of what we learnt for the medical centres generally known as detoxification centres proposed in the 1972 Criminal Justice Act. The most obvious factor is that, although the majority of the men were habitual drunkenness offenders, by no means all felt that they had a drinking problem. They therefore might regard a detoxification centre as equally irrelevant to their situation as a court appearance. Our defining the men as having certain problems is of little value unless it coincides to some degree with their own perceptions. Equally important is that very few of the men seem to require, admittedly on a superficial examination, serious and immediate medical attention or psychiatric help. The few where it was required were given it fairly quickly at the local hospital. This would indicate that a medical centre may have few serious demands made upon its medical expertise. Of course, it may be that currently the more serious medical cases go direct to hospital and do not come to court, so we would not have seen this type of case. Taking that into consideration, the majority of drunkenness offenders, as seen on this exercise, did not require medical or psychiatric attention. This would clearly indicate that the social work element in a drying-out centre is equally as important as the medical. This would be especially so when a large percentage of the drunkenness offenders are homeless.

Although in terms of immediate impact upon a group of drunkenness offenders the exercise was disappointing, it none the less provided information for discussion for the agencies involved with the problem. The general view was that the evidence we obtained supports the argument that we should try to keep the drunk out of the court system because there is virtually no sensible or satisfactory way of intervening at that point to make positive use of the situation. On the other hand, we should be careful about the nature of the detoxification centres that are intended to be established, otherwise they, too, may become equally inappropriate, perceived by the clients as cynically as they now perceive a night in the cells and an appearance in court. We must always guard against developing a system that is not strictly planned to meet the needs of the client; the tendency is often in such circumstances to blame the client rather than the system if the desired goals are not achieved. The general experience of the Project with the courts confirms the specific experience of the court exercises that we conducted. Initial contact at the court rarely produces an ongoing relationship and the court process for the habitual drunkenness offender remains a futile parade, known to be such to all involved and yet seemingly impervious to any change.

(ii)   *Prison*

If the courts seem to offer little chance of effectively contacting the drunkenness offender, then prison would seem to offer even less. It seems ironic that the more the drunkenness offender becomes enmeshed into the correctional system, the less able it is to devise ways of assisting him. In 1970 in Pentonville Prison, a large London local prison, offenders serving less than three months were not seen as of right by the welfare officers but only if they asked to be seen. This meant that most offenders who were in for being drunk and disorderly or non-payment of fines for drunkenness, were rarely if ever seen on a regular basis. While most men and most prison officials said in conversation that fourteen days in prison saved men's lives and was generally good for them, little use was made of the time by staff or prisoners. It was always possible that nothing could be done, given the high turnover in prison and the complexity of the men's problems, but it seemed worth while to explore the matter further.

In September 1970 it was agreed that the Project staff and the Inner London probation officer liaising with Pentonville, would together attempt to find out more about the after-care needs of all the men leaving the prison during one week in November (Cook, 1971). The Project was principally concerned with those men who had drinking problems, whilst the probation officer concerned himself with the other offenders. We wished to know what proportion of the men in Pentonville had been in touch with alcoholic treatment facilities, whether they knew how to contact the services that were available, and if more could be done in prison to give them information as to what was available. Considerable assistance was given to us by prison staff, as well as essential outside services such as the local offices of the

Department of Health and Social Security. Pre-release interviews were conducted to build up an outline picture of the after-care needs of the men. Ninety-five men were released in the week but only eighty-three were adequately interviewed. Of these, forty were serving less than three months, meaning that on this sentence at least no formal interview had been offered them. Homelessness was a common problem as forty-five men had no fixed address on release, and all but six of these were staying in London.

Drinking was an admitted problem in thirty-four instances, though these men were not exactly the same as those men serving sentences for a drunkenness offence. One or two men who were in for maintenance debts admitted that drinking was the root of their problems. A few men serving the umpteenth sentence for drunkenness still felt it was just bad luck that they were arrested. Further, it is worth noting that of the twenty-six cases which were followed up with the probation service outside London, nine later mentioned drink as a problem, though five of them had not referred to it in the pre-release interview. In summary, 40 per cent of the men admitted drink was a problem, while a few others admitted it subsequently, or continued to deny it despite the evidence of their record. Despite the relatively high percentage of men with drinking problems, we were soon aware of the ignorance about alcoholism, its nature and its consequences. Only nine men said that they had ever had treatment, medical or social, for alcoholism. The amount of after-care that we were able to provide was no more than that usually available. We did, however, offer all men a bacon-and-egg breakfast but only sixteen availed themselves of it! Almost all the alcoholics drifted away and made little contact with the Project on the day of release. After a three-month period twelve men contacted the Project, eight were seen once, two twice, and two were given more substantial help. The results of the probation officer with the non-alcoholics were very similar.

As a result of this exercise, we felt strongly that the system of court reports, pre-sentence enquiries, prison welfare and after-care was not meeting the needs of many short-term offenders. An army of social workers, even if that were the answer, will never be available to tackle the problem. We therefore have to ask whether a non-system can be made into a system by offering a minimum of help to all. The alternative is to offer a lot of help to a few, but on what basis of selection? There was certainly a need for some system of regularly seeing men, however short the sentence, as, clearly, a once-only after-care exercise, such as we conducted, was not going to alter radically a man's well-entrenched life-style. Despite the limited nature of the Pentonville experiment, we were soon to learn from a much wider survey (Walmsley, 1972) that the figures and problems we revealed reflected the national picture quite accurately. Revealing a problem is one task. Quite another is knowing how to proceed from that revelation. As far as the Project was concerned, we committed ourselves for at least one year to providing a worker, himself a recovered alcoholic, to go into Pentonville one or two mornings a week. This was to see men serving one month or less, sent to Pentonville from either of the two magistrates' courts in Southwark. At the same time, the prison staff introduced an induction scheme which now included the under three-months men, so that every man at least had the opportunity to discuss after-care with someone, should he so wish.

We would not presume to comment in detail on the prison view of the exercise except to say that at no time were serious efforts made by the prison authorities to release the prison officers involved to visit outside facilities relevant to the after-care of the men inside. This meant that, at times, relationships between outside services and the prison became strained often because of a basic lack of understanding, for example, of the nature of the hostels. Until regular visits to alcoholic hostels are made by prison staff there will continue to be some mis-understanding. Are the hostels really full, too selective, or awkward? If these relationships are not satisfactory, then prison staff will soon become disillusioned about trying to place men from Pentonville in suitable after-care facilities.

However, the Project's work in the prison should perhaps lead one to be cautious about how easy it is for the alcoholic himself to leave the prison after fourteen days and go straight to a residential alcoholic unit or hostel. The Project worker in Pentonville was a man of immense experience and skill, well known both to the men and the outside agencies. Yet he too found considerable difficulties in linking many men direct from the prison to an after-care alcoholic hostel. In his first six months he saw ninety-one men. Of these, fifty-one never took up any after-care appointment; twenty-six subsequently came to see one of the Project staff, while the remaining fourteen were already known to the Project prior to the prison interview. In the next twelve months just over 350 men were seen in Pentonville but only one in ten of these ever made contact with the Project when released. Few even of these found their way into alcoholic hostels. Facts such as these cannot be explained away, but need to be faced head on for the challenge that they clearly present.

The Project's evidence and experience confirms that of others, namely that prison for the short-term drunkenness offender is as futile a place as the court to attempt much serious rehabilitation. The culture within the prison workshops where the drunks work together militates against serious discussion of sobriety on release. No one ever really makes it anyway, so why try? Men are often discharged with drinking mates, so why trade the uncertainty of an interview with a social worker for their time-honoured, time-trusted company? In any event after fourteen days in prison 'you owe yourself a drunk' (Spradley, 1970). On the outside, men in the alcoholic hostels regard it as a great achievement if a man arrives sober on the day of his release from prison, however short or long the sentence. Practical evidence suggests that it is. Although the Project had a number of factors in its favour, it was still unable to make any significant impact upon the habitual drunkenness offender either in the prison or directly on his release from it. Once again, there seem to be present the elements of a system that in itself serves little purpose and yet defeats most attempts to change it. Imprisoning drunks is expensive. It is also a cumbersome process to deal with a problem of social nuisance. Worse, it would seem that it prevents, by its very culture, effective ways of helping ever being realized. Physically, it may at times be a life-saving process but it could be argued that in every other way it is a life-denying process.

(iii) *Lodging houses*

The lodging houses have always been as inseparable a part of the revolving door as courts and prisons. Men pour through them in their hundreds. To live in them or to visit them is still to experience being part of another world, nineteenth century in outlook and flavour (Orwell, 1932; Turner, 1960). Yet for too long many services, statutory and voluntary, have sent men to the lodging houses requesting that they come back in a week to keep an appointment or to be told that they may soon have an appointment. Sometimes social workers wonder why the clients do not stay in the lodging house. To visit such places is to wonder no more. It is still worrying, however, how few social workers and others do actually visit, other than fleetingly, the kind of places where many of their homeless clients have to stay.

The Project, along with a local senior probation officer, felt that some effort should be made to contact men in the lodging houses, to go to them, and to be available in their setting, rather than ours. The local Salvation Army Hostel Captain was enthusiastic to co-operate in any such exercise and committed himself to assisting us. It was decided that several people would be involved and that a group discussion would be held in a small room of the main dining/TV area. Such a

7

weekly meeting was held for over a year. It was open to anyone who wished to come. As the probation service was also involved, it was not restricted to men with drinking problems. Posters announcing the weekly meeting were displayed. Once the weekly meetings began it was found that the staff of the hostel were encouraged by the fact that at least something was going on in the hostel; their own isolation from other social services was reduced. Another by-product of the meetings was that, both before and after them, men who had not attended stopped the social worker with numerous requests, indicating that the permanent presence of a social worker in the lodging house might be of benefit. With regard to the meetings themselves, the numbers attending were small, rarely more than ten, even though the total population in the lodging house was over 400.

The one question that clearly needed to be asked was why only ten men out of 400 attended the weekly meeting. To an outsider it may well have seemed disappointing that so few ever came to the group, but to anyone familiar with lodging houses it was perhaps surprising that anyone came at all. Even medical services are not readily taken up by lodging-house residents (Brickner, 1972). The apathy and despair engendered by simply living in lodging houses is at times overwhelming, making it difficult for positive decisions to be made, even to decide to go into a small side-room for a weekly discussion. Added to this is the sub-cultural pressure against being involved either with your fellow man or other agencies such as visiting social workers. Almost all aspects of the lodging-house existence seem designed to prevent men reaching out to anything more hopeful. It is not uncommon to talk to men who came to a lodging house for a few weeks after some domestic crisis and with a view to moving to their own room afterwards; but they have stayed on in the lodging houses for years, retaining the hope that one day they would obtain their own room or flat. In a lodging house waiting for Godot takes on many forms. We would say, therefore, that with yet another part of the skid row system there are institutions which, given their present size and history, are not possible to alter radically. The reaching-out process that the Project has tried suggests that, once in the lodging houses, it requires great individual strength to break clear of them. They are for too many men a tomb rather than a temporary stage on the way back into normal society.

(iv)   *Hospitals*

Just over one in four alcoholics seen by the Project staff are admitted into general or psychiatric hospitals within one month of contacting us, though not necessarily as a direct result of our endeavours, nor necessarily specifically for treatment for alcoholism. Naturally hospitals' willingness to admit homeless alcoholics varies and we have sought to understand some of the reasons that make some doctors resistant to involvement with the down-and-out alcoholic. With this aim in view we sought to work alongside the services both in a psychiatric emergency clinic and in a general casualty department. With regard to the latter, we were unable to create an opportunity even to try an experimental scheme. As far as the psychiatric emergency clinic was concerned, an opportunity to involve ourselves occurred when anxiety was expressed by the doctors that too many vagrant alcoholics were coming to the clinic, especially on a Friday evening when the figure of twenty was actually mentioned by one doctor. We therefore offered for a series of six Friday evenings to be available in the clinic to see if a specialist worker on hand could in any way alleviate the problem. Eagerly we attended the clinic, fearing the worst, only to find that over the six evenings only two homeless alcoholics actually appeared. Other psychiatric emergencies were however frequent enough. It was unfortunate that so few alcoholics did appear, as, clearly, the numbers attending would seem to be less than twenty a night and more than an average of one every three nights. Two features, however, did emerge which were instructive.

First, by witnessing the duty doctor deal with other psychiatric emergencies, we were better able to understand the pressures on the clinic and how a difficult drunken patient can present demands that make the duty doctors feel angry when faced with other pressing emergencies. The homeless alcoholic who attends the clinic late at night presents many problems which may well have little obvious psychiatric content. This is the second feature. One interview between a doctor and a homeless alcoholic centred on three interesting points. The first was that the alcoholic had been a regular visitor to the clinic for over ten years and made it clear to the doctor that he knew as much, if not more, about the services, so if the doctor would just do as requested all would be well! As the alcoholic said, 'Look, I've been coming here for ten years. . . .' The second was the bargaining that took place over how many pills should be prescribed. The initial demand was for fifty, the original offer nil. The result was three. This bargaining took a lot of time and seemed unrelated to the problems of either the clinic or the man. The third point was that, just as the man was about to leave, came his real request, namely, 'Look, doctor, I've nowhere to stay tonight, can you give me ten bob?' Are psychiatric emergency clinics welfare centres or not? In this instance not, and the man left without money. It

seems likely that similar encounters occur quite frequently; obviously
they pose problems for a psychiatric emergency service in an area
where homeless alcoholics are certain to make use of the service for
reasons other than those for which it was established. If, of course, the
medical profession is saying that alcoholism is an illness, then it is only
to be expected that alcoholics, homeless or not, call at hospitals for help.
But the medical model does not, possibly cannot, take fully into account
the life-style of the homeless alcoholic who has in a sense overloaded
the concept that alcoholism is an illness. Unless the sub-culture of the
homeless alcoholic is better understood, doctors and alcoholics may just
continue to get drawn into games that serve mainly to confirm the
rather jaundiced view that each already has of the other.

The houses

The early history of the houses within the Project has been given in
chapter two. I would now wish to look at some aspects of their development which were affected by the growth of the wider work of the Project.
First, however, I shall examine the establishment of a third house
opened late in 1971, which was intended to meet a specific need of the
Project social workers.

We had found that for the men coming sober to the shop fronts
seeking help, it was increasingly difficult to ask them to wait for two
to three weeks in, for example, a lodging house prior to admission into
a long-term alcoholic centre. For some men, once sober, immediate
assistance was necessary if they were to have any real chance of sustaining this sobriety. At this time we were offered a short-life property
which would accommodate four men. It was a small terrace house due
for demolition in three years. We accepted it with a view to using it as a
short-stay house for men who were sober and who we felt needed
breathing-space before moving to more long-term accommodation. It
was not intended to be a formal assessment unit though some assessment
took place; we noticed how men lived while there, which in turn
influenced decisions about which units they would eventually go to.
Also, of course, men who left drinking generally selected themselves
out of any immediate consideration for a place in a longer-term rehabilitation centre. Finally, a psychiatrist visited weekly to talk informally with the residents and to see privately any individual on whom
we wished to have a psychiatric opinion. The house was staffed initially
by a recovered alcoholic (a former resident of Rathcoole) and has been
staffed since either by recovered alcoholics or by Community Service
Volunteers. The rule of no drinking generally applied; men were

expected to stay from two to four weeks. They were not expected to obtain work, indeed this was positively discouraged, for it was felt important for the residents to think about their situation rather than escape into work. They were also asked to keep in daily contact with the shop-front workers. All referrals to the house came from within the Project with the referring social worker having the responsibility to make subsequent arrangements for the alcoholic.

In the first two years of its operation ninety-two men were admitted, including fourteen re-admissions. Of these, thirty-two left drinking, eleven failed to return, thirty-five men moved to the Project's own long-term houses, eight men to other alcoholic centres and six to home or hospital. The average length of stay was nineteen days. In operating the first-stage house, we learned a number of things. Even though help had been given virtually immediately as requested, 35 per cent of the admissions still departed drinking within a few days. On the other hand, for those that stayed, we found that the very smallness of the house produced very affectionate feelings about it and ex-residents have regularly revisited the house, even though they had only been there two to three weeks. Since leaving home, some men had rarely lived in anything but the larger type of institutions. Further, as the turnover was fast, a man quickly became the senior resident, having to let others know where the eggs were for breakfast or answering the telephone. Even in the space of a few weeks we saw some remarkable social changes in a proportion of the residents, brought on by the psychological warmth of the house and the challenge of some immediate responsibility. The possibilities of this increased when it was decided to have the staff living away from the premises, as happened in the other houses. But it has also meant that we are very dependent on the residents' being able to move rapidly from, for example, the prison setting to a position of some considerable trust and responsibility. For some, the absence of residential staff has proved too great a strain, particularly when in a short-stay house there are no long-term residents to carry the culture and provide the essential stability. Finally, and perhaps most important of all, was the fact that the turnover and relapse rate were very similar to other first-stage houses which operated with a more intensive and more obvious treatment programme (Armstrong, 1972).

In writing about short- and long-term houses, we should be careful not to suggest that the road to recovery for the alcoholic necessarily lies in a logically progressive system. There can be a danger that such a system has administrative appeal and suits social workers' needs without necessarily meeting the men's needs. Not all men want a cradle-to-the-grave system of caring, for so much depends on their previous attempts to stay sober and what they have learnt from them, if indeed there have been any. It was consideration of this last point that led us to modify the criteria for admission to Lynette Avenue, one of the two long-stay houses in the Project. In 1969 we were running the two houses Rathcoole and Lynette Avenue as identical houses, and men would go to either depending on where there was a vacancy. This policy continued for a further two years (1969–71). It proved eventually to be rather unsatisfactory as, in practice, no two houses can be identical. Even the physical layout of rooms can determine the atmosphere to some degree. Also, staff could simply not give equal attention to both houses, with the result that at times Lynette Avenue residents tended to feel neglected. After discussion it was agreed that Lynette Avenue should be a house for alcoholics who had at some previous stage experienced a period of sobriety of at least six months in a residential establishment. This meant that the residents at Lynette Avenue would all be familiar with the problems of living in a community and would not require quite such a degree of support. Also, by being encouraged to be more independent, they were building on their previous residential experience rather than merely returning to it and repeating it. Since this rather loose policy has been adopted, the house has operated much more satisfactorily and has been of greater benefit to residents. By 1973 the residents in Lynette Avenue asked to operate without any social worker involvement in matters as varied as the weekly house meetings and the collection of the rents. To this we readily agreed.

There did, however, begin to develop in 1972 some staff feeling that although the houses were the original part of the Project, they were now the less exciting part, that though once experimental they were now stable and established. This meant that they were discussed less at staff meetings than say the problem of the shop fronts. The tendency not to discuss the houses was reinforced by the fact that I had been the social worker at the houses for three years. This meant that matters concerning the houses were discussed with me individually, as I was seen as the repository of knowledge on the houses. Gradually therefore the detailed discussion on the residential work seemed to take place away from the rest of the staff. A sense of division between residential and non-residential workers was also increased by the fact that the Project staff were generally involved with individuals in the houses, rather than with the house as a whole. 'How is Bill doing?' would be the question asked rather than, 'How is the house going?' This was not to say that there was not a commitment to the house as a unit, but rather that in the end the emphasis was different. It was even suggested at one stage that the Project had a vested interest in keeping the houses quiet and safe and not wanting too much change in them. This arose because it was felt that the staff went to a great deal of effort to help a man stop drinking and obtain a place in a house; so that once in the house they did not wish the resident to be subject to too much challenge and to too many difficulties. It was not easy to say whether these perceptions were totally accurate, but certainly they served to highlight some of the problems caused by the close proximity of residential and non-residential work in the same Project.

At the same time there were some definite advantages in having a number of social workers concerned with a residential establishment in addition to the one worker with the major responsibility. It meant for example that at times of crisis several people were involved in supporting the residents, and in providing suggestions as to the causes and resolution of the crisis. Individual residents, if they left drinking, were more easily able to maintain contact with the visiting shop-front social worker, feeling too guilty to re-establish contact immediately with the house itself. For some residents the fact that the house was part of a wider project reduced the feeling that they had been passed on to yet another agency. The visits of the Project social worker gave the men opportunities to be seen in a setting other than on the street, drinking or in a state of disarray. Some witnesses to their progress were at times needed. Finally, it could be said that the demands on the residential worker were made more tolerable and realistic by the fact that some men made use of the non-residential workers to work at some of their problems. This was not felt to be manipulative or divisive, but a proper use of the resources that were legitimately available to the residents.

Some problems developed, however, which were inherent in the way the houses were run rather than related to the setting of the work in the total Project. These arose out of the still unusual role of a non-residential worker having sole responsibility for a residential unit. Few units have developed this kind of management, though where it has been tried it seems to have been reasonably successful and by no means as wearing on staff as full residential work. But it does require the worker to be able to pick up very quickly the nuances and undertones of the residential community, although he may only be visiting it for certain hours every day, and will generally be away from it much more than he is there. It also produces varying expectations in the residents themselves; some may want him to be the more traditional warden on the spot the whole time, others may feel that he should only call as required and not be too obtrusive. For some he will be the buddy, for others the social worker, and for others the man in charge (Rubington, 1965). Problems in this area are enhanced by the fact that the social worker is the sole person with official responsibility, so that rules cannot be divided up among staff. One-man working is an exciting but demanding challenge for both residents and the one staff member.

Whatever the difficulties and uncertainties, the houses in their turnover rate and in length of stay showed improvement as the Project progressed. For example, in the two years 1971–3 there were sixty-six residents admitted to Rathcoole and Lynette Avenue, of whom seventeen (25·8 per cent) stayed for more than six months. In the first two years of the houses, 1966–8, there were 121 residents admitted, of whom six (4·9 per cent) stayed over six months. There now seemed with some residents and the staff to be a growing sense of being together as members of the Project, not divided as clients or social workers. At times residents have felt that they had some kind of responsibility to contribute something to the work of the Project. These feelings found practical expression in the residents' request to have representatives on the Project management committee. This was welcomed and each house duly elected its representative. Certainly the houses should never again be the fortresses and isolated units that they once were. We would ourselves feel it difficult to advocate the setting-up of a house for alcoholics unless it was to be accompanied by other facilities supporting and feeding it, these in turn supported by the house itself.

Information service

It is perhaps not surprising, albeit a little alarming, that in London there is no Alcoholism Information Centre. To establish one in London would require a great deal of co-operation among local, national and voluntary authorities and it would need to be a particularly large and well-manned centre. So far, no such centre has emerged from the drawing board other than for two brief spells in the mid-1960s. Outside London, information centres do exist in a few cities, providing both a counselling and information service. Given the wide and varied type of facilities available for the homeless alcoholic and the co-ordinating role of the Project, it was to be expected that, in the absence of a central London information service, we would receive a number of requests for information about services in general and advice on individuals in particular. Even so, we were surprised at the demands that were made on us in this area of work. They undoubtedly revealed a need for a central information point which could provide accurate and detailed advice on the homeless alcoholic and the facilities available for him. From 1970 to 1972 we had 212 substantial enquiries about individuals previously unknown to us and what might be done to help them. We use the word 'substantial' to indicate an enquiry in which we were not asked to see the alcoholic but rather to advise on a course of action. This contrasts with casual enquiries which, for example, merely requested the address of the nearest alcoholic hostel or hospital unit.

Table 5   Sources of enquiries to the Project, 1 May 1970–30 April 1972

Inner London probation and after-care service	77
Probation and after-care service – outside London	11
Hospitals	44
Self	18
Local authority social services	17
Prisons	17
Churches	5
General practitioners	3
Relatives	3
Voluntary organizations	3
Police	1
Miscellaneous	13
Total	212

The majority of these 212 enquiries came in 1972 when the Project was better known and they have continued to increase. In 1973 we had 150 enquiries. It is to be noted that over a third of all the 1970–2 enquiries came from the probation and after-care service; most of these from the Inner London service. It seems extraordinary that one small voluntary organization should be seen as providing such an information service to a statutory organization with ample resources to establish such a service itself. So far, however, the Inner London probation service has been unwilling to commit resources in this direction, despite requests from the Project to do so. From our experience it is clear that, compared with local authority social services, the probation service is still heavily involved with the homeless alcoholic and will continue to be so whatever happens to the recommendations of the report.

Another form of information that the Project began to provide was related to general issues such as the setting-up of a hostel or the concern of residents about the vagrant alcoholics in an area. The Project's involvement in these broader issues has been welcomed by us as it increases opportunities for influencing developments elsewhere and is a way of preventing the Project becoming too parochial in outlook. Several London boroughs have sought our advice, as well as cities outside London. Our contribution has often been quite minor and we would not wish to overstress it except to point to our own awareness of the national scene and the role that we may be able to play in its development.

Co-ordination

We have referred already to the problems surrounding the task of co-ordination. It is some consolation to us to know that it is not only in South London that co-ordination is difficult to achieve. Shandler (1972, p. 2) has stated the Philadelphia problem:

[In 1969] I reported on Philadelphia's progress in moving toward a comprehensive alcoholism program and made the prediction that within two years that program would be developed. Now three years later Philadelphia still lacks a well defined, well co-ordinated city-wide program.

The movement towards and need for co-ordination is usually expressed in rather general terms, but it is rare in any discussion on the alcoholic for the topic to be omitted. Few would wish, in this or other health fields, to return to the days of splendid isolation, one agency from another, one department from another. Yet at the same time we are unsure as to what is truly involved in a degree of worthwhile and positive co-ordination. Agencies are always assured that there will be no 'loss of identity and control over their own affairs' (Home Office, 1971, p. 135), which can mean that there is no real power and authority in the co-ordination proposed. Cahn (1970, p. 198) has stated that American efforts at co-ordinating alcoholism programmes are 'still too often timid or theoretical'. Warren (1973, p. 358) sees co-ordination simply becoming an 'idle intellectual game', unless there are means for a plan's implementation.

But why try to co-ordinate anyway? Are not agencies best left to themselves? There are two ways of answering this type of question. First, there is the rather negative answer that we wish to co-operate in order to prevent abuse. Anderson (1923, p. 261) wrote that 'in perhaps no other field of social work is there more overlapping and duplication of effort or so low standards of service . . . a constructive programme for rehabilitation demands the co-ordination of the efforts of all agencies now engaged in serving his needs.' The Manhattan Bowery Project (1970) reported that 'services currently available to the Bowery man are surprisingly numerous. . . . There is, moreover, considerable duplication of services by private and public agencies.' The second answer is more positive and is best expressed by the report (Home Office, 1971, pp. 139–40):

It seems to us axiomatic that the three fields (medical, social and penal) and the statutory services and voluntary agencies which they embrace must aim at operating as different elements of one treatment service with the capacity to absorb the habitual drunken offender into a part of it which is most appropriate to his needs at the time, and to provide therefore care which is both continuous and adjustable in response to changes in his needs.

It was primarily for the latter reasons that the Project set as one of its main tasks the goal of co-ordinating the facilities in the locality so that there should be a better system of helping and reaching out to the homeless alcoholic.

At the same time, we were concerned along with other agencies in the area to try to establish just how much abuse of agency services existed. We therefore took a sample of twenty-six men, being the total of two months' referrals to us early in 1972. We then enquired of all the principal agencies in the area of their contact with these men in a six-month period prior to being referred to the Project, and of any contact subsequent to the men becoming linked to the Project. The evidence from this small sample was that there was almost no degree of overlap and certainly not the abuse that we had expected, and that once the Project became involved there was a still further reduction of overlap. The men it seemed were not abusing the services, even though lack of co-ordination makes abuse possible. Alcoholics were really giving us a fair deal. Some evidence to support this came from a paper which among other things looked at agencies in Camberwell, and the vagrant alcoholics they reported as known to them in 1966 (Edwards, 1972). Here, too, going the rounds of all the facilities was not the problem we so often fear. Maybe we should not fear it anyway, as the alcoholic may feel he has the right to shop for whatever facility he most feels he needs at a particular time. If clients can be seen more as customers, the issue is perhaps less emotive and threatening.

Returning to the more positive reasons for co-ordination, the Project found a number of basic problems inherent in its efforts to produce a system of helping rather than a lottery for assistance. Not all agencies are at the same stage of thinking about the problem of the homeless alcoholic, so that to talk about co-ordination to some is to introduce a strange and threatening concept while to others it is seen as supremely relevant. This means that, unless there is some power or authority to summon agencies together to discuss the issues, as opposed to telling these agencies what to do in their daily work, the work of co-ordination proceeds very slowly and disjointedly (Warren, 1973). To proceed at the pace of the swiftest or the slowest is to isolate a few agencies at one end of the spectrum or the other and to make any future consolidation of progress extremely difficult. The power to summon can rarely be held by a single voluntary organization and such a summons is probably best performed by the relevant central government department. Yet it is a task central government is reluctant to take on in the light of the historically unhappy relationships between statutory and voluntary services in this field. The result tends to be that agencies stay separate or seek to co-operate on fairly neutral topics. Frequently we found pressure to set up a comprehensive case register of alcoholics known to a variety of agencies even though there is not even a central record of drunkenness offenders. (The offence does not qualify for recording by the criminal records office.) Even if practicable, this action would have soon turned the Project into almost nothing but a centre of information, while still leaving many wider questions unresolved. The absence of the power to co-ordinate is of course related to finance. Cahn (1970, p. 207) comments that 'advisory, research and planning bodies can indeed point out weakness and inadequacies in existing programs: without some financial authority behind them, their recommendations will rarely be acted on.' Central government does however give considerable sums of money to voluntary work in this field and the responsibility that goes with it is surely to involve itself more directly with the recipients of the money.

One of the ways over some of these difficulties seemed to be to bring together representatives of various agencies in an Action Group which was to examine together some specific problems. This the Project attempted to do in 1970 and such an action group was formed: it produced two documents outlining the need for first a detoxification centre and second an alcoholism information bureau. The group was however *ad hoc* and was not accountable to any body fully representative of all the agencies in the area. While efforts were made by the Project to press for the establishment of both the facilities required, either the impetus was insufficient or the climate unreceptive. Yet, with the publication in 1971 of the report, there now seemed more to 'bite on' – at least no one could procrastinate by saying, 'Let's wait to see what the report says.'

A proposal was put by the Project in 1971 to the Southwark Council of Social Service, which had already organized a one-day conference on the subject of the report, that it should establish a Southwark Standing Conference on Homeless Alcoholics. Some of the developments that were occurring in the area certainly seemed to warrant some kind of standing committee. The Department of Health and Social Security (hereafter referred to as the DHSS) wanted to establish a detoxification centre in South London; a community psychiatric service was being planned; the work of the Camberwell Reception Centre was being reviewed; the local authority had started to establish social services area teams; plans were being made by the probation service to tackle the problem of the homeless ex-offender, and some voluntary bodies such as the Project itself were reviewing the role they had to play. Late in 1971, a large meeting of local statutory and voluntary agencies called by the Southwark Council of Social Service gave authority to the Standing Conference to create a permanent forum in Southwark to look at the problem of co-ordination and integration of the services, general and specific, being provided for and used by the vagrant alcoholic. The Conference met regularly and had as one of its main tasks the pressing for the establishment of a detoxification centre. There seemed at the time a possibility that the Standing Conference would succeed, as it had certain live issues to tackle, some limited authority vested in it, and a realization of the time-scale involved in any co-ordinating effort. Unfortunately by the end of 1973 the Southwark Standing Conference had not succeeded in producing sufficient pressure to establish a south-east London detoxification centre. The forces of inertia seemed to win another victory. This time the inertia seemed to lie with government departments, while the voluntary bodies were never more in harmony. Co-ordination of effort to establish and manage a project such as a detoxification centre made sense, but when the latter could not be established, the purpose of co-ordination lost its significance.

Finally, we should look at the implications for co-ordination of the fact that the homeless alcoholic is only part of a complex skid row system which in turn involves only part of the whole problem of the homeless single person. In looking at the solution of the skid row problems Cahn (1970, p. 204) has said, 'There is a need to focus on a total way-of-life, on the total socioeconomic and psychological complex in which skid row men live rather than on the problem of alcoholism alone.' Given this position, and it is not one from which I would fundamentally disagree, there is clearly a need to see efforts at co-ordination among alcoholic agencies in a much wider context. Locally in south-east London this has been done through the experimental Consortium of Community Endeavours (Braithwaite, 1972); nationally it is being tried through the Campaign for the Homeless and Rootless (CHAR). It remains to be seen whether either of these bodies triumphs where others have failed, and whether they obtain teeth and authority where others have been toothless and powerless.

At a national level, co-ordination over a field as multi-faceted as that of the homeless single person is an awesome undertaking. Early in 1973 CHAR was officially formed to try to do just that. Its broad object is the promotion of the interests of homeless and rootless people and, through a range of both short- and long-term objectives, to place administrative and financial responsibility for these people on central and local government. This would leave the voluntary bodies in a better position to perform their essential role of contact, support and re-habilitation of the homeless. It is too early yet to state how this latest attempt at national co-operation will progress. At least in 1974 the issue of the homeless is a live and politically potent one; circulars have been issued on the problem, the ten-year plans of local authorities should hopefully include provision for the single homeless, and grass-roots frustration is as strong as ever about the passing of the buck. The only dangers here are that, in the grand sweep of a campaign, too much attention may be given to the quantity of provision rather than its quality: and that, while a few large organizations talk and act together at national level, the smaller organizations in the field still fail to talk to one another. Worse still, it may be found easier to agree on the need for 1,000 extra beds for single homeless people in London than on how the facilities providing these beds should be run, by which staff, and to what end. The real difficulties in fact seem to occur when a particular organization is being asked to do something in the way of co-ordination as opposed to that organization's committee expressing the general belief that we should all communicate better and co-operate. If at the end of the day an organization stands alone, no sanctions can be brought to bear.

Essentially, it is true to say that the Alcoholics Recovery Project has found the achieving of a *system* of help for the homeless alcoholic its most difficult task. It has not been possible to establish a card-index system concerning the vagrant alcoholics in the area, although over the years we built up information on over 1,000 people. The same could probably be said of several other agencies also, so much so that we could all spend time interviewing the files, not the people to whom they refer! On the other hand, the Project has gone out of its way to work closely with all other facilities; indeed, in our shop fronts we have depended almost entirely upon other agencies to effect our work. Still, however, any sense of achievement we have in the field of co-ordination remains diluted. Much has to be done before a truly co-ordinated system of help can be seen and felt to exist both by staff and by alcoholics.

The alcoholic as helper

One of the aims of the Project has been to explore and understand more about the so-called skid row sub-culture. The main method of achieving this was to deploy a research worker in the field, or rather out on the streets. Some of the data from this are reported in chapter 7. Complementary to that, however, we believed it important to involve the former users of the skid row system in the daily work of the Project. We have already described how the concept of Rathcoole was only fully developed when the residents' views were sought and when they participated in the decision-making within the house. The whole notion of the therapeutic community means that residents and staff play equally important, albeit different, roles in effecting therapy and hence changes in individuals. Alcoholics Anonymous's astonishing rate of growth since its inception in America in 1935 is further evidence of the power of the ex-client, be he a recovering patient or ex-prisoner, as an agent of help and change. Set alongside this is the stark fact that professional workers will never be able to meet all the problems that are presented to them, nor indeed should they alone try. The realization of the potential of the client, along with the accepted bankruptcy of much orthodox social work endeavours led to the growth of the 'new careers' movement in the United States in the 1960s (Pearl, 1965; Gartner, 1971). This movement implied that people in the position of the helped were to be trained to become helpers and were to be offered not just a menial job in social work but an exciting career. In this section we would like to examine this concept as it has developed in the Project.

The idea that recovering skid row alcoholics could be employed to assist others still on skid row is not entirely new. Rubington (1967) outlined a different approach towards the control of alcoholism on skid row. 'I suggest that alcoholics can rehabilitate themselves when they are paid to keep the skid row peace. This proposal, then, is about a rescue service staffed by homeless alcoholics who are paid to rescue other alcoholics.' He concludes that 'applying existing skills in public service for private gain is more apt to lead to status and lengthier periods of sobriety than learning new vocational skills which would be practised in an unfamiliar environment'. It is none the less a very big step from men helping each other in a residential community to becoming paid social work colleagues involved in a professional service, with the considerable increase of responsibility and accountability which that involves. Too many people have been conditioned into believing that the down-trodden cannot do anything of great importance:

most crucial of all, the down-trodden come to believe it. 'What can I do? I'm only a peasant' (Freire, 1972, p. 37). I have lost count of the number of occasions I said at house meetings, 'The trouble is I have more confidence in you than you have in yourselves.'

The Project, through its hard-won experience at Rathcoole and Lynette Avenue and through the evidence of the Manhattan Bowery Project (1970), believed it essential to obtain the services of a recovered skid row alcoholic to work on the staff from the beginning. Accordingly in May 1970 we successfully submitted a proposal to the Chase Charity, who provided the salary for such a worker. In the proposal we stated:

There is a very large gap between the vagrant alcoholic on the street and the ultimate help available. This gap is as much psychological as physical. This means that the vagrant alcoholic is unable to conceive of himself as being anything other than a vagrant alcoholic and that the help available – be it hospital, hostel or whatever – is not suitable for him. To overcome this gap it is believed that a recovered skid row alcoholic can be effective. He is able to empathise immediately with the vagrant alcoholic and to provide visible proof that recovery is possible. The Project would, therefore, like to employ a recovered skid row alcoholic to work alongside the team of four social workers. We feel this would be of great benefit, not only to the men who are seeking help, but also to our own social workers, and, indeed, other agencies.

Since then, the Project has always employed at least one recovered alcoholic and this has proved a stimulating experience from which all concerned have learnt a great deal. In describing what we see as the benefits, we are aware that not too many generalizations should be made from a few individual experiences; but other projects' limited experience supports our own. For example, Buckley (1972, p. 25) states:

Project Re-Entry is based on a number of important assumptions: that the successful ex-inmate is an excellent resource in helping prisoners; that he can help men in prison examine the attitudes that fostered their criminal behaviour; that he can provide them with a positive figure with whom to identify; that he can offer them a measure of hope for the future in spite of the prison experience and the difficulties of adjusting to life outside.

It is instructive to examine the value of this work for the recovered alcoholic and his problems in undertaking it in two main areas, namely his relationships with the men, and with his social work colleagues on the Alcoholics Recovery Project and in other agencies. The men themselves seem in conflict between the feelings that social workers do not understand 'men like us' – 'What do *you* know about alcoholism?' –

and yet resenting one of their own who is now in some position of influence in the alcoholic world. Consistency is however not necessarily a virtue, and the co-existence of these feelings serves to highlight the men's own uncertainty as to who they are and what they want. The recovered alcoholic worker needs of course to be near to the drinking alcoholics in order to be of value and it is in this bridging of the gap that difficulties can arise. To be 'elevated' too soon from the ranks can be a disaster course, but to have been too long sober may create the response, 'You were never an alcoholic'; for veterans on skid row, sobriety is viewed as impossible so that a man who is several years sober cannot by definition be an alcoholic! Of the four men we have actually employed up to 1973 one had been sober for five years, two for one year and one for six months. All experienced divided loyalties, but in the last case these were far more acute, eventually causing him to feel that he should cease working for us. In part the loyalty to other men needs to be retained and be seen to be retained; while at the same time the worker must be able to communicate to all the other agencies the true experience of the men still on skid row.

It is by no means easy for drinking alcoholics to appreciate that their sober, erstwhile drinking mates may not be able to place them immediately in a hostel or may not feel it wise to try to do so. For some men to have an interview with the recovered alcoholic is merely a quicker way on to the rehabilitation circuit, which avoids confrontation with another social worker. Effecting change in the orientation of one or two sober skid row men carries with it a challenge to the remainder to change their orientation too. Members of a drinking school may, for example, still see sober ex-members as having 'chickened out' or 'thrown in the towel', rather than seeing these ex-members in a position of some strength to assist them should they themselves require this. If however the position can be accepted (and more often than not it is), the alcoholic employee can then relate in a direct and vital way to men coming forward for help. There is less need for pretence on the part of the men; less need to play the familiar alcoholic games; and more instant communication about what is really required. The alcoholic who has been through the mill himself is able to insist that the man returns sober in the morning with a passionate sympathy that might be clouded with guilt in the social worker insisting on the same thing. This is not the same as the sober alcoholic saying, 'I did it, therefore you can,' which can be a very judgmental attitude. Rather, what is being said is 'Our total experience tells us that what I am saying is not nonsense and I will help you when I see you sober in the morning.'

One incident best illustrates the use of directness and of a common

8

language. Jack was an alcoholic constantly seeking help, yet always claiming he received none. Most of us thought there was little that could be done to help him anyway. The alcoholic worker decided to devote a whole week totally to Jack and first to seek to place him in a residential centre. Jack continued to call, usually only half-sober, still complaining that no one would help. Eventually an 'interview' was begun in which the alcoholic was told to stop complaining and was informed that one of them would go out through the window unless Jack sat and listened seriously. He did. He remained sober for eighteen months.

For another group of men the alcoholic worker provides a source of continuous comradeship, especially when they are in prison and are visited regularly each week. 'Having a crack' with no other motive is for some men a way of accepting the worker, leaving unstated the fact that help is available when the right moment came. But the 'crack' is a method of keeping contact which might be difficult for ordinary social workers to perform.

With regard to colleagues on the Project, other aspects manifested themselves. Most important, the alcoholic employees were basically doers, not talkers, who did not always see lengthy staff meetings analysing the Project's position as relevant to the core work of the Project. There is room for both action and talk, but the tendency of the majority of the staff to be introspective was brought home to us by the comments of the alcoholic workers. This attitude had another result, namely that the alcoholics seemed more able to perceive the difference between a man seeking help but who was being 'mucked about' by the system and a man demanding the impossible, then being angry when he could not have this. Doctors would be told if necessary that 'This man is very sick and I want you to get him into hospital'. Unnecessary prevarication by hospitals was severely dealt with by the recovered alcoholics, but from such a position of experience and understanding that no complaints have ever been received by the Project from other agencies about the vigour of their approach.

Many of us talk about 'cutting through the red tape', but often we are too diplomatic actually to effect this. The alcoholic who can feel more acutely the client's needs is in a strong position to break down unnecessary resistance. On occasions such resistance is due to lack of knowledge about the problem, and in these cases the alcoholic is able to perform an educative function with the agency or worker concerned. In this way, the reception of future alcoholic referrals is likely to be improved. For the staff on the Project itself, daily involvement with the alcoholic worker meant that we were wary of underestimating the potential of any clients we saw. For example, the second alcoholic worker employed was first contacted in the court in which he was appearing for the 'nth' time; in outward appearance he was the stereotype 'derelict drunk'. Two years later this man was still sober, having worked for six months as an extremely valuable colleague. The presence of the alcoholic worker increases awareness of the development of potential, rather than leaving it in the realm of wishful thinking. The alcoholics' own understanding of any other alcoholic's position is different in kind from that of the social worker. This daily contact has subjected the staff's judgments to critical comment from a viewpoint not usually available in social work agencies. Such comment was not automatically 'right' because it was made by an alcoholic, but it was comment that needed to be taken into account.

Whatever the strengths actually brought to the Project by the alcoholic worker, we felt these were never as great as they could have been. This worker was only one in a group of more orthodox social workers, and his future prospects as a social worker were virtually nil outside the Project. The support offered to the alcoholic worker tended to be of the same degree as that given to the rest of the staff, which was by no means always effective. One alcoholic was troubled by meeting alone with me to discuss issues, claiming this felt like being 'called up to see the Prison Governor'! Clearly there was a need here for a more appropriate support mechanism. A team of alcoholic workers was we felt a better idea and would enable a more sustained contribution to be made by this group.

Early in 1973 we therefore decided to build up such a team of at least four men filling vacancies left by orthodox workers. We were fortunate to obtain in 1973 a three-year grant from the Wates Foundation to enable us to appoint an organizer for the establishment and sustaining of this team, which was selected early in 1974. We believed that in recruiting this team it was essential that its members did not just come to do short-term jobs with us but rather to embark upon a new career. This meant that someone on the Project was to be responsible for training and supporting these men, not in becoming just like other social workers, but in fully developing their own particular skills and aptitudes to the full as a new careers team. In this way the men concerned might be in a better position to seek out other posts, after a year or two's experience with us. If this is not possible, they will remain second-class workers, unable to progress in the way open to more formally educated Project colleagues. The first alcoholic worker was with us for over two years and then wanted to continue working as a prison welfare officer with alcoholics in the prison setting. No one was willing to offer him that opportunity despite the fact that for two years he had been seeing alcoholics in a prison regularly each week. He was given interviews, but he felt that delaying tactics were used before the negative decision was finally made. The interviews, he said, were like bad apple trees, 'all blossom and no fruit'. We would not wish a scheme of employing recovered alcoholics to be similarly so fruitless. We are grateful to the experience our first four workers have given us as colleagues and hope this should in future ensure better opportunities for their fellow alcoholics, when fruit and blossom will exist in the right proportions.

6 DETOXIFICATION CENTRES

I decided to single out detoxification centres for particular attention for a number of reasons. The Project has become increasingly concerned about the proposed establishment of these centres, and has consequently devoted considerable time and energy to consideration of the problems involved. The possibility of their being established has informed a great deal of our activity since 1972. One member of the staff, Joan Walley, visited detoxification centres in North America (Walley, 1972). Much of the discussion about these centres raises basic issues such as to how we define or redefine the homeless alcoholic for whom they are intended to cater and what form of help it is hoped to be able to offer. Questions of the politics of responsibility are also involved. Some fear that detoxification centres may in practice prove to be unworkable and eventually as inappropriate as the old inebriate retreats of the last century. On the other hand, they may be the next vital step forward in tackling the skid row problem. What is certain is that they have become part of everybody's thinking and are a dominating feature of any current discussion on the treatment of the homeless alcoholic.

The report was bold enough to claim that 'Some form of special arrangement for detoxification will be indispensable to any future system which attempts to deal comprehensively with public drunkenness' (Home Office, 1971, p. 144). But just what is the aim of such an arrangement? In Poland they are viewed merely as 'sobering up stations' (ibid., p. 145) while in America they seek to play a more positive role in the whole treatment process (ibid., p. 145). The report stresses that in this country they should be 'demonstrably medical and social work facilities with a clearly therapeutic purpose' (ibid., p. 152). Nimmer (1970) has most clearly conceptualized the detoxification process, identifying five objectives of this new system. These are the removal of the criminal label; the provision of humane and sanitary shelter; the provision of expert medical help; the reduction of the burden on the criminal agencies; and the introduction of the potentiality of rehabilitative therapy or referral. The last is especially important as 'none of the operating detoxification programs challenges the assumption that rehabilitation is a proper goal' (ibid., p. 7). Nimmer

(1971) has since looked in detail at some of the problems arising from such a multiplicity of objectives. We, too, through our own Camberwell Court study (Hershon, 1974) and other experiences have come to look more critically at the current proposals for detoxification centres in this country. Certainly we would not yet share the Swedish optimism which claimed that their two pilot experiments 'revealed unequivocally that the detoxification clinic concept is not only fully workable but that it also creates entirely new premises for an active and effective socio-medical treatment of drunks' (Ministry of Justice, Stockholm, 1968). The Project has always pressed for the establishment of a detoxification centre in South London as part of the Project's policy to close the gaps in the services provided, at the same time there has been a growing realization that the issues involved are more complex than seemed at first sight.

The first such issue is that 'whatever the original stimulus for the setting-up of the centres, it has certain consequences for the operation of those centres' (Walley, p. 19). In England much of the pressure for the centres has come about because of dissatisfaction with the present legal system and its handling of the drunk. It is even worth pondering whether the report itself would have been produced if prisons had not been so full and the drunks an obvious group that could be dealt with somewhere else. We need to separate our desire to reform the Criminal Justice system from the need to establish new treatment services for skid row men. If this division is not clearly made, the result can be that we merely facilitate prevention of arrests by providing an alternative process to satisfy community interests, which is in essence a system of 'acceptable harassment' (Nimmer, 1971, p. 144). Arrests are outlawed and then relabelled.

What are the implications of the new approach? It is intended that the police will still be involved, as they will be taking the drunks to the detoxification centres; so that in essence an agency of social control is defining the target population for a socio-medical, therapeutic facility. Tatham (1969) describes the operation of one detoxification centre where the police are asked to distinguish between 'happy drunks' and 'dangerous drunks'. The consequences of this are either that the police should be involved in a programme of re-education for this new role, or, if not, the centre will only function in accordance with existing police perceptions. In our court study, for example, we found on one morning eight men had been arrested by the same policeman, a young constable, and most of these arrests were felt to be 'inappropriate' by the jailers. If too many men were to be taken to the detoxification centre by policemen unfamiliar with what it can do, then there could easily be a breakdown in relations between the police and the centre, as has happened with some detoxification centres in North America. In St Louis this resulted on occasions in no men being taken to the centre and the centre's director asking for drunks to be brought into the centre (Nimmer, 1970, p. 18). We would argue that the police need to be involved in the planning and preparation of the centre to avoid their continuing to see dealing with drunks as a second-class activity warranting less attention than others. As one policeman remarked to us, 'Believe you me we do not go along with the social work ideas that are being introduced into the police force . . . we'd rather not have anything to do at all with drunks.'

For the men themselves, will being taken by the police to a medical unit be seen as more acceptable than going to court? For the new system to work it is surely important that the men do have some perception that they are ill and in need of the treatment being offered. The court-prison system fails to work with this group, not because it is inhumane and brutal but because it is simply irrelevant to the needs and problems of the drunkenness offender. Will detoxification centres be seen as kind and friendly, but still irrelevant places? Of habitual drunkenness offenders going through the courts there is only a small percentage who are ill at the time and see themselves as ill, generally because of delirium tremens, shakes and other clearly-defined symptoms. The majority do not have a clear perception that they are alcoholics who are ill and need socio-medical treatment and care. In other words the disease concept has by no means penetrated the skid row sub-culture, and for the setting-up of a detoxification centre this will present problems. It may mean that more education than medical care will be needed in the centre. Even so, we should be careful about persuading everyone they have an illness, as there is growing concern among professionals about the real appropriateness of the disease concept of alcoholism (Robinson, 1972). While this concept is an improvement on the old moralistic and punitive concept, it none the less has some inherent problems on its own account, not least of which is the non-medical content of most of the treatment that is actually provided. It is arguable that, if the men do not see themselves as ill, we should not push them towards that view. Why change the stigmatized offender into a passive patient? It may be that the police will only bring in those who are manifestly ill, but this again presupposes a greater degree of actual medical competence by the police than is fair. American evidence also suggests that the police do not seek out the most ill, but rather those who are most available or most unsightly (Nimmer, 1971, p. 56). If then we assume that the majority of those

being brought to a detoxification centre will not be acutely ill or even
see themselves as ill at all, should we stress the medical content of the
centre?

This raises one of the central issues that so far seems to have perplexed
those who run most centres. Where does the medicine end and the
social work begin? Should the centre be based on a medical model and
sited in a hospital? How far will the balance of medical versus social
workers affect length of stay and discharge procedure? The report
foresaw the centre as being 'under medical direction' (Home Office,
1971, p. 154) and having the 'features of a good hospital ward' (ibid.,
p. 155). This perhaps puts too much emphasis on the medical model.
It does, however, seem that in England and Scotland most of the pilot
detoxification centres are to be sited in hospitals with a consequent
stress on the medical model of operation. This is likely to produce
major difficulties for the social workers at the centre. Most of the people
being admitted will be homeless, and yet most will only stay at the
centres about seven days. If the unit is too medically biased, then
clients could be discharged medically fit before they have any place to
stay, thus serving only to add another stage to the revolving door
process. It seems clear that unless there is a massive social work
involvement co-operating with a network of after-care facilities, many
men will simply return to the street whence they came. Nimmer (1971,
p. 122) noted that such was the turnover at one centre in Washington
that in six months 1,282 men were referred on to an Alcoholic
Rehabilitation Clinic, of whom only sixteen arrived. There has been
recognition that the detoxification centre is only part of a total programme.

There is little reason to believe that the chronic offender will change
a life pattern of drinking after a few days of sobriety and care at a
public health unit. The detoxification unit should therefore be
supplemented by a network of co-ordinated aftercare facilities. Such
a program might well begin with the mobilization of existing
community resources (US Task Force Report, 1967, p. 5).

The Home Office report (1971, p. 155) went further, envisaging the
possibility of the centre being 'the hub around which all activity for the
management of the habitual drunken offender should be arranged'.
Despite these hopes, Walley (1972, p. 7) observed that in America at
least, 'the concept of the unit was seen too often as an alternative to all
existing resources'.

One of the ways of overcoming this situation would be for all agencies
concerned to be involved in the preliminary planning of the centres.
This however becomes difficult when the principal agency involved is

a hospital and many of the others involved are voluntary organizations, which run the majority of hostels that will be essential if any centre is to have even half a chance of functioning adequately. This means that hospitals may have to cast themselves in a new role, at least as far as their involvement with the drunkenness 'offender' is concerned. Even though the centres may be sited in hospitals, the American experience is that 'in all instances a huge medical and nursing staff ratio has gradually been reduced' (ibid., p. 25). It is obviously essential that the tensions between medical and social work staff are kept to a minimum. It is fine to list the advantages of the centre over the old system as including 'more encouragement for patient utilization of supportive community health and social welfare resources upon discharges' (Tatham, 1969, p. 48), but not so fine if this merely masks inadequate hostel provision and failure to make best use of what there is because of the low status of social workers in the centre.

Wherever the centres are placed and however they are staffed, experience indicates that they must be accepted as experimental and must therefore be evaluated. The report (1971, pp. 157–8) stressed the need for limited pilot experiments to be tried out. No one should be encouraged to view the detoxification centre as the latest panacea for the ills of skid row. Drawing attention to the unknown quantity in the exercise should prevent too many false hopes being dashed. 'It is vital not to over-promise and under-perform' (Nimmer, 1971, p. 98). If this danger is not avoided it tends to be the alcoholic who is then dismissed as 'hopeless' rather than the method being described as 'inappropriate'. Part of the experiment should surely involve a variety of different methods of running centres. These would for instance include some centres which took self-referrals as well as those from the police; some which were placed outside a hospital; some with a non-medical director – hopefully one such centre will be established by the DHSS. As the early experiments get under way, it is important that they are continuously evaluated so that some true assessment can be made. Walley's (1972, p. 26) comments on the American centres should be noted:

There were masses of figures relating to the number of admissions but little attempt to see how effective all the work really was. It almost seemed as if once a busy centre was underway, everyone became so busy 'doing' that time for evaluation was not set aside for fear of it demonstrating how unproductive all the doing was. Yet some centres had been set up with a clear commitment to evaluation.

We would hope that in England the research element would be seen, not as an optional extra, but as a necessity.

The St Louis detoxification centre has probably been subject to as much critical comment as any. It has been suggested that it does not show that the criminal process can be reformed by the detoxification centre, but rather demonstrates the difficulties inherent in this approach to reform (Nimmer, 1971, p. 98). The data so far do not indicate that the rate of success is very high (Nimmer, 1970, pp. 22–4). But the issue is more complex than was thought initially, in that it has too often been assumed 'in some ill-defined way, that the drunkenness arrestee population represents a unique grouping, both in terms of immediate needs and rehabilitative potential' (ibid.). In essence, the conclusion about St Louis was 'not that the detoxification model should be abandoned but that its use and structure should be subjected to more incisive scrutiny' (ibid.).

Though much of what has been said so far applies to North America, there is little doubt that the issues apply with equal relevance to the proposed development of detoxification centres in this country. Because of the problems and complexities involved, the Project has constantly sought both on its own and through others to present these issues to responsible authorities and further, to seek representation on the planning body for the centres. The final responsibility for these centres was a problem that was briefly mentioned in the report (Home Office, 1971, p. 158) but was left unresolved. Fortunately, the DHSS undertook this responsibility in 1972. But they, in turn, are dependent on hospitals showing an interest in siting or supporting a detoxification centre, since they are not able to compel any hospital to develop such a centre. It has always seemed to us that, given the general view held by the medical profession of the homeless alcoholic, hospitals were not likely to be too willing to have such centres. One way of reducing hospital anxieties is surely to involve all the other actors in the drama, including the police and voluntary rehabilitation agencies, at the planning stage. It is clearly among the latter that much skill and energy lie, yet it is so often just this group that are not involved except when their direct services are required. So it is that, with a challenging new development such as detoxification centres, it is found difficult for voluntary and statutory services to come together effectively at the crucial stages. The twin problems of responsibility and co-ordination reappear. Just who is responsible for ensuring that all relevant agencies in a given area are involved in planning the centre; and who is accountable to whom if they are not so involved? Why is the issue of co-ordination so difficult to resolve even where there is one very specific task to perform? Such questions need to be answered if the concept of detoxification centres is to become a reality and centres are then to multiply. Of the four pilot detoxification centres proposed for England, none is likely to open before 1975 and even that seems an optimistic date.

In view of all the efforts made by the staff of the Project to try to set up a detoxification centre, it is not without irony that the city whose services most impressed our staff member on the visit to America was Philadelphia (Walley, 1972, p. 6). Here there was no detoxification centre but there was a Diagnostic and Rehabilitation Centre which secured official working agreements for detoxification with all the hospitals in the city area. This means that alcoholics do not receive any special attention in the hospitals but are integrated into wards of the general hospital. The belief of the Diagnostic Centre is that the general hospitals should not be allowed to refuse admission to one category of sick people, and that possibly the existence of a detoxification centre would tend to reinforce a man's alcoholic behaviour pattern (Shandler, 1967). In this arrangement, it is the concept of detoxification which has been adopted rather than a specific unit being established. There are obvious advantages with such an arrangement, in that the problem of the drunk has not been 'hived off' to some specialist unit as if it were something that did not really concern the medical profession as a whole. Further, this situation forces some degree of co-ordination upon services and increases the possibility of wider community participation owing to more hospitals being involved. It would be exciting if some such arrangement could also be worked out in England, rather than our feeling that at all costs we must be wedded to the notion that detoxification centres alone can do the job of taking the drunken man or woman off the street and into the rehabilitation circuit. If detoxification centres are going to take so long to establish, even as pilot schemes, and then have to be evaluated, it is surely imperative to be thinking of parallel developments. These also could seek to divert the drunkenness offender from the courts.

All the efforts to remove homeless alcoholic men and women from the court process are no doubt laudable. Yet the men we have talked with express world-weary reservations about the proposed procedures. 'The police will just arrest you for begging instead or get you on "sus" ' is a common observation. A change in police practice is by no means to be discounted. Leigh (1974) has highlighted the looseness of the vagrancy laws, the ease with which arrests can be made under them and the powerlessness of the vagrants to withstand this. Local arrest rates for drunkenness and begging vary considerably from month to month. All this strengthens the case for well-thought-out police involvement in any new schemes.

Whatever the practical problems of any new procedure, there

probably has to be some belief that it can be made to work. No one is satisfied with the present 'revolving door'. Other than simply ceasing to operate the court system for drunkenness offenders without providing any alternative – which is one argument put forward – we are forced to work hard on a genuinely effective alternative. I only wish we could hurry up about it.

7 VIEWS FROM THE OTHER SIDE

Assisted by Peter Archard

Part of the task of the Project has been to try to understand more about the sub-culture of the homeless alcoholic as it is manifested in some areas of London. We are not attempting to define the term sub-culture or defend our choice of the term. That would be a study in itself, and the concept has been throughly analysed by others (Arnold, 1970). A sociologist on the staff, Peter Archard, undertook one year's participant observation study in order to try to gain some notion of how the alcoholic on the streets viewed the activities of the helping agencies in the area (Archard, 1972). We include here some comments and views mainly arising out of Archard's field notes that seem relevant to those in the helping professions. Already in this report we have on a number of occasions alluded to the disparity between our intentions and the alcoholics' actual situation which produces a poor social work outcome. This unsatisfactory outcome has been noted in results of surveys in courts, lodging houses and prisons. We are persuaded therefore of the urgent need to understand better and take account of the alcoholics' own views.

Though this chapter will be descriptive rather than analytical, a few general comments are essential. Investigators have tended to agree that 'skid rows maintain a "loose" sub-culture or "rudimentary" community life' (Bahr, 1968, p. 19). This is a life 'dominated by group norms, moves and folk-ways' (Ross, 1970, p. 15) and according to Wallace (1965, p. 144) it is the 'most deviant community in the United States'. This sub-culture has been examined by Rubington (1958), who enumerated some of the features of any sub-culture, namely that it 'provides a solution to problems. It disseminates a shared way of acting, thinking and feeling as a response to the challenge of a special situation. This special situation raises its own problems. The sub-culture defines the solution' (ibid., p. 51). Of course in some ways solutions in turn create secondary problems, but the immediate ones at least have been resolved. Skid row, claims Rubington, offers a solution to 'the problems which confront the homeless, jobless and the alienated' (ibid., p. 53). Workable solutions, though short-term, seem available for these desperate problems within it. Skid row can then almost seem to offer an extended kinship system and – even more important – a 'defence against the hostile conventional world' (ibid., p. 55). There is an alternative system of values which suggests that 'if all is not quite right with the respectable social world, then all is not quite wrong with the skid row world' (ibid.). We need to know more about this in order to find the answer to the really difficult question, 'What does it mean when you try to get someone to get out of this way of life?' (ibid., p. 52). If, as Wallace (1965, p. 156) claims, it is true that 'to the skid rower the social worker is *persona non grata*', then to answer this question seems virtually impossible. Fortunately, however, our experience suggests that the sub-culture, though very strong, is not quite as tight as this. Skid row residents at times need social workers and the facilities they have to offer even though it may well not be for quite the same reasons as the social workers hope they are needed. When there is no contact at all will be the time to worry. Additionally the sub-culture is not fixed and isolated: men can be on the fringes of it. One study (Blumberg, 1971) suggested that only a third of skid row residents were truly part of the skid row community. Phillimore (1973) has explored the role of sub-groups within the total sub-culture and the lack of rigid boundaries between the vagrant and non-vagrant worlds.

Let us then examine some of the attitudes of the homeless alcoholics to their world, attitudes with which we are perhaps less familiar and which we would be wise not to ignore. We do not view the vagrant world as homogeneous, and therefore need to stress that the participation study, from which most of the following material is drawn, was restricted to certain areas in South London. Further, we should explain that remarks made by the alcoholics and reported here were spontaneous and unsolicited. Both the strengths and weaknesses of such spontaneity are apparent.

The alcoholic's own condition and position

We have already had occasion to remark that the drunkenness offender does not generally see himself as a sick alcoholic in need of treatment at hospital. There is in some men a genuine ambivalence about their own condition:

'I wouldn't say I was an alcoholic. A drunkard, yes . . . a few years ago you never heard of the word alcoholic. We were all drunkards. But now all these doctors keep telling us about being alcoholics, I don't know so much about that.'

Yet the same man can define a drunkard as someone who must be working, whereas an alcoholic essentially does not work, sleeps rough and 'does not give a fuck about his appearance'. By that definition the speaker himself would be an alcoholic. The full-blown medical model will however be used by the men if need dictates. One man told a court he was suffering from a disease: once he had alcohol inside him he 'could not do anything' about his behaviour. The label of 'being an alcoholic' is a valuable part of the skid row survival kit.

Such discussion as there is among alcoholics about the nature of their problems tends to centre on three beliefs: first, the alcoholic cannot be cured and there is no answer to the problem of alcoholism. Second, any attempt to come off the drink has to come from the man himself, who will however inevitably slip! Third, the genuine alcoholic is someone who 'wants more and more drink' – the man who recognizes no ceiling to the quantity he can drink. To the outsider these views seem to reinforce feelings of both hopelessness and togetherness. They are an outcast group of genuine alcoholics who cannot be cured, and who blame themselves for their failure to obtain sobriety. The drinking alcoholics seem almost relieved to learn there is no 'cure': such a group asked an alcoholic, sober for six years, whether he regarded himself as 'cured' and he said 'no'.

There can however be a virulent rejection of other alcoholics, such as middle-class alcoholics, with whom some men have been involved in hospital alcoholic units. The home-based, though not necessarily middle-class, alcoholic, talks in group meetings about hiding bottles from his family. The skid row man reports back to the drinking school, 'When I heard that crack, I told them "any real alcoholic wouldn't give a fuck about having to hide his bottles".' If further proof is needed of the pathetic nature of the other hospital alcoholic patients it is readily supplied. 'Some of these fellows can't be alcoholics . . . they asked me what "jack" and "skippering" are. They'd never heard of them.' The extremities of this antagonism were related by one man who told how in his hospital unit the park drinkers 'form a sort of protection circle. We don't reveal everything in the meetings – we exchange information amongst ourselves, but we don't let it out to the other patients.'

Whatever the skid row man may feel about other alcoholics, there is little doubt that they see themselves as better than many of the 'non-alcoholics' on skid row. The alcoholics are certainly not 'natural born bums', they have worked in the past and will work again. They still have life in them. Alcoholics are 'sick of places like the Sally and the Spike, in those places most inmates are being led by the neck – this is not the case with the alcoholic'.

'There is no man with a livelier mind than an alcoholic dosser –
especially the "toby man" whose wheels are always working. It's only
when you are very, very drunk . . . that you might not be able to
think straight . . . even when a man is very drunk, his instinct makes
him alert to the presence of the law.'

These are real men compared with 'those bums down at the Crypt who
just sit around and drink tea'.

Within the drinking groups themselves there is some indication that
methylated spirit drinking is something quite different again.

'It's a big step down. You feel that you are degrading yourself.
Since when you are a cider drinker you realize you have not quite
got to "rock bottom", but then when you begin drinking "the jack" you
have to join the "rough boys". Then of course our attitudes to the
cider drinkers change and they are condemned. You see the cider
drinkers and say "fuck them" and don't bother with them any longer.'

The view the meths drinkers have of themselves perhaps suggests why
they are viewed, as a group, as being difficult to help, not because they
drink meths, but because of the attitudes that accompany this step. If
it's a big step down, it's a big step up.

The men's attitudes to their homelessness is also interesting. An
alcoholic only recently made homeless said he felt 'low and depressed'.

'I haven't got as low as these boys [the other drinkers]. Mind you
I'm feeling it more. I'll tell you what I would like most at this very
moment: a hot bath. These boys are used to skippering. I only come
into this park because I have nowhere else to go. I know it's the only
place I can get a drink.'

The fact of homelessness is less worrying to the more experienced skid
row alcoholic. The first break away from formal responsibilities can be
'frightening' but thereafter can come a tremendous sense of freedom.
To be 'on the tramp' is happiness – for a time. Men will recount how
people who gave them lifts in cars wanted to leave their car and go on
with them!

Once homeless, how does it feel to be on public view, as it were,
most of the time? One man said that when he became a dosser:

'I was aware that I was under the boot of anyone – it could be the
street cleaner, the copper, anyone. The dossers are aware that when
you are in public you are a public football – and you have no
come-back. Even if you are in a cubicle in a doss-house, that's not
really private – you can hear everything going on around you.'

The location of 'skippers' is kept secret because this is one of the few
chances to obtain a semblance of privacy. The totally public life is not
seen as presenting too many problems.

'You don't pay much heed to these problems – you learn how to cope with these things. Yes sometimes you want to get away from it all – that's when you become a "toby man". You get some kind of privacy when you're on the tramp . . . you see, the dosser is going to the same situation which he's leaving: but by moving the dosser feels very much that he is making plans – even if they don't come to anything . . . when you're moving you feel you're doing something about yourself – you get away from all the "crack".'

But, despite this optimism, are the men institutionalized by the round of form filling, queuing and the rest of the routine which is required of them because of their homeless, rootless situation? For the alcoholic dosser the spark exists that may prevent this happening.

'The alcoholic dosser never really becomes institutionalized like some of the men that use the doss houses. For example, the police are never out of Marshalsea Road [a Social Security office for homeless men] because the drunkard is always throwing his arms up, is always having the same old questions asked of him, the dosser is always rearing up on the men in there, and the staff are rearing up on him. It's funny, but in a sense the alcoholic dosser has not yet got a chance to be institutionalized in a sense he is denied being institutionalized. I've seen many tramps get a "knock back" at Marshalsea Road and the man just accepts it – well you won't get this from a drunkard. The drunkard won't take a "knock back" drunk or sober, especially when he's sober, the man cannot stand it, his nerves cannot take it.'

For some men at any rate it is possible to survive in a situation many outsiders would deem as almost impossible.

Recovery

We have noted that these men see alcoholism as incurable; though this may reflect the view that a return to social drinking rather than permanent sobriety will never be possible. In general, relatively little discussion about recovery seems to occur, which may indicate that the immediate needs of getting the bottle and the bed are so paramount that time for philosophical reflection on long-term needs is simply not available. Attitudes to the attempted recovery of others are generally rather cynical; some men go so far as to entice the recovering alcoholic back on to skid row. At times it seems as if a sixth sense operates among the drinking men in that they estimate when others will break out and, more important, how much money the men concerned will be bringing with them. As one man, who had relapsed, said: 'They knew to a penny how much I'd saved and all I'd done was to work for them buggers to drink my money.'

9

The existence of rehabilitation agencies and of alcoholics living in them does present problems. One recovered alcoholic, now a social worker, put it this way:

'I've planted a crossroads in their mind – I'm presenting them with an alternative. In other words I've created a problem for them – it sets the wheels in motion again about there being an alternative to the type of life they're leading. Mentioning Rathcoole, Maudsley Hospital, presents the men with an inward battle.'

This man went on to illustrate this from his own drinking history:

'Till the day I went to Cane Hill Hospital I did not think I had a problem – I accepted my way of life – but Cane Hill Hospital put the seed in my mind. I didn't recognize any problem until then – I didn't have any as far as I could see. I knew hundreds of men in my position who didn't think about their life as a problem – nobody set any panic stations about the way we lived.'

While some men regard rehabilitation facilities as 'all a big lemon' they do none the less exist in some state of tension between a continuous drinking situation and a projected state of future affairs defined as sobriety.

The border between these two states is not however a rigid one that is crossed only when the man has motivation: 'coming off the beer' is a complex process. The men talk of 'turning' long before any actual move is made towards a rehabilitation facility: suggesting that motivation may build up over a period as long as a year, rather than being suddenly acquired in order to get a man through his hostel interview. One man, months before he finally stopped drinking, began to say, 'One has to get moving' and to claim that he was 'browned off' with the drinking scene. The feeling of having to get moving was brought on as much by the low level of drinking activity in the park as by the attraction of a sober life. A month or two later the same phrase would be used again, 'One's got to help one's self. You've got to get moving.' Later still, feelings of being 'ashamed' of himself emerged together with a dislike of 'skippering'. Soon he stated that he was 'beginning to turn' and he must start 'getting a room and a job'. Only some months after this did he gain admission to an alcoholic rehabilitation facility.

Once involved in a facility that aims to rehabilitate a man, a distinction is made between simply being 'off the beer' and being 'sober'.

'Paddy has been off the drink for a long time now but he hasn't gained sobriety at all – he's still immature – he's still the same old Paddy – he's far from sobriety, he hasn't grown up. I can tell you the man who hasn't gained sobriety – his whole "patter" is all about the drink, what he did in the past with the men. In the hostels all they talk about is the telly, the job, the suit they've just bought – they never develop any outside interests. It's good to see them this way but they're not moving towards sobriety.'

It seems as if the men 'can go so far in their development, then stop. They can't take any more.' As one recovered alcoholic put it, 'Many men think there's a plateau and you shouldn't go beyond it – buying a car for example is really taking recovery too far.' But 'sobriety has to do with bettering yourself – finding outside interests. Coming off the drink is only the very first step towards sobriety.' When social workers say a man 'is doing all right' they all too often simply mean 'he's keeping off the beer'. 'It's no good social workers learning about a man's weaknesses – that's no good – if the man hasn't realized his own weakness himself. It doesn't surprise me if men go on the drink after two or three years keeping off the beer.' The alcoholic's perception of what constitutes real progress is usually astute. I remember two men talking of another, and one commented, 'He's doing well, he's well dressed.' 'But', asked the other, 'what about the inner man?' On another occasion a man said to me that of all the sober ex-skid row alcoholics he knew, 'not one had a relationship with a female.' And where do you find a decent woman if you want something more than picking up 'a stray at the bingo'?

Social workers

It will probably be no surprise for most social workers to learn that they are not the most revered section of the population as far as skid row alcoholics are concerned. Social workers are of course needed from time to time, and perhaps the realization that social workers cannot in practice be universally written off creates an awkward ambivalence that in turn produces the anger and frustration of needing the people you despise. Some hostility is however only part of a wider resentment.

'Society has got the boot in and is going to run your face into the ground. The only satisfaction you get in prison is that you know the tax payer is paying for it and that since your attitude is "fuck society" . . . you do get that small satisfaction when you're in prison.'

This universal resentment can lead a man to a position where he resents 'the man running for the bus who you think is an overfed bastard who doesn't give a fuck about you and is only prepared to give you two bob in order to get rid of you'. Men with no shoes will beg car drivers who give them money, the men return to their mates denouncing the 'idiots' who gave them money and who now drive off leaving behind the shoeless men!

It is at the practical level that social workers tend to be judged. For example, there is little room in the men's view for any concept of balance between short-term and long-term needs.

'The social worker at the hospital wouldn't give me ten shillings to pay the fine for damping down my bed at the Sally Ann. Unless I paid that fine I was forced to sleep rough – but I did all right in the end because I went to see another social worker a couple of days later and she gave me the money. She is all right.'

A female alcoholic relates how at another hospital

'there is a social worker who has done me a good turn. I'd been in for taking an overdose of tablets. When I explained I had no fixed address, she fixed me up with a voucher for a hostel in the West End for the next seven days. Well, I did all right there, didn't I?'

Sadly, the probation and after-care service is viewed by many alcoholics as 'nothing but a hand-out'. They do have money to give out so 'why not to me today?' can be the cry which thus determines the nature of the help provided. One man explained:

'I asked another dosser where the probation offices were. But I only managed to get two bob off them. I thought I might get ten bob – the woman who gave it to me asked me if I drank, and then tried to smell my breath. She made me sign for the money. I bought five woodies, but it wasn't worth the bother. Being skint is a problem – I think I'll give Borough High Street probation office a try tomorrow – maybe I'll have better luck there.'

The probation service is seen as being there 'to provide a few bob or a bed voucher or a room', yet a 'knock back' is used by the alcoholic as cause for a statement about his being stigmatized.

'The officer at Borough High Street refused to give me any money because he said I would drink it. They never give you anything there – they know you'll spend it on drink. Mind you, they'll give money to a boy out of borstal. But once you've got a name for yourself – once they know you're an alcoholic – that's it, you're stigmatized. Everywhere they treat you the same.'

Even striking lucky can carry with it some penalties and may not always be worth while in terms of self-respect. One man recounted:

'Nine out of ten times some young probation officer who is all dressed up ends up telling you what you've done wrong, how you've got on the wrong foot; and instead of getting help you get all confused. You end up "rearing up" inside yourself because of his fancy office and job. Eventually he offers you five bob and you end up telling him to stuff it. It makes you realize that this world is a jungle, a shit, and that everyone is just out to get what they can take,

so there's no reason why I should not go and do some screwing.
You soon learn it's not worth turning to the probation service for
help or any other of the charities.'

A service that only gets seen as a hand-out faces tremendous problems
as some men do in fact want more assistance than that. The skill of the
probation officer can turn the situation to good effect. 'I only went in to
beg him for a pair of socks and we ended up talking about my drinking
problem.'

Too often whatever is suggested is seen merely as a plot or game
devised by social workers to outwit the alcoholic. A man who is given an
appointment at 4 p.m. on a particular day sees this as a move by the
social worker to stop him drinking during the day so that he will turn
up sober for the appointment. No alternative explanation of the time
offered is considered. The constraints and practical realities governing
the working conditions of the social workers are not readily invoked as
a means of explanation. 'They earn lots of money, have seven holidays
a year, and aren't even very good at their job.' Demands that are made
upon the alcoholic by the social worker are used to devalue the helper
and sustain the drinking.

'The social worker was prepared to listen to me. I told her that I was
wanting to get a place in a hostel but she is asking me to keep sober
for three weeks till she gets me a bed. That's asking too much of a
man – you can't stay sober while you're skippering and hanging
around the park all day . . . social workers don't understand what it's
like to be down here in this park every day.'

Worse still is the fact that 'social workers don't help the genuine skid
row alcoholic; they give too much time to men who can afford rooms
and flats.'

Placed, it seems, in a position of powerlessness, the man invariably
devalues the helper and 'tears a strip off him', preferably in the presence
of as many other people as possible. A man may well relate how he
'told the social worker a thing or two', though in reality nothing was
said at all. The recovered alcoholic worker, too, comes in for his share
of criticism.

'It's a waste of time going down to see – when he doesn't really
want to help you. He asked me to stop drinking for seven days to
show I was really serious . . . how can a man do that when he is
skippering? . . . All I get from that man was that he used to be in the
Merchant Navy. I don't care what he was – he's no different from me.
He's not cured yet – he never will be. For all you know he might be
down in this park tomorrow begging us for a drink.'

Similarly, when men are out of the rehabilitation houses and back with their drinking mates they can display a considerable degree of derision about the houses, which incidentally may turn into laudatory comments if there is any possibility of a return.

'When I was in – some of the men were drinking slightly and telling the warden the next morning that everything was O.K. These social workers are no good – they earn good money for doing nothing, and all you have is the residents pulling the wool over their eyes.'

At times it seems as if the distance between social worker and homeless alcoholic is so vast that it is a wonder it is ever bridged.

The medical profession

Doctors are not always used by the skid row man in quite the way for which doctors underwent prolonged training. For the men not yet concerned with taking a 'cure', doctors are mainly judged by two criteria. First, will they readily supply pills or tablets? Some drugs do have an intoxicating power which augments the effect of alcohol; and 'good doctors' are those who provide a flow of tablets. Second, doctors who are readily prepared to write out official sickness certificates are viewed favourably also. With such a certificate the alcoholic knows that the Social Security office is obliged to give him money without too close an examination of the overall social and economic circumstances of the claimant.

'When I was in a hostel last time I registered with a doctor. I could get a sickness certificate from him easily enough. Every two weeks I used to get a certificate. On one occasion he got fed up with me so that the last time he gave me one for four weeks and told me not to bother him for a month. That suits me all right.'

The men are often suspicious of hospitals in a way that reflects again their sense of being powerless outcasts. One man who had been hospitalized for liver trouble commented:

'The trouble with doctors is that once they know you're an alcoholic they class you as shit. They know they can't cure you, all they are interested in is operating on you to show the medical students how to save others in the future. But I'm only interested in them saving me. No fucking doctors are going to cut me up for some other geyser.'

Horror at the idea of being experimented upon is not uncommon. 'Mental hospitals treat patients as guinea pigs.' Regrettably, many of the men have to dry out in mental hospitals – a milieu with which the man can rarely identify. 'I don't know why they put me into that hospital – it's full of nut cases in there. I may be an alcoholic but I'm not a head case.' The presence of locked wards leads some men to state that 'there's no difference between staff in the hospitals and screws in the nick'. Sometimes the attempt of a man to get admitted into hospital leads him instead direct to the police. 'I went up to the hospital drunk. But they didn't help me there because all I got was two injections and then they called the police.' Doctors, like social workers, are not thought to understand the social predicament of the homeless alcoholic. In many cases this is true, though it may not make them any the less able as doctors. 'The trouble with doctors and psychiatrists is that they don't fully understand the problems of drinking in parks. No man will have his problems cured by any doctor unless he is removed totally from his drinking environment.' The men also feel that the hospitals would not understand their general state, and at times they avoid hospitals altogether because of their dishevelled condition. 'I'm not going to hospital in this condition. I'm too dirty. They don't really want to help you when they know you haven't got a fixed address.' One man in a bad state with the shakes forced himself to clean up before presenting to the hospital to which he was immediately admitted.

While alcoholism has come to be accepted under the medical umbrella, the high observed relapse rate of alcoholics (and skid row alcoholics in particular) produces an ambivalence on the part of doctors about the whole hospital treatment setting. This ambivalence in its turn filters down to the alcoholic. He wants medical help yet criticizes medical institutions and their personnel.

'I saw another new psychiatrist at the hospital the other day. He told me straight that there is not much hope for me because of my severe alcoholism. They're bloody useless – you see it's no good keeping an alcoholic in hospital just for three months – what one needs is at least a year as an inpatient at an alcoholic unit.'

With all those middle-class alcoholics!

Involvement with psychiatrists is for many men restricted to the contact during a remand in custody for medical reports. Of this situation they are critical in the extreme. In general the inadequate reports that emerge after their fourteen days in custody would tend to bear out the prisoners' criticisms. The part psychiatry can play is in any event limited, but it is unfortunate that these men's frequent experience of psychiatry is so superficial and unfruitful.

Correctional agencies

For most homeless alcoholics, encounters with the police are a feature or hazard of everyday life. Men may be asked to 'move on', warned off the railway station and, most inconvenient of all, arrested, usually for drunkenness. For everyone involved in the process of an arrest for drunkenness there is a strong feeling of valuelessness about the whole procedure. There is little doubt that the police do not view drunks as criminals and that they represent a 'residual' element in the offender population. The men's accounts of arrest, jail and court procedure clearly reflect the perfunctory nature of the business in hand.

Homeless alcoholics are on occasions arrested for drunkenness when sober – it happened to the research worker himself – and they accept it, as it is unwise to create too much protest for fear of becoming too well known to the police in the area. When arrested it is always the men's advice to 'play it sober' (even if you actually are!). Pleading not guilty is rare, as this again causes attention to be drawn to the man who only wants to get through the court as quickly and unobtrusively as possible. In the police cells drunks claim they are rarely visited half-hourly as police regulations state. In general the police are said by the men not even to charge them properly – charge sheets have the wrong dates, one man who had not been charged asked for a charge sheet and surprised the police by his insistence on having one! Some men are 'old hands' and will greet the police officers in the cells with, 'How are you keeping then?' The policemen respond, 'All the worse for seeing you in here again.' Arrest is more often an interference with the men's usual routine than a major crisis.

There seems among the men an acceptance that if you are a habitual drunkard, drink in public frequently and are known to the police, then being caught in a general 'clean-up' operation is a risk you run. You become resigned to the whole arrest-court process and do your best to avoid prisons but otherwise go along with the scenario. One man expressed this position quite clearly:

'It's no good calling witnesses when you get done for begging – by the time you get to court, you believe you were actually begging, because you've been up before the same magistrate so many times and you were sometimes genuinely drunk and genuinely begging, and sometimes were not. If the magistrate already knows you, it doesn't matter what you say, he won't believe you . . . we always plead guilty.'

Efforts are made in court to 'fool' the magistrates – obtaining a clean shirt, producing long forgotten letters from doctors and social workers, standing to attention and saying 'sir' – so that little of serious consequence will result from the court appearance. An illustration of the wish the men have to avoid hassle in the court occurred in a case when the defendant had pleaded guilty and, when asked if he had anything to say, replied, 'Yes, your honour – ten bob – I'd like to be fined ten bob.'

The magistrate said, 'I haven't sentenced you yet, Mr. R., I was asking you if you had anything to say for yourself as to being found drunk.'

'No, your honour, if I could pay ten bob.'

'Fifty pence or one day.'

All the drunkenness offenders who go to prison for non-payment of their fines or for minor offences such as begging in fact go at present to Pentonville Prison, which takes all men serving twelve months or less from London courts. To many of the men and to the prison officers as well, the prison now seems like a 'glorified doss house', not a 'real prison' at all. It is 'the Dossers' Retreat'. In any case, 'Prison isn't the place to cure people with these problems – we must be honest about this and face it.' The other prisoners don't welcome the dossers either: 'They're awful beggars – there's no other word for them.'

For most men the fact that prison is too short a time for anyone to try to offer much help means that Pentonville is just a minor irritation. It is regarded as better than the doss houses, although 'the performance in reception' annoys them, as indeed does 'the performance of the sentence. And it is a performance!' These men do not see themselves as criminals: 'We bring the outside world into the nick, the only difference is that we haven't got a bottle in here.' Because all the short-term drunks are put in the rag shop, this is 'like getting round the bonfire in a skipper – you know everything what is going on, who's been into prison, who's about to go out, and you hear about fellows who are drinking in other manors'. While it is agreed that 'if they were to open a wing here for dossers, voluntary-like, they'd all be in here', this doesn't prevent fierce complaints about some aspects of the prison.

Prison officers are quite well regarded – 'You can talk to some of them as if they're your own brother.' Some of the younger ones are thought to consider that 'the job consists of bawling at people', but that is the worst anyone has to encounter. The prison officers who work in welfare are respected for what they try to do, even though it is seen as a 'bloody hopeless job'. 'The men who work in welfare have the kind of personality which can cope at a gut level with some of the blokes you find in here.'

Despite efforts made by any of the staff, attempts at rehabilitation programmes are not well regarded by the men. They resent young girls who come in to try to 'educate us'. Staff who begin with high hopes of this particular development become cynical. 'There's a woman in

Welfare whom I knew when she first started – she was good to all of the men – but some of the geezers fucked her about and then she began to change – she's now changed completely.' Men go to Alcoholics Anonymous 'just for cigarettes and to get out of their cells'. The issue of rehabilitation was summed up by one man:

'There's no rehabilitation in here – it's only on paper. There may be some facilities, but you've got to look for them. In any case, nobody can help you unless you start to help yourself. They ask you if you have any problems, and if you have you might tell them, but you've got to start it off yourself.'

In the end the 'performance' of a short prison sentence remains very much a performance. No one can take it too seriously. For all concerned, prison is the wrong place for the wrong people. Thus for the senior welfare officer the alcoholics are a problem for 'medical specialization'. For the doctors 'they are a social not a medical problem'. For the prison officers they are dossers, not criminals. For the man after fourteen days in Pentonville 'you need a drink!'

Lodging houses

Many of the hardened alcoholics on skid row will not use the lodging houses by choice or are barred from them. We have noted earlier that some men at least see it as important not to become institutionalized into the lodging-house culture. Groups of drinkers will use some of the lodging houses 'for a bit of heat', to beg cigarettes or food, as a dry place to drink, or to wash and shave, but will not book a bed in the more accepted manner. One man who went in for the heat was questioned by the porters and reacted by saying he would rather skipper than stay in a lodging house: 'You have more freedom when you're in a skipper. Fuck this heavy gang (the porters) – you don't have any of this crack when you're in a skipper. In these places you always have the porters telling you what to do.' This response is extremely common amongst the alcoholics and is in some ways a tribute to their spirit. They feel that their 'life has been taken out of their hands', when they are with several hundreds of men in a lodging house. Even Pentonville is viewed as 'miles better' than the common lodging houses.

Archard spent periods of three weeks in each of two lodging houses and experienced situations that certainly lend credence to many of the views held by the men; though it never seemed to him quite as filthy as had been portrayed. 'It's a dirty hole that place' is a frequent comment, indicating that the prevailing conditions mean 'you can't leave off the stuff (alcohol)'. General human degradation is apparent – epileptics having fits surrounded by applauding men, obsessional behaviour (an hour to cut a sausage), men continually scratching themselves, men eating scraps from the floor and from other men's plates. It is this kind of atmosphere that produces such reactions as:

'When I go to the NAB after coming out of nick I do so to get money for drinking. If they give me a voucher for the Salvation Army, I just tear it up – it's no good to anyone, not even for flogging because who would go to the Salvation Army? . . . I wouldn't go there if you paid me.'

Salvation Army Hostels are none the less always full.

These attitudes to lodging houses are time-honoured: since Orwell (1932) and others described the prevailing scene, little has fundamentally altered and the lodging house is still the most fearsome part of the alcoholic dossers' treadmill. They are not yet regarded by the men as the 'inns of healing' so described by one lodging-house authority.

The local community

The very homelessness of the vagrant alcoholic means that much more of his life is lived in public than would be true of other sections of the community. The result of this public exposure is vastly to increase the opportunities for contact with the local residents who also visit the parks frequented by the drinking schools. Further, men purchase their wine from local shops and at times beg from passers-by. Letters in the South London newspapers testify to some degree to the (mainly angry) feelings of people who are subjected to begging from alcoholics or who witness their drinking in public spaces. Some of the fears of the local public are understandable. One experienced community worker explained:

'We cannot underestimate, or for that matter overestimate, the problem. I, myself, don't believe the homeless alcoholic to be a violent person but I certainly wouldn't believe it if I was a housewife constantly being tapped for money and experiencing a very real fear for my children using local parks frequented by homeless alcoholics.'

Some 'violence' can be experienced by the men as when a local shop-keeper shouts at them, 'You meths drinkers' when they are simply walking home to a 'skipper'.

But it is with the children that the major problem occurs. Fears of children being assaulted or of seeing men drunk are a natural concern of the local community. The alcoholics' attitude to the children is in fact one of some concern in that, despite provocation from them, they make every effort not to chase or touch the children, partly of course for fear of creating even more serious trouble for themselves. Children will throw stones at the men in the parks and on occasions three or four of them, generally aged about ten or eleven, will bump into the men on purpose, seeking to enrage them. One housewife admitted that the children are 'naturally curious about the alcoholics drinking in the square' and that they poke them to tease them. The fear is, will the alcoholic turn round and poke the children? So far this does not seem to have happened.

At firework time the men receive their share of attack with lighted fireworks thrown by local children. Again, the men restrain each other from retaliation as they do not want to get 'knocked off'. A more subtle form of attack is when the children throw empty cider bottles into their own play area, leaving large quantities of broken glass, hoping that the alcoholics will be blamed. The men feel they can do nothing. 'We get it in the end for that kind of behaviour' is the view of all the men. Such behaviour by the children is in a way quite natural, but it raises questions about the nature of the threat posed by the vagrant alcoholics. The end of the spectrum that begins with stone throwing is the vagrant alcoholic being actually beaten to death as a worthless human being, which in fact happened to one client of the Project who was killed by a teenager in a church porch in Bletchley during the summer of 1973.

It would be too easy simply to blame the children who call and throw stones; they too, possibly living in the high-rise flats, are part of the problem of inner city life. It seems as if each section of the community finds a scapegoat for the difficulties in which it finds itself. This is natural. In essence, the attitudes of the homeless, down-and-out alcoholic seem no less responsible and hostile than the attitudes of other sections of the community towards him.

Social Security

Although nearly 2,500 applicants a week go to the two London Social Security offices catering especially for the homeless single person, a surprising number of alcoholics only use Social Security when they leave prison. Ever after, until the next sentence, they may never go near the office. Certainly our own observations suggest they use it less than they may be entitled to do. When they do go to the offices, the officers' view seems to be that they will tell tales: 'The better the tale this type of bloke can tell the more money he is going to get'. Stereotypes again exist on both sides: time and pressure of numbers both make it easier for everyone to rely on such stereotypes rather than penetrate beneath the surface.

For the men who do attend, the long wait – often up to three hours – the bleak conditions, the nature of the interviews and the consequent aggravation, can make begging an easier and often surer means of raising money than battling with Social Security – 'no wonder they call it the SS', as one man put it. Again, whatever the realities, this is how many men actually feel about it. At the Social Security office itself the men know that the 'real crack' takes place at the interview booths, that in some booths they 'really put you through it', while at others you have a better chance. This now becomes a game, with the 'screws' in the booths trying to trip you up. To cope with this you have to

'keep your wits about you . . . weigh the situation up, keep your eyes and ears open . . . keep your cool. It is fatal to lose your head, I've seen too many men do it and not get anything out of it. It is essential to have a ready answer for anything he asks you about.'

But of course the pressures are such that men do rear up. 'You can't help it sometimes; this place is enough to drive you crackers.' The best laid plans can go wrong – an interview that's going well is spoilt by another drunken and angry client butting in. When this happened to one man he said: 'This has now spoilt it for me . . . I felt like hitting the bastard.' Once the money is obtained, a man is then a 'live-wire' (a dosser with money on him) and it is essential to escape without being begged or followed.

It is perhaps not surprising that the men themselves find the Social Security offices such a trial as even staff in the other Social Security offices put across a fairly poor opinion of the offices for the homeless. 'Get yourself down to the dossers' assistance, son' is how one young alcoholic described his reception at the usual Social Security office. 'No one ever called me a "dosser" before, I turned away to let my mind settle down a bit.'

Attitudes to the Reception Centres, the DHSS's major provision for homeless men and women, were difficult to establish. This was mainly because Archard was not able to undertake a participation observer study in any of the centres, unless he had done it illegally. The drinking alcoholics view the 'spike', as reception centres are called, more favourably now than they did a few years ago. 'It gives a man a chance', but on the other hand 'it's no place to stay sober for long'. Individual welfare staff are highly praised far more than many social workers in other agencies, though some men feel the staff's efforts are 'wasted on that lot'. For the hard core of skid row drinkers the Camberwell 'spike' can still represent the final downfall. As one hard-liner put it: 'I felt sick, really sick, sick from drink, sick from "skippering", and sick of

life. In fact I felt so bad that I walked from the East End to the "spike".
That was really admitting defeat.'

Conclusions

In this chapter we have tried to give some indication as to how some
aspects of the services are viewed by the men they are designed to
serve. We would not expect everyone on either side to agree with the
views expressed. Yet they are views fiercely held and represent strong
feelings, even if the reality is not always exactly as described. We would
urge, however, against too hasty a dismissal of the underdog's view.
'I'm surprised you pay attention to what these men say' is a reaction we
have had from some officials: but to ignore entirely what the men
actually feel and therefore report seems an untenable position. Case-
workers listen intently to a man's views about his parents. Why
shouldn't we listen equally sensitively to his views about the agencies
which serve him? It is, after all, with these views, attitudes and feelings
that the homeless alcoholic navigates the various agencies which have
been in theory placed to assist and befriend him.

It goes without saying that the study of participant observation on
which we have drawn was done among men who were, at the moment
of study, drinking alcoholics, not 'successes' in the eyes of the helping
agencies. This would colour their views of agencies such as halfway
houses, but not necessarily of everything. Indeed, sober residents of
halfway houses tend to share very much the views given above of
prisons, lodging houses, courts, doctors and social workers.

In the final analysis, we believe strongly that there is ample evidence
to demonstrate the gap in understanding and trust between the homeless alcoholics and the helping agencies. Exhortation on the one side
and training on the other will not of themselves bridge that gap. We
still need to listen and learn a great deal more about each other. Unfortunately the alcoholic in court, office, prison or church crypt has
ample opportunity to hear our view, often given as immoderately as
his own: one judge remarked – 'If crime is committed when you are
drunk, the answer is simple, stop drinking.' As yet we afford ourselves
little enough opportunity to listen to a different view of the alcoholics'
own world. Even if we hear it, can we then be sure that we understand it?

8 ASSESSMENT AND EVALUATION

All social workers, whether working as individuals or as members of teams, know well the difficulty of answering the justifiable question, 'How successful are you?': the questioner often adding, 'I know it is difficult to give precise numbers', when of course that is just what he wants. After all, why talk about a 'recovery' project if you are unable to say how many alcoholics you have recovered? If on the Project we try to give exact numbers of men whom we think have been 'successes', are we merely playing along with the evaluation game? If, on the other hand, we avoid giving any statement about numbers, admitting that 'it's impossible to know what counts as "success" for any man', are we merely avoiding facing the issues of evaluation; retreating into social work jargon without daring to ask whether what we do is effective? In this chapter I shall attempt answers to some of the questions relating to the effectiveness of the Project. Wolins (1960, p. 247) has said that 'to pursue effectiveness in social work is to attempt to catch a chirping cricket in a totally dark room'! With that warning well in mind, I shall try to catch a cricket.

This chapter treats assessment and evaluation as two rather different concepts. The assessment I shall give is subjective and not essentially concerned with statistical analysis. The evaluation was a separate exercise involving a greater degree of objectivity. In any discussion of assessment, it is important to know who is asking the questions and for whom the answers are intended. For example, it may be that local authorities see the value of the Project in the number of men it takes off the streets; while government funders may see the worth of hostels in their high occupancy rate; clients see success in terms of how many men remain sober; and other agencies assess the value of the Project according to our degree of co-operation with them. An extreme statement of this kind of dilemma is given by Marris (1967, p. 46):

Where there are few obvious criteria of performance an institution must turn to indirect symbols of achievement especially those which earn public acclaim. But good public relations material for middle class backers may have little to do with the authentic ideals of the service. An institution can become so preoccupied with marginal activities which enhance its prestige that it neglects the less visible work which makes up its true purpose.

How far do we think we have achieved that which we originally intended in 1969? We are asking the question of ourselves, though we trust that others are listening to the answer. It would be easy to claim that because, from October 1972, we obtained funding from local and central government to continue the Project for a further three years, we therefore must have been seen to have been successful. This would be a neat way of answering the question, but it in fact only tells us something about the government's wish that someone tackles the problem of homeless alcoholics, and our powers of persuasion that we, among others, should be the tacklers.

In the original programme drawn up in 1970 we listed some of the areas in which we felt we would need to assess the effectiveness of the Project. Reviewing that list now only serves to show how naive we were and how complex the task is. We had hoped to study the effect the Project had on other agencies, but the number of variables involved was so great that the task became unrealistic. For example, we had hoped to see whether there would be an improvement in co-operation between agencies and also whether the referrals made both to and by the agencies were more appropriate and more effective. While most agencies informally report more co-operation between them than in 1969, this is not necessarily related to any specific efforts of the Project. With referrals there needs to be a great degree of common agreement on the language used when describing alcoholics. Such an educational function has not been within our remit, but unless it is carried out it is difficult to decide whether referrals are more or less 'appropriate'. Increasingly we ourselves welcomed self-referrals, as these seemed to reduce the element of false expectations that can occur when one agency refers someone to another.

It had also been suggested to us that we could measure our effectiveness by finding out whether there had been any marked change in the local police arrest rates for drunkenness. This had a superficially neat attraction but, again, it soon became apparent that this was not to measure the Project's effectiveness. One obvious reason was that, twelve months after we began the Project, the courts in the district changed their catchment area, so that the number of court appearances for drunkenness altered dramatically, but only because of administrative reorganization. A more fundamental reason for our decision not to use arrest rates was that men are known to be arrested for many reasons that are subsumed under the heading of drunkenness: the homeless man is highly visible, drunk or not, and changing police policy affects arrest rates more than the acts of other agencies (Bittner, 1967). Finally, the numbers of men that we could adequately cope with were so slight compared with the total number of drunkenness arrests that the police could not use our services in any way to reduce significantly their arrest figures. It was therefore impossible to use police figures to measure our effectiveness.

In the early stages of the Project we had also intended to see whether we could reduce the element of public nuisance and at the same time increase public interest in the problem. Clearly, a greater public interest might well reduce the nuisance, in that people might become more tolerant; while there might be an actual increase in behaviour previously felt to be offensive. Here, too, assessment became virtually impossible, as we lacked the basic resources with which to conduct a thorough survey on these issues. More worrying from the staff point of view was the decision as to whether the local people should be helped to be more tolerant – how much do inner city twilight zone inhabitants have to tolerate? – or rather, whether they should be encouraged to show more anger, working with us to pressurize for more facilities. In the event, we found ourselves possessing insufficient community work expertise to tackle these issues. With regard to the local community, we had to rest content with an informing rather than a catalytic function.

After due consideration had been given to several other ways of assessing the Project's effectiveness, we felt in the last analysis that we could at least try to examine whether we had helped men achieve increased periods of sobriety, employment and residential stability. It did then seem that we had been forced back on to mere counts of 'successes', though this at least necessitated some further thinking about the criteria used to measure 'success'. We know that approximately 20 per cent of the men who contact us become involved in such a way that clear improvements can be claimed to have been made in their life-style, generally centring on such tangibles as work record, and length of periods off drink. Without a control group, it is impossible to state that this would not have happened by spontaneous remission, though it is unlikely. It is, however, the only figure that we have at present. This remains unsatisfactory because it is a rather 'neutral' figure, concealing other ways of measuring success and failure. Figures so far produced fail to tell us for example how the men themselves measure their own success; or what is the base from which men start: as there are different baseline points, the measurement of actual success is less subject to generalization.

The first point, concerning a man's own view of his success, was brought home to me when, in one week, I met separately two well-established skid row alcoholics, both known to me over many years. Quite independently, both men drew attention to their feelings that they had done well over the past few years in that they had not been in prison (both had previously very long prison records). Both men had, however, been drinking and living on skid row in much the same way as before. They were unable to explain why they had been arrested less frequently and had not been sent to prison. Yet for each of them some 'success' had been achieved in the past year or so: they had had infrequent contact with helping agencies, so their 'success' was self-attained. Had these two men been in regular contact with the Project, we would not ourselves have described them as 'successes', but if we had, we might have been tempted to claim their success was partly due to the Project's activity. In either event we would have been doing a disservice to the truth.

The fact that different men come to us at different stages represents a problem for which Rowan (1973) has sought to provide an answer. He has suggested that we attempt to develop a table on the following lines:

(i)   On the floor, unable to cope, unable to look at the future, no hope.
(ii) Some glimmer of hope, some idea of future. Possible to discuss limited aims.
(iii) Off alcohol, but needing much support in sorting out head.
(iv) Off alcohol and motivated to take up work and love.
(v)   In work and relationships, but needing support in maintaining gains.
(vi) Going beyond work to ecstasy and self-actualization.

If such a continuum were agreed, then, clearly, an agency taking in people at stage (iv) might well have a better 'success' rate than agencies taking men at stages (i) and (ii). Certainly the lay public and fund givers paying little attention to the stage of entry might well be more impressed with the actual numbers at stage (vi). The Project in fact has men coming in at all stages, except (vi), with the majority in stages (ii) and (iii). So far, we have not related success rates to this concept of stages: we merely mention it to indicate how dangerous it is to make categorical statements about success without reference to the base line from which that success is being measured.

But even this neat outline raises two further difficulties. What do the men themselves perceive as change and what is the time scale involved? I think we have to guard against too much stress on change, desirable though in some instances that might be. Social workers might sincerely feel that an individual needs to change his whole outlook but, as one man said, 'Isn't coming off the streets and stopping drinking change enough?' It often is for a while, which then raises the question of time scale. Most men whom I honestly believe to have finally broken from skid row have usually taken at least two years of hard struggle, and in some instances it is seven or eight years before the confidence of the man is really secure. I mention these points to illustrate how complex the task of evaluation can be, but not as a way of avoiding that task.

We return then to our figure of 20 per cent of men in touch with the Project as being the best indicator of success we have at present. In so doing, we are fully conscious that current critics of social work would see us as merely having taken drunks who are striking a blow for freedom and turned them into conforming, disorientated factory-fodder. Heraud (1970, p. 212) makes this point strongly:

Social work agencies . . . measure 'success' by the extent to which clients have been helped to achieve the minimum standards necessary in a market-dominated economy. Thus while comforting the failures, social work acts also as a bridge back into a race which most of its clients cannot hope to win.

This view raises hotly-debated issues way beyond the scope of this book. We would only say that, for many of the men with whom we have been concerned, achieving the minimum standards necessary has seemed to be what they themselves wanted. We cannot in reality offer them hopes of a more exciting society, albeit through 'new careers' some, at least, can see a more challenging prospect than labouring. We would, however, not want to forget the destructive nature of their former addiction to alcohol and the gains to be had in everyday life when freed from that addiction and the consequences of it.

In some respects at least it is easier to measure the success rate of the houses. The success can be first looked at in terms of the length of stay and sobriety while a man is at the house. This we have attempted to do in chapter three. Without a control group, it is not really possible to state conclusively that men who stay at the houses are doing better than a sample of men who are not residents. However, practical experience suggests very strongly that for most homeless alcoholics a stay in some residential unit is essential if any recovery is to be achieved. We have noted that over a third of the men can stay sober in residence for at least four months and a small group stay for over twelve months. But as no one has yet decided to stay for ever, we need also to look at success in terms of life after the house. There is, significantly enough, a dearth of follow-up studies of residents of halfway houses or hostels of a therapeutic intent. Partly this could be due to lack of resources to conduct a follow-up, partly to the inherent problems of follow-up with such a group, and partly to wishing to continue in blind faith that residential provision must be a good thing because of all the work we have put into it! It is also more encouraging to look at the figures for occupancy than for follow-up. We should also note the 'tendency in alcoholism treatment to continue programmes of dubious value, apparently because of inertia and the feeling that one should be doing something' (Bahr, 1973, p. 253).

From 1 May 1971 to 30 April 1973 there was a combined total of admissions into the two long-term houses (Rathcoole and Lynette) of sixty-six men, which included thirteen men who had previously been residents prior to 1971. Over a quarter (25·8 per cent) stayed for more than six months and 12·7 per cent stayed for over a year. Certainly that degree of stability marks considerable achievement on the part of the men. But what happens when men leave the houses? As yet the Project has not obtained its own flatlets, though we are now keen to do so, in order that men who leave sober do not have to go into rooms, which can be isolating and rather soul-destroying. Some landlords are more restrictive than the houses that they have left – where is the progress in that situation? We can rightly make any number of qualifications to the final statement about successful long-term sobriety, but none the less we would wish to make some attempt at such a statement. If we take the total of 218 men admitted into Rathcoole and Lynette from 1966 to 1973, we found as at 1 May 1974 that sixteen have since died in drink. These are men that we personally have known about. Clearly there are likely to be other deaths unknown to us. Five men died sober when still resident, and two of these men had been with us for over two years. Twenty-three men are still in regular contact with us even though they are still drinking. Nineteen men are still sober after leaving the houses. Seven men are still in residence after at least one year.

I would offer three comments on these figures. First, they show clearly the relatively small numbers that will be permanently helped away from skid row and the compelling need to look continually at new ways of tackling the problem. It is a reminder that, as one resident said, 'Skid row for the most part will not come to us, nor submit tamely to our experiment, nor our scheme.' Second, the figures, spread as they are over seven years, mask the improvement that has steadily been occurring over the years. This meant that in the first two years, 1966–8, the number of men who were successful on leaving the house was barely 2 per cent, whereas in the two years, 1971–3, this figure is nearly 20 per cent. Third, none of the statistics given takes account of the residents in whose recovery the houses may have played a part, but not the final part. For example, a number of men have 'failed' while with us, but the knowledge gained of them and their continuing relationship with us has enabled us to place each man in another centre more appropriate to his needs and where he has flourished. Conversely, of course, some of the men whom we might list as 'successes' are only such because of what they have learnt in other settings prior to coming to us. Merely touching on issues like this indicates how complicated and even unwise it is to say how a man recovered from his alcoholism, and how dangerous it is for one agency to claim any credit for such recoveries. In the end one is often left with the feeling that many men have a time when they are likely to recover and some agency happens to be about at that time. The nature of any given agency may not be as important as sometimes we like to believe. Bahr (1973, p. 282) goes so far as to say:

It probably does not matter much what kind of treatment is given. If he [the skid row alcoholic] believes in it, and if those administering the treatment believe in it, the results are likely to be as positive as would result from any other treatment mode now available.

It would be unrealistic to expect many alcoholic agencies to under-state their contribution to an individual's recovery. We are probably no exception. But even if we like to believe that what is going on in our particular house is in fact producing the alleged success rate, do we always know exactly 'what is going on' and are our perceptions of it the same as the residents'? Partly to tease out this aspect of things, we taped a number of interviews with residents and one of the cooks to find out how they felt about the houses. As a result of these interviews, it seemed fairly clear that some residents do not always invest their stay at the house with the same weight and significance that staff give it. The transitory nature of much of their earlier experiences no doubt guards them against an over-investment or commitment to the houses. In some instances their perceptions of the role of the staff and the house for example is at total variance with the staff's own perception.

'I don't care who comes as staff, he's only the rent collector. I do everything I'm supposed to do, I'm off the drink and I come in before twelve o'clock. I don't argue or shout with anyone in the House, and I don't ask for anything.'

On the other hand, another resident can say:

'The aim of the house, apart from a guy keeping sober, is to try and let him get something out of his life that he's been missing before he came to the house. It's very difficult to put into words. It's for me more of a feeling . . . I've never had a thing about social workers. Never at any time because I know that if it wasn't for social workers, none of us would be here.'

With such varied responses from two well-established residents, it is surely difficult to state just what the house is offering except that it is a number of different things to a number of different people. To the cook at Lynette Avenue the value and meaning of the house is expressed as:

'This is their home, isn't it? I wouldn't mind doing the cleaning, even if they said to me, do you think you could go and clean the bathroom out? I wouldn't mind at all, but I never have because I think it's private. That's their domain up there. I've heard the men say they've painted the room up, and I think, ah that's good – I've curiosity obviously, a woman's always curious! But I think oh that's nice, they're doing their rooms out, Ian's doing his television, or he says he's going upstairs to play the records – I know what they're all doing. To me it's like home here, if you know what I mean.'

It would, I hope, be apparent that we still know far too little about just how and why some men are 'successful' now and some later. The likelihood of what the houses offer coinciding with what the men want and need seems increasingly hard to obtain. We still believe the houses to be providing a valuable service to homeless alcoholics, but in the last analysis have to declare it as a belief rather than state it as proof.

How effective the Project has been in its intervention compared with other processes that intervene in the lives of the men was the question we examined in a separate evaluation study, outlined below. In thinking about an evaluation study, we were struck partly by the problems of follow-up, but even more by the absence of previous follow-up attempts with homeless alcoholics. This led me to ponder on the question – whatever happened to last year's drunkenness offender? We know that the survey problems of early attempts at follow-up studies of non-vagrant alcoholics are very considerable (Lemere, 1953) and it is therefore reasonable to assume they would be of even more alarming dimensions in the case of vagrant alcoholics. One of the few certainties about all groups of alcoholics is their exceptionally high mortality rate. One study concludes (Schmidt, 1972): 'Our results confirm that alcoholism is associated with a high rate of fatal somatic disease, accidents and suicides.' For the skid row alcoholic the situation is even worse. Wiseman (1970, p. 237) came to the conclusion that there are only three major ways off skid row, one of which is to die. The others were to become a live-in servant for an institution and to go into alcoholic rehabilitation as a profession. We have referred already to the death rate of ex-residents of Lynette Avenue and Rathcoole House, a rate significantly far in excess of other populations of similar age range. Even so, not all skid row alcoholics die quite so rapidly and we were interested to find out whether the homeless alcoholics who were 'on the circuit' in London several years ago were still there in 1973.

It seemed important to attempt some preliminary answers to this question, as, clearly, in the past decade London's skid row population had not grown to take on the dimensions of the nineteenth-century's 'dangerous classes'. Could it be that many men simply leave London after a few years on skid row, either having been helped to rehabilitate themselves or, more likely, returning 'home' not significantly affected by skid row, or by its agencies of control or reform? Is there a central core of homeless alcoholics, augmented marginally each year, who form the basis of most of the work of relevant agencies? The Camberwell Reception Centre admits each year 2,000 vagrant alcoholics. Of these 500 are new cases to the Centre and 1,500 are already known to the Centre. What happens to the larger proportion of the 500 who, clearly, do not all reappear as 'known' cases in the following year? Answers to this type of question are essential if we are seriously to try to understand the total scene of the homeless alcoholic.

Regrettably, with the limited resources available, we could only highlight the importance of the questions with some raw data, leaving the final answers still in the realm of speculation. From 1969 to 1972 the Project acquired information on over 1,000 homeless alcoholics who were either referred directly to us or about whom other social workers sought advice. We also had a list of 617 vagrant alcoholics who had been assisted by the Royal London Prisoners' Aid Society from 1960 to 1965. We examined how much overlap there was between the two groups. Only seventy-one men were on both lists. Various enquiries produced information about another 117. What has happened to the remaining 429? Are they all on skid row somewhere else or all sober? Who is where?

It has been said that professional workers complain that they 'keep seeing the same guys over and over again' (Wiseman, 1970, p. 52). This certainly is not the whole truth. Indeed, the reverse could well be the case in that the professionals do not necessarily keep seeing the same men, but rather hosts of different ones. These cursory examinations of the records suggest that we should look very closely at the differences between men who 'try the rehabilitation circuit' once or twice and those who do so repeatedly. Others may frequent the hospital circuit. Why and how do these patterns of behaviour occur? We would suggest that a lot more needs to be known about these patterns, otherwise we shall too readily accept such generalizations as 'homeless alcoholics just "use" the agencies' or 'most of the men we've seen are back drinking'.

An evaluation study

We believed it was most important that, within our resources, we should attempt some evaluative study of the shop fronts, seeing them as a key feature of the work we had been engaged upon. We felt that a limited statistical enquiry might give some indication of the degree of effectiveness of intervention by the Project in the lives of some men. But we also wished to see whether other groups of homeless alcoholics were being equally well assisted without any specialist intervention at all. Late in 1971 we obtained three random samples of thirty homeless male alcoholics.

Sample A: Thirty homeless male alcoholics selected consecutively from the records of a London magistrate's court located in an area which is also serviced by one of the shop fronts as well as hostels and hospitals which treat alcoholics.

Sample B: Thirty homeless male alcoholics selected consecutively from the records of our three shop-front offices situated in different areas but generally with access to hostels and hospitals.

Sample C: Thirty homeless male alcoholics selected consecutively from the records of a London magistrates' court located in an area without shop fronts and especially noted for its marked lack of any treatment facilities for homeless alcoholics.

Both samples A and C, drawn from the two magistrates' courts, consisted of men who had three or more convictions for drunkenness (during the first eight months of 1971) in the court from which they were selected in the last four months of 1971. Sample B – drawn from the shop-front offices – consisted of the first thirty men who visited the offices from 1 September 1971 and who had not previously had any contact with the Project. The shop-front social workers were not informed that these men were part of the sample, in order to avoid these alcoholics' receiving any special attention. Although we did not set out to control for factors other than alcoholism and homelessness, we did find that the average age of each of the three samples was also consistent: sample A 45·1 years; sample B 45·4 years; sample C 44·0 years. (All surveys of homeless alcoholics show that their average age is around the mid-forties.)

Our hypotheses were basically two. First, that involvement with treatment facilities would vary, with sample B being most involved, then sample A and with sample C being least involved. Second, that involvement with penal facilities would be the reverse, with sample C being the most involved, then sample A and with sample B being least involved. It seemed likely that alcoholics appearing voluntarily at the shop fronts would have better admission rates to hospitals and hostels than alcoholics being compulsorily processed through the courts, whether the court was located in an area of treatment facilities or not. It seemed better for homeless alcoholics to be in contact with social work agencies – a shop front – rather than penal agencies. Further, the shop front offered specialist skills which we felt the alcoholics required and which were not available, for example, in probation offices, where the social workers dealt with a wide range of social problems. We were of the opinion that shop fronts should be a major facility in assisting men into hospitals and hostels and away from the penal system. If shop fronts were not substantially involved with referrals to hospitals and hostels, then we would have expected the admission rates for sample B to be similar to that for sample A, as both samples were drawn from the same geographical area.

Early in 1973 we sought information from a number of selected agencies as to the number of occasions each of the agencies were in contact with the men during the twelve months of 1972. By 'in contact' we mean that men in the three samples were admitted to a hostel, hospital, prison, were resident in the reception centre, appeared and were convicted in a magistrates' court, or were interviewed by a referral agency or probation officer. Information was sought, under the usual terms of absolute confidentiality, from ten alcoholic hostels, five probation offices, five mental hospitals, four magistrates' courts, three referral agencies and non-residential social work centres, one prison and the Camberwell Reception Centre. All these facilities were in London. Also, we obtained information from the Criminal Records Office and the Central Hospital Index. Again, this was, of course, subject to strict legal safeguards.

In Table 6 we show the specific findings of the study. We should make it clear that the figures do not refer to recovery or sobriety, as we were only concerned to assess the value of the shop-front endeavour. Shop-front workers cannot themselves direct the therapeutic programme of a hospital alcoholic unit or a rehabilitation centre. The measurement of long-term sobriety is essentially an evaluation of the efforts of the other facilities beyond the shop front. Table 6, column II, shows the percentage of each sample of thirty that was involved on at least one occasion with the various agencies that are part of the lives of skid row alcoholics. It is clear from this general perspective that between samples A and C there are no major differences (except that sample A made greater use of the Reception Centre, whereas sample C was more

Table 6 Shop-front evaluation study

Samples		I No. of men*	II % of men*	III Total of 'events'	IV Range†	V Median
Court	A	22	73	122	1–18	4
convictions	B	14	46	75	1–15	1
	C	19	63	139	1–26	4
Prison	A	8	27	21	1–6	2
sentences	B	8	27	12	1–3	1
	C	15	50	47	1–11	2
Probation	A	9	30	17	1–4	2
offices:	B	6	20	18	2–6	2
visits	C	11	37	28	1–8	2
Referral	A	5	17	37	1–32	1
agencies:	B	29	97	155	1–30	3
contacts	C	7	23	18	1–8	1
Reception	A	6	20	8	1–2	1
Centre: stays	B	10	23	20	1–3	2
in residence	C	2	7	2	1–1	1
Hospitals:	A	2	7	2	1–1	1
admissions	B	6	20	13	1–3	2
	C	0	0			
Alcoholic	A	3	10	5	1–2	1
hostels:	B	12	40	17	1–2	1
admissions	C	4	13	8	1–2	1

* Men involved at least once.
† Excluding men who have had no contact at all.

frequently sent to prison). We had expected greater differences between
the two samples. The fact that a sample of homeless alcoholics habitually
in an area where there are no rehabilitation facilities fared no worse
than a sample from an area where there were facilities, was surprising.
Among other things it suggests that the relationship between the
agencies and homeless alcoholics is a complex one; that agencies may
not always attract clients to an area – for the clients would surely use
the agency if they had been attracted into the area by it. The relative
non-use of facilities by sample A may also indicate the inabilities of
the general social work agencies to refer on to the specialist agencies.
At the same time it may indicate that men who do go to shop fronts
and other relevant facilities may have overcome the biggest hurdle of
all: the decision to talk to someone about 'the drink'. Whatever the
surface reasons for alcoholics going to the shop fronts, some self-
selection would seem to have taken place with sample B.

If these assumptions are correct, it is most important to show that at least the men who did go to shop fronts made greater demands on the hospital and hostel facilities than the other two groups. This would seem to be so. Twenty per cent of sample B were admitted one or more times into psychiatric hospitals for alcoholism treatment, compared with 6·7 per cent of sample A and 0 per cent of sample C: for alcoholic hostel admissions the respective percentages were 40, 10 and 13·3 per cent. These differences in rates of admission to hostels and hospitals are significant. At the other end of the spectrum, we hoped to find that sample B was less involved with courts and prisons than A or C. This was the case with courts where only 46·7 per cent of sample B appeared in court, at least once, compared with 73 per cent and 63 per cent in A and C. Sample C received twice as many prison sentences as each of the other samples.

There was a less certain area of rehabilitation activity relating to the involvement with probation offices, the shop fronts and other referral agencies such as St Martin-in-the-Fields and residence in the Reception Centre at Camberwell. No group had any major involvement with the probation service, a third being the highest proportion. Apart from shop fronts, which were almost by definition heavily used by the shop-front sample, other referral agencies figure hardly at all for any of the three samples. The Reception Centre was barely used by group C, which was geographically the most distant from it; it was used more frequently by shop-front men compared with the court men in sample A, though both groups were physically equally close to it. Line II therefore outlines the overall pattern which supports the contention that sample B contributed the largest percentage of admissions to alcoholic hostels, which we believe to be the major rehabilitation facility. Hospitals were also more often used by group B, which also used the Reception Centre more and went less to prison. There was no major difference between these percentages in the other two groups.

Lines III–V attempt to spell out in more detail the percentages of the second column. We list the total number of events with any one agency, the range that represents and the median number of events. We excluded those men who made no contact at all with the agency. We felt it important to give these three pieces of information so that the most complete picture possible of the activity of the homeless alcoholics could be presented. The total number gives some idea of the cumulative effect on any one agency of any of the three samples. The range of events that the individuals contributed at least shows the most extreme activities of some individuals. The median shows any agency's involvement in perhaps a more realistic perspective.

Apart from examining whether our hypotheses were upheld or not, we would draw attention to some interesting implications:

(1) In spite of recommendations embodied in the Report and a general acceptance that homeless alcoholics should be removed from the circuit of arrest, trial and imprisonment, it is quite evident that law enforcement remains the dominant model by which habitual public drunkenness is controlled.

(2) The probation and after-care service, in spite of being officially the 'treatment arm' of the law enforcement model, has little effective contact with homeless alcoholics in terms of enabling men to be admitted to treatment facilities. It may be that hostels turn down probation service referrals even where contact is made, though we had no hard evidence to support this view.

(3) Hospitals and hostels do not as yet constitute major alternatives to law enforcement agencies for the majority of homeless alcoholics, even for those alcoholics in sample B.

(4) It would appear that homeless alcoholics are not as geographically mobile as is generally thought since we discovered that it was rare for men to be known to agencies outside the particular areas from which the samples were originally drawn.

(5) The claim that it is difficult to 'follow-up' the movement of men who are habitually of no fixed abode and have a high alcoholic relapse rate is not substantiated. A well prepared study could certainly extend the scope and validity of this pilot exercise.

With regard to our original hypotheses, the figures only supported the parts of the hypotheses relating directly to sample B, namely that this sample would have greater involvement with treatment facilities and less involvement with penal facilities than either of the other samples. Samples A and C were not markedly different in any important respect.

Most research tends to raise more questions than it provides answers. This pilot investigation is no exception. We do know that of the men who go to the shop fronts there is more than a one-in-three chance that they will eventually be admitted into an alcoholic rehabilitation hostel. This is not the position with men who are in contact with other referral agencies. Indeed, we should point out that in sample A, two of the three men admitted into alcoholic hostels did so through the shop fronts, although originally the men were in the court sample. We do believe that the evidence presented is sufficiently persuasive to indicate the value of more shop fronts in London; the more so because the men do not move readily into another area just because there is a facility there. A distinctive specialist role seems to have emerged for shop fronts.

Conclusion

So far we have stated the difficulties of assessment in contexts other than our work with individuals. None the less, this does not obviate the task of looking at the aims with which we began the Project in 1969 and stating fairly subjectively whether we seem to have achieved them. We are still far from the ideal of a comprehensive treatment service which effectively utilizes all resources; but we are a great deal nearer to understanding the blockages which prevent the creation of such a service. We are still travelling hopefully. Some of the long-range goals we set ourselves have been successfully accomplished: the establishment of shop fronts; and of some other new facilities such as the short-stay house at Cranmer Road; a clear services commitment to social and medical agencies in the area; the development of the Project as a central referral point for information about clients and services. On the other hand we have not been at all successful in helping to bring about the establishment of drying-out facilities, or in creating a sustained local public interest in the homeless alcoholic. Finally, the effective development of a system of help rather than chance use or misuse of facilities has so far eluded us.

Any assessment of course tends to be a static one. Unforeseen developments occur, and almost overnight breakthroughs take place or old developments cease. The Project's influence may often be minimal for good or bad. More powerful forces are continually at work, some of which we may hardly be aware of until their effect is visible to all. Assessment of the Project at this stage inevitably feels rather like an end-of-term report: mildly encouraging to parent and pupil alike; criticism of the school is thus forestalled, but reading between the lines I hope it is clear that there is not only room for improvement but also the potential to make that improvement.

9 CONCLUDING CONSIDERATIONS

In this final chapter I wish to try to set out what seem to me to be the lessons or underlying themes of the work of the Project. This will lead on to some recommendations that hopefully might fall on less stony ground than the recommendations of the report. The various themes that I have singled out are important at a number of levels and all of them are crucial if we agree with the report's final statement: 'We believe there is a duty to act constructively and to act now' (Home Office, 1971, p. 193).

The politics of responsibility

It is clear by now that one key issue in the field of vagrant alcoholics is the absence of action, which partly arises because no one is sure who should act. The social historian would be hard pressed to find a group more subject to 'buck passing' than the vagrant. I have attempted to gain a hospital bed for an alcoholic of 'no fixed abode' at a time when 'catchment areas' were of even more concern than usual. For the hospital to assess whether it had any commitment to this particular man, I was asked what streets he had walked the previous night! The 'boundary' problem may now be even more important with the reorganization of local government areas and the establishment of regional and area health authorities on 1 April 1974.

But long before any modern reorganization Gray (1931, p. 119) was able to point to one of the main difficulties in trying to pin anyone down to accepting the responsibility.

Authorities are not exactly anxious to take readily a step which may throw upon the locality an enduring charge and obligation in a matter in which they have no greater concern than any other locality. As the vagrancy law of the past admittedly failed, so must any law which seeks to throw a national burden upon a locality and leaves it to the locality to determine whether it will accept the burden.

Gray's comment raises one of the central issues in trying to determine the question of responsibility for the vagrant, namely: when is a problem local and when is it national? If it is a local problem, then local government should solve it. In 1906, a Dr Cooper of the London

County Council felt that that authority had a direct responsibility for the homeless poor who were then sleeping on the streets (Higgs, 1906, p. 49). 'No civic community', he said, 'ought to allow what is going on at the present time . . . the whole of the outcasts should be absorbed into LCC shelters.' There has so far been little evidence that civic communities feel that degree of concern. Vagrants from the north of England sleeping rough in London are not seen as the local borough's problem ('we didn't invite them here'), are not always even viewed as London's problem, but are definitely seen as the national government's problem.

The national government, while accepting some responsibility for destitute persons under the 1948 National Assistance Act and while providing facilities in its twenty reception centres, none the less does not seem to accept an overall responsibility for the wider aspects of the problem. This is partly because, even within central government, it is not clear which department has what responsibility. The homeless alcoholic offender has now come to rest with the DHSS, but only after a long battle with the Home Office, who seemed reluctant to relinquish responsibility for a problem about which they had done little for 150 years. Any person or organization approaching central government soon finds that the Department of the Environment, the Home Office and the DHSS are all involved, and that what is needed is a central co-ordinating department, or a unified and responsible department. One report has called for just this (National Association for Mental Health, 1972). Local authorities, however, still have to be involved in the provision of rehabilitation facilities and the like. In this respect it was ominous that the Department of Health's report on the reorganization of local authority personal social services (1968) totally failed to mention the problem of the homeless single person. But then it was never asked to do so by the agencies concerned with this problem who, better organized, might have campaigned to have the terms of reference altered. None the less, the failure of such reports even to refer to the problem leads almost inevitably to voluntary bodies filling the gap.

The question of responsibility is a core element of the problem of the down-and-out. Part of the problem is certainly the man lying drunk and infected on the Thames embankment, part of it is the hospitals' reluctance to admit people of no fixed abode, but part of it is also the publication of reports with little or no action following. When government enquiries and committees have made recommendations on, for example, the treatment of the habitual drunken offender and little has occurred as a consequence, it is crucial to ask why this is so. Castigating civil servants can be too popular a pastime and of little avail unless deeper issues are also examined. I should make it clear that, in the discussion which follows, I have not restricted myself solely to debate on the homeless alcoholic, but I have looked at the larger field of the homeless single person. This better illustrates the problems, and also it is the context within which much provision for the homeless alcoholic will eventually be made.

From the grass roots upwards no one seems to feel that they are really involved with the problem, or have clear responsibility to do anything about it. A spokesman for off-licencees in South London has said:

Even if we were in the same position as pubs and could turn people away simply because we didn't like the way they were dressed, I don't see we have any social responsibility to do so . . . if a man comes in with a bottle of methylated spirits hanging out of his pocket what right have we to turn him away? (*South London Press*, 24 September 1971)

That attitude may be all right, but in what kind of position does it leave park-keepers, parents and rehabilitation services in the same area?

Local attitudes are crucial when it comes to serious efforts to establish facilities for the homeless single person. Efforts have been made since the late 1960s to replace the gigantic Camberwell Reception Centre by smaller units in other parts of London. An attempt to establish one in a drill hall in Tottenham, in North London, failed. The member for the area told the House of Commons (Butler, 1969, col. 1758) that not only was the building unsuitable, 'It is in the wrong place.' She went on to say: 'I assure my Hon. Friend that the suburbs of London are not just places where Ministry establishments can be placed without regard to local interests.' Perhaps most revealing of all was the statement that the Ministry had assured her that the men using the proposed centre would not be 'meths drinkers or other undesirables' (ibid., col. 1759).

A number of vital issues were raised, none of which was ever answered or even scrutinized very carefully. First, where is the 'right place' for reception centres for the homeless? Children's protection is always going to be involved as vagrants lurk in the shadows! No locality will demand that it has a reception centre as a desirable amenity but, if no locality is the right one, do we reach a situation where vagrants cease to exist because every area is the wrong place for them? Second, there is the problem facing a ministry wishing to assist and yet not being able to insist on the establishment required actually being established. The responsibility in this instance has been assumed, but there are limited powers to act upon it. It is also worrying to see how a phrase like 'ministry establishments' suggests the people in them are not related to local residents but rather a different breed. Third, it is perturbing to speculate that there is still some notion of 'undesirables' (which includes alcoholics) and that this group will not be going to some areas. Who are they? Where will they go? These seem two questions needing elucidation. Surely no one is claiming that even among the 'undeserving' there are some still more undeserving than others? Unfortunately, it seems that someone is saying just that.

Let us now look at a slightly different situation where there was an existing facility for homeless men, namely Butterwick House in West London. On this occasion, however, the facility (a lodging house) was being demolished for redevelopment schemes. The problem here was that of responsibility for providing alternative accommodation for the 750 residents, given that Butterwick House was owned by a private company, Rowton Houses Ltd. The problem was debated in the House of Commons on 24 March 1972. Again, the question of responsibility floated in the rarified air but rarely seemed to rest anywhere for long. The MP for the area in question rightly made it clear that

It is not purely a Hammersmith problem. It will be quite impossible for a borough of the size of the London Borough of Hammersmith suddenly to rehouse 750 men who require single accommodation. It could not be done. No one . . . could expect an individual local authority to do that (Richard, 1972, col. 1954).

He went on to state that 'It may be that the GLC is the proper authority to solve the problem' (ibid., col. 1955). On this occasion the reply came from the Under-Secretary of State for the Environment who referred to reports on aspects of homelessness being prepared both by his own department and by the DHSS (Channon, 1972, col. 1962). There was little evidence to suggest that anyone had any very specific responsibility. Sympathy and concern for those falling 'prey to home-lessness' were expressed and voluntary bodies were to be consulted about ways of alleviating the problem, but a true line of accountability was not established. Surprisingly, press comment on this episode was outspoken and critical. The Child Poverty Action Group stated that 'Both the Supplementary Benefits Commission and the Secretary of State seem gripped by a common paralysis when it comes to enforcing Section 21' (*The Times*, 28 April 1972). Their Director made proposals which sought to balance the interests of all three parties, government, local councils and the homeless. In the end Butterwick House was demolished and although *ad hoc* arrangements were made for some of the men, the fundamental problems remained untouched.

'Post-Butterwick' attention was focused on the Hayes Wharf re-development, a proposed Thameside development scheme in South-wark. Here lodging houses and other rented accommodation will be lost if the £300 million scheme goes through (*Guardian*, 30 August 1972). The issues involved in this scheme are intricate and emotive, but at least we are shown again that benefit for some is hardship for others: but it is particularly hard for these 'others' if their future is assured by no one, being no one's clearly defined responsibility. While this particular development was being discussed, the former 700-bedded Parkview House (another Rowton House) in Southwark became a tourist hotel. Later, the managing director of Rowton Houses Ltd called on the Government to deal with the mounting problems of homeless single people (*South London Press*, 8 December 1972). In the meantime a 74-year-old pensioner was told to leave his £2·50 a week room and tramp the streets looking for cheap alternative lodgings (*South London Press*, 16 June 1972). He certainly must have wondered what was going on.

Who then should do something about the problem? Exhortations come from all sides and in many forms. On the Butterwick House issue one journal (*New Statesman*, 3 March 1972) claimed that 'The moral responsibility for these men belongs to all the surrounding boroughs.' A councillor of the borough in question reiterated his belief 'that it was a problem which should be solved on a national level' (*Post-Mercury*, 2 April 1972). The concept of national responsibility is the one most generally urged. The National Association for Mental Health (1972) recommended:

Central policy-making responsibility must be accepted by the Government, preferably by the Department of Health and Social Security, with the full backing of the Department of the Environment (with its responsibility for housing), the Department of Employment and the Home Office.

An article in a national newspaper (*Daily Telegraph*, 6 September 1972) concluded:

As the down and out problem is a national one it is absurd that it should be catered for in the present haphazard and unsatisfactory manner.What is required is for the Department of Health and Social Security to accept the overall responsibility, using outside agencies as it sees fit, for the problem must be dealt with on a national basis by a body with the resources to succeed. All the money should come from the Exchequer, so relieving the demands on local rate-payers and voluntary contributions.

We ourselves have always advocated some form of national commission and continue to do so. Others, too, have called for 'planning on an informed national basis' as the only viable response to the problem (*Lancet*, 1970, II, p. 139).

Yet in these suggestions there often resides one of the thorniest questions of all, namely multi-Ministry involvement. This is clearly seen in the proposal of the National Association for Mental Health which lists four ministries hoping they will give each other 'full backing'. The difficulties of several ministries being in any way involved require little spelling out here. Two ministries cannot answer in the same debate. This can lead to the feeling of never really knowing whose door it is best or wisest to knock on.

Mr Greville Janner asked the Secretary of State for the Home Department how many homeless people were prosecuted for vagrancy or for other similar offences in 1961 and 1971.
Mr Carlisle: I regret that this information is not available. The number of persons prosecuted for 'sleeping rough' under Section 4 of the Vagrancy Act 1824 was 950 in 1961 and 401 in 1971.
Mr Janner: Does the Hon. and learned gentleman agree with the view expressed in *The Times* today . . . that it is wrong to stigmatise many of the young homeless as mere vagrants, drifters or drop-outs and that they need care and concern and above all homes? What do the Government propose to do about it?
Mr Carlisle: As the Hon. and learned gentleman probably knows, the law of vagrancy and street offences is under review by the Department. Housing for the homeless is a matter for my Right Hon. Friends the Secretary of State for the Environment and the Secretary of State for Social Services, to whom questions on it should be addressed (Janner 1972b, cols 1644-5).

Some weeks before the above exchange took place, the Prime Minister himself had been asked whether he was 'satisfied with the co-ordination between the Department of Health and Social Security and the Department of the Environment on policy towards single homeless people' (Barnes, 1972, cols 229-30). He replied that he was and that he knew of no difficulties 'from practical experience' that had occurred in co-ordinating efforts made by the two departments (ibid., col. 230). The issue is surely partly the difficulties that occur between the departments and partly those with outside agencies seeking to obtain access to the appropriate department at the right time. An illustration of the former seems to be contained in the Department of the Environment's Consultation Paper on Grants for Hostels and similar accommodation for Single People (1973). In that document are listed all the government departments that were consulted in order to produce some suggestions on the issue of accommodation for the single homeless. The departments even included the Department of Education and Science but, *mirabile dictu*, the Home Office is not mentioned! Ten thousand homeless men leave prisons each year. What extraordinary reasoning led the Home Office not to partake in the Department of Environment discussions?

In a subsequent debate the Under-Secretary of State for Health and Social Security took up the challenge by avoiding it (Dean, 1972, col. 682).

What we want is not so much one Minister as a comprehensive co-ordinated effort. From my personal involvement in the problem, I believe that the co-ordination and co-operation of both government departments concerned, and between them and the local authorities and voluntary organizations, is becoming closer and more effective than it has been hitherto. I am not saying that it is yet anything like right, but as we become more aware of the problem so the will for more effective co-operation will come increasingly to the surface.

The weaknesses of this kind of approach, as the history of the problem abundantly shows, are that general appeals for co-ordination rarely penetrate at the depth necessary to bite into the problem. Further, the approach still fails to make it clear just who is responsible and hence accountable for wrong action or non-action. Above all, the duty to act is not clearly vested in anyone. This absence of mandatory duty is crucial. Later in this same debate the Under-Secretary referred (ibid., col. 690) to the Mental Health Act 1959, yet this failed dramatically to provide hostels for the mentally ill, mainly because local authorities were given permissive powers, not mandatory duties. He then referred (ibid., col. 691) to the Housing Act 1967 which 'gives authorities all the powers they need to provide whatever housing is needed, including lodging houses and hostels in their area'. Again, these powers are ghost-like. So that any local authority can still claim that 'vagrancy is not a local problem but a national one and national problems require national solutions.'

This pinpoints the other area in which the ball bounces back and forth, this time between local authorities and central government. The Prime Minister was asked in the Commons (Janner, 1972a, cols 705–6) 'whether the government can give more direct advice to local authorities in helping the homeless and rootless'. He replied that a circular was on its way to local authorities 'about the social service needs of single adults who cannot cope with problems of everyday life'. Circulars and advice again fail to home in on the problem. The groping for some kind of clearly defined arrangement is well illustrated by a report on homelessness in the south-west of England (DHSS,

1972c, p. 22). In writing of the homeless single person this report said:

There remain those whose needs are such that unsupported accommodation is evidently inadequate. As we have remarked, a national response is not yet in sight and purely empirical solutions face the same difficulty of hyper-mobility with the added difficulty of intolerance which inhibits official action. It may be that the first approach will need to be in the undemanding atmosphere that a voluntary service can offer. We understand that the Department of Health and Social Security are discussing these matters with the associations of local authorities as a national policy issue and we consider it preferable to await a statement of general import rather than attempt to formulate one for application in this area. We draw attention, however, to the possibilities of voluntary action and to the financial and other support which local authorities can give to it.

The message seems to be that, as a national response is not in sight, we must rely on discussions, goodwill and the *deus ex machina*, voluntary bodies. The circle is now complete. Voluntary bodies press for central government to define their responsibility. Local authorities are then involved and circularized. The nature of the problem suggests that voluntary bodies have a prime role. It all sounds so reasonable, but for two hundred years this eminently reasonable solution has failed to deliver the goods.

Relationships between local authorities and voluntary organizations are variable at the best of times. And they present special difficulties when the client involved is the homeless, rootless man or woman who has not paid rates and is low on most authorities' priorities. There is too often too much reliance on good will and other nebulous qualities; too little on clear direction. A circular from the DHSS (1972a) sought to obtain ten-year development plans for 1973–83 from local authority social services departments. Voluntary organizations were referred to: 'It is very desirable that planning of the personal social services should take account of the views of voluntary organizations, which in many fields supplement and support the statutory services.' Some directors will consider consulting voluntary bodies, some will not. Where does the traditional pat on the back end and real partnership begin?

In this context it should be noted that the DHSS (Seebohm) report (1968, p. 34) had clear views on divided responsibility.

Organizational issues are of crucial importance when considering the effects of divided responsibility upon policy, use of resources, public accessibility, accountability and co-ordination. The more fragmented the responsibility for the provision of personal social services, the more pronounced these problems become.

Though that committee was only asked to look at the changes desirable 'to secure an effective family service', they themselves went on to say when defining what is a family, 'we could only make sense of our task by considering also childless couples and individuals without any close relatives: in other words, everybody' (ibid., p. 18). How was it then that homeless individuals without any close relatives, or even with them, were not ever seen as legitimately the province of the personal social services? Responsibility for these groups remained divided, with all the consequences the Seebohm Committee itself predicted would occur.

An encouraging but still limited step forward came with the DHSS Circular (1972b) on Homeless Single Persons in Need of Care and Support. Although now there was some clear initiative being taken by a government department, at the end of the day doubt remained as to who would actually do what and when. That circular made it clear, for example, that the Supplementary Benefits Commission, part of the DHSS, had a duty to make provision for people without a settled way of life to be influenced to lead a more settled way of life, and reception centres were to be provided accordingly. Yet the commission does not have powers to provide 'long-term accommodation for people in need of care and support'. They further admit that the general problem is exacerbated by the shortage of cheaper accommodation for single people, yet 'this is a problem for the housing authority'. The department in this circular therefore seeks to encourage local authorities to make some provision for the homeless single adult. They may need to 'mobilise or co-operate with voluntary effort' and 'it may also be useful for neighbouring authorities to consult together about ways of taking joint action to meet the combined need in their areas, either directly or through a voluntary body'. It is accepted that any provision in this field 'will be a new venture for many local authorities'. Now it is accepted that circulars sow seeds rather than set up projects, so that too much should not be expected of any one circular. None the less it still seems unsatisfactory that there should be such lack of direction together with over-reliance on the voluntary organizations, who may or may not be consulted by either central or local authorities, for the facilities that will be needed.

If we turn to the specific area of the homeless alcoholic, it is probably true to say that, here again, no one has really decided who is responsible and how any responsibility that does exist can most effectively be implemented. In 1967 the House of Commons had an impassioned plea from the member for Bethnal Green in the East End of London (Hilton, 1967, col. 1556). He stated forcibly:

Some of the residents have asked me 'why cannot the council do something about the problem of crude spirit drinkers?' Naturally, the first thought of any ratepayer is about action by his local authority. He thinks that they ought to be able to do something when he is suffering a social evil in this way. In fact the local authority are powerless. They have no powers even to clean a methylated spirits drinker. . . . Local authorities can do nothing about this problem except go to the government department concerned, put the problem before them as forcibly as possible and ask them to accept their responsibilities.

One might well ask 'what responsibilities?' The speaker was wise to anticipate some general evasive answer about co-operation with voluntary bodies by saying that 'any voluntary body which tries to tackle a problem which is too serious for it to tackle successfully, a problem which is completely beyond its resources in terms of manpower or money, ceases to be helpful and becomes irresponsible' (ibid., col. 1558). But who is irresponsible if the voluntary bodies are left to do the work? 'It is a public scandal that in 1971 we should rely on the vision and dedication of voluntary organizations to provide for some of the most distressed people around us' (*South London Press*, 25 June 1971). In the same debate, one member trod the same old path when he said the problem should be tackled by every organization to hand!: 'It is a job both for government departments and the local authorities . . . and also for voluntary organizations' (Macleod, 1967, col. 1562). The reply by the Ministry of Health's representative went so far as to say that 'Somewhere along the line we must regard this matter nationally and see if we can find a proper formula' (Snow, 1967, col. 1568). We still await the formula.

It was natural to have hoped that some form of national direction would have come from the Home Office Report on Habitual Drunken Offenders (1971). But the report's very terms of reference revealed the problem. The terms were 'to consider the treatment, within the penal system, of offenders who habitually commit offences involving drunkenness'. The phrase 'within the penal system' showed the confusion which still existed as to who should hold responsibility for the treatment of habitual drunken offenders. It seemed odd that the treatment of people, who are in the majority of cases defined as medically ill through alcoholism, should be within a penal framework. However, after the publication of this report in 1971 the attitude of the DHSS dramatically changed and eventually that department accepted responsibility for implementing most of the report's recommendations.

This was known to have followed some internal debate between the Home Office and the DHSS. The delay that this caused to even initiating the implementation of the report was considerable. This was perhaps not so surprising, for the report had yet again failed to come to grips with who was to do what.

The present working party's report is in fact weak when it comes to the practicalities of action, and seems rather piously to hope that vastly complex organizational problems need to be matched by no very special or imaginative efforts. Nevertheless 'co-ordination' must become more than a hopeful slogan. The Department of Health is presumably going to share some partnership with the Home Office . . . and a host of voluntary organizations with strong traditions of individuality are also going to have to be brought into the scheme (*British Medical Journal*, 20 March 1971, p. 621).

Just how is the report weak on the 'practicalities of action'? The majority of the working party members made the following statement on co-operation between the treatment services.

We would accordingly hope that it might be possible to consider the formation of a standing advisory body which could similarly combine the range of membership which our working party has enjoyed and could continue to concentrate on the development of facilities for habitual drunken offenders, possibly within the framework of the Advisory Council for Probation and After-Care (Home Office, 1971, p. 141).

However, four members of the working party, all of whom worked outside government departments, considered 'that something more than this would be required' and urged that the 'responsibility for co-ordinating action is concentrated in a single body' (ibid., p. 142). They proposed the formation of a Commission (ibid., pp. 238–40).

The Commission, with an initial three year life, would be charged with the responsibility of determining that in the shortest time possible there was set up throughout England and Wales a network of services to deal with the chronic drunkenness offender in ways alternative to imprisonment. Its terms of reference would emphasize that the Commission's job was not further debate but the actual solution of a social problem which has been discussed for too long, but which has up to now remained intractable perhaps largely because of there being no one spearhead organization charged with forcing through a real programme of action.

The fears of the minority who recommended the Commission have to some extent been warranted. The role of the Advisory Council for Probation and After-Care with regard to this problem ceased to be relevant when the DHSS took on major responsibility, yet there was no other similar body in the health field that could undertake the role recommended by the majority of the Home Office Working Party. No spearhead organization has yet come into existence and the arguments against it expressed in the report (ibid., p. 142) seem, as the years go by, to carry little weight, given the overwhelming need to establish a visible, strong, central body responsible for action in this field. Voluntary organizations continue to feel frustrated at the lack of any national response to the problems, be they those of the homeless alcoholic in particular or the homeless single person in general. The absence of any Commission means that there is no regularized partnership between voluntary and statutory service. While, for example, the DHSS is concerned to develop detoxification centres, it can only effectively do this if the many voluntary bodies provide ancillary support and after-care for these centres. Yet at present there is no established forum where such groups can meet to plan these facilities, so leaving voluntary bodies 'out on a limb' despite the fact that, for all their limitations, it is the voluntary agencies that have been the main pioneers in working with the potential clients of detoxification centres.

A long-awaited circular was issued in 1973 on community services for alcoholics (DHSS, 1973). Rumours of its coming had been floating about for months beforehand and possibly too much was expected from it. It certainly had a lot to commend it, in particular its lack of emphasis on the medical model of alcoholism and its treatment. But on the vital issues of who had responsibility for the proposed community services, difficulties abounded.

To develop these services a partnership between local authority and voluntary effort will be needed, and it is to be hoped that local authorities will use all the means available to them to help voluntary bodies which are trying to develop services for the alcoholics in their areas.

A move towards partnership and away from patronage is welcome. But in reality local authorities can only be exhorted to take action, to consult and to co-operate. A large element of luck is needed if the hoped-for partnership comes into being in the majority of areas. Already there are small signs of the troubles that lie ahead. The circular makes generous provision from central government to enable alcoholic hostels to be established, on the understanding that within five years' time the local authorities will take over the financial responsibility. One London borough's social service committee has been reported (*South London Press*, 3 July 1973) as complaining that 'it seemed an increasing trend by the Government to expect local authorities to take on extra work in the social work field but not give them the money for this'. Who does what for whom and how? That is the painfully unresolved question running through this and other similar statements in this field of concern.

For many voluntary organizations the issue of responsibility finds its most concrete expression in the problem of funding. From what sources should bodies such as the Project obtain the money to carry out the work that government has said should be done? In London, at least, this question can appear at times totally unanswerable. In the end we have been fortunate in so far as funding has eventually always been obtained, but not without a great expenditure of time and energy. The particular problem of London is that any single borough can claim that vagrants are a London problem and therefore funding should come from the London Boroughs Association. But within that body the outer London boroughs (where there are no vagrants) wonder why they should contribute money for a problem that is the concern of only a few inner London boroughs. The logic then is to say that 'it's not a London problem, it's a national problem.' The astonishing fact is that, through all this maze, funds do emerge. The sad fact is that it is such hard work. As one Project committee member said: 'I'm tired of going to meetings of voluntary organizations where half the time is spent discussing just how to raise the money to continue in business.' We always hoped the day would come when at least some voluntary bodies would be seen as agents of central government, doing their work, and accordingly funded as of right rather than after interminable negotiations.

Overall, then, too much is left to chance, with relationships developing on an *ad hoc* basis as particular pressure points occur. The strategy of 'muddling through' (Maddox, 1971) is all too apparent. It could be argued that there are other problems where several government departments are involved – the absence of clearly defined central responsibility in this field is not unique. I would not wish to claim that it was. What I would say is that there is every evidence to show that a fundamental part of the total problem is the inability, unwillingness or impossibility for any one agency or Ministry to seize the problem and to be totally accountable for its resolution or non-resolution. As long as we remain trapped in the uncertain area of argument as to whether vagrants are a local or a national problem, and then of defining what is local and what national, of relying on permissive rather than mandatory legislation, of hoping piously that local and central government and voluntary bodies will somehow all get together in a spirit of co-opera-tion – as long as that continues we shall be forced to admit that the vagrants are only part of the existing problem. The other part is ourselves.

Chance and growth

It is common to read references in the literature on the planning of services to the phenomenon of the 'unplanned plan'. This has certainly been illustrated by the development of the Project. At the start, few of us could have possibly anticipated the vital upsurge of interest in the alcoholic that was to be taken by the DHSS. The publication of the report early in 1971 and the DHSS circulars in 1972 and 1973 on homeless single persons and alcoholics led many of us into thinking that much was about to happen. As I have tried to show, it did not work out quite as well as we might have hoped. For the Project, there have been important lessons which taught us something about how difficult it is in this field to plan the growth of a service.

We soon learned that impending publication of any official statement prevents in the meantime any action being taken. 'We are waiting to see what the circular has to say' was a theme tune of many officials whom we approached when we sought, for example, to involve local authority social services departments in our particular sphere of work. Circulars are intended to be a stimulus to action, but until they actually appear they can be very constipating. On the other hand, when reports are published it is possible to argue that this gives agencies such as the Project an opportunity to pressurize official bodies.

But many documents are published on a host of problems, some far more 'deserving' than the vagrant alcoholic. When the report was published, one journal pleaded that the report should not be 'read, praised and forgotten' (*New Society*, 11 March 1971). Again, procrastination occurred when statutory agencies waited to see what the 'official' line was to be. When it seemed likely that the DHSS would have some responsibility for implementing the report, the probation and after-care service was reluctant to undertake any commitment in this field, even though it was never suggested that all drunks would cease to be offenders. A few of us on the Project certainly felt in the heady days after the publication of the report that we were now 'on the way'. It was not to be. A similar reaction occurred among many alcoholism service workers when the DHSS Circular 21/73 on Community Services for Alcoholics was issued. Circular '21/73' was talked about in almost reverential tones – everyone seemed drunk with the achievements that were just around the corner.

What all these various documents did, however, was to help change the climate, particularly in local authorities, and to give us half a chance to present ourselves as relevant, rather than as a nuisance. This meant that in the borough of Lambeth, for example, an imaginative social services department offered us an opportunity as from 1973 to be their 'agent' in developing alcoholism services in the borough. Initially we were given a grant for the salary of an extra social worker who, though working with vagrant alcoholics, would also be a source of advice and information on other alcoholic problems. This working relationship between a voluntary body and a local authority has exciting possibilities. It is also realistic in that in inner London it will be some while before alcoholics, vagrant or not, become a high priority for the social services.

This kind of development took a different turn with the borough of Lewisham. Our involvement in that area best illustrates how the Project has tried to use valuable growth points. When we conducted our survey of drunkenness offenders at the Camberwell magistrates' court (Hershon, 1974) we discovered that nearly 40 per cent of these offenders had in fact been arrested in one small area of Lewisham. We decided therefore to release one social worker to explore the problem of the homeless alcoholic in Lewisham. This took several months, but led to the setting-up of a Lewisham working party on the vagrant alcoholic. The Lewisham social service department already had a senior social worker with responsibility for alcoholism and drug addiction, so as a borough it was sympathetic to the problem. The working party met regularly for nearly a year. The outcome of it all was that in April 1974 the Project was officially invited by the council to work in the borough and to establish a scheme to assist the homeless alcoholics.

This invitation came at a time when the new careers team had just been recruited. We thus found ourselves in 1974 in a position to ask the new careers team to undertake the project in Lewisham. A chance had now been made whereby a team of four ex-skid row alcoholics could try to establish what they saw as the best way to assist the vagrant alcoholic. Bahr (1973, p. 294) actually raises a question that addresses itself directly to our scheme in Lewisham.

If the skid row men had a say in the kind of facilities and treatment available to them, what would they choose? What would be the effects of giving them, as a group, some say in the direction of the changes now, for the most part, imposed on them?

We believe that some realistic answers to these questions may emerge from our work in Lewisham.

While much that has occurred on the Project has not been carefully planned in advance, it is also fair to say that we have not lurched from one idea to another. 'We must have more beds' has at times been the heart-felt cry of the shop-front workers. It has been my job to try to strike a balance between providing a reasonable service and becoming an accommodation agency that tries to 'soak up' skid row. I believe that we have sought to attain our goals by a process of mounting an initial exploration, intelligently examining this early stage and then moving on to provide a coherent framework within which to maintain and support the earlier development. Some growth has been rather haphazard. At all times it has been the director's task to ensure that the Project continued to head in the right direction.

Some myths of skid row; the individual's potential

I have already made several references to the fact that much of the Project's growth from the early Rathcoole experience onwards was related to our increasing realization that the skid row man had more potential than his commonly-accepted stereotype allowed. Employment of ex-skid row alcoholics and the formal development in 1973 of a New Careers Scheme were then the logical outcome of early moves we made to give full responsibility to residents in all houses. It is fair to say that many areas of social work are at last awakening to the potential of so-called 'hopeless' clients and, while the Project has been ahead of many agencies in the attention it has given to this potential, it has been by no means unique.

In this section I wish to stress once more the possibilities of growth latent in the skid row man. Probably more than any other person, he has been viewed as a hopeless case with little interest in anything other than the 'easy touch' and the next source of the drink. Some of these views may be true of some men some of the time but they cannot, we believe, be sustained as universally applicable views. Some aspects of the stereotype that many agencies apparently hold is due to at best a mis-reading, at worst a total ignorance of the skid row situation. Unless there can be greater understanding of the true nature of skid row itself, it is likely that agencies will continue to act in accordance with their own preconceptions, thus frequently producing self-fulfilling prophecies. For example, when we were recruiting our new careers team of recovered alcoholics, one rehabilitation agency took the view that none of their men was suitable as 'they are mainly Scots and Irish with a labouring background'. What is the limit being placed on their growth? Or again, if any agency believes every down-and-out will spend any money given to him on drink, how does any man reach a position where he is trusted to exercise a choice? I am certainly not so naive as to suggest that a better understanding will have miraculously successful

results; certainly, however, no progress at all will be made until efforts
are intensified to achieve some understanding.

What then are the most powerful myths that we believe cloud our
understanding of skid row alcoholics? The men have arrived on skid
row through a variety of circumstances. Many initially came to England
from Ireland and Scotland to work. They have not been continuously
on skid row, but have spent many years in hard labouring jobs such as
hydro-electric schemes or motorways. To hear magistrates tell such
men that they are a drain on this country is a travesty of the truth,
totally denying the laudable reasons for their coming here in the first
place. Work records of men on skid row are many and varied, but our
experience suggests that the men are far from being a work-shy bunch,
whatever their immediate appearance might suggest.

Helping agencies tend to see the skid row man as being out to
exploit every opportunity to his own advantage and their own game is
to prevent that. In practice however it appears that, while men are
begging from passers-by at the railway station, they are not at the same
time drawing weekly benefit from the local Social Security office. Many
indeed seem not to draw any state benefit from one week to the next.
Nor are they always going the rounds of the numerous agencies open to
them. Hand-outs are used, but there is no evidence to support the view
that men from one area flock into another as soon as a new hand-out is
rumoured to be on offer. A few men are of course highly mobile and
appear everywhere, but not the majority. We need to hesitate in ascrib-
ing patterns of behaviour to men generally on the evidence of the wiles
and ruses of a small minority. Our own shop-front evaluation study
showed for example that the homeless alcoholics of North London
were barely known to agencies elsewhere in London.

While social workers are too ready to write off men as hopeless and
inadequate, we wonder if this judgment is not sometimes made at a
distance from the client, when closer examination might produce a less
pessimistic view. The word 'illiterate', for example, tends to be bandied
about as a derogatory description of men about whom no attempt has
been made to check the facts. It is used synonymously with 'poorly
educated', but carries with it pejorative undertones of a dismissive
nature. Words such as 'inadequate', 'weak', 'mentally unstable', flow
through social workers' reports on men referred to us, which suggests
that the mere fact of being alcoholic and homeless is proof of the
characteristics mentioned: 'He is an inadequate man and his many
drunkenness offences seem to be symptomatic of this inadequacy.'
Frequently wild generalizations are given as further 'evidence': 'Mr W.
is an alcoholic who, as seems to be the case with many other alcoholics,

also suffers from mental illness.' These 'judgments at a distance' do not reflect in any way the qualities the men need to survive on skid row. The resourcefulness and energy required on skid row can at times be considerable, and hordes of the passively inadequate men described could not survive at all. It is therefore essential to spell out in what ways a man is inadequate but, even more important, to look at the ways in which he does cope. There are positive qualities to be detected among skid row alcoholics; notions of self-help for example are strong and should be given more attention. Nor is it really realized that for the men, telling lies is acceptable, whereas being a fraud is not. It is possible that on occasions the men's hatred of 'phoniness' is described by us as 'belligerent unco-operativeness'. It may be disconcerting for us to find that men can quickly discern the gap between an agency's stated intentions and its agents' actual practice!

One area in which much more demythologizing needs to take place is that surrounding the concept of 'motivation'. Referrals are made to the Project that contain phrases such as 'poorly motivated', 'not very well motivated', 'lacks motivation' or, rarely, 'highly motivated' – to stop drinking. Yet we have noted how men may take many months to build up to the decision even to try to stop drinking. Further, the ways in which an agency is organized can affect the level of 'motivation', suggesting that it is not entirely a matter of the individual alcoholic's personal inclination (Chafetz, 1961). Too great a stress on personal inclination can lead to condemnatory statements as to just how unmotivated a person is if he later returns to drinking after a stay in a hostel or hospital. There is need to recognize much more forcefully the degree to which others can contribute to an individual's motivation. Thus it is clear motivation can change almost daily. Certainly it is rarely so fixed that we are in a position to say someone has or has not got it, or that he will or will not 'do well', i.e. stay sober.

It is only fair to point out that some of the myths of skid row work to a man's advantage, at least temporarily, although in the end they are almost bound to cloud reality. The view still exists that the down-and-out, alcoholic or otherwise, is really a fun-loving soul who has decided to leave the rat race for others and who is now the last 'free' man. The happy tramp with his bread in a red spotted handkerchief is the predecessor of them all. Few studies have however revealed the existence today of such happy tramps: few alcoholics see themselves as making political statements by their very existence. To hold such a view of the men on skid row is, however, to make it easier for oneself to withdraw help or even to cease seriously concerning oneself with their condition. There are some echoes of this in the view that drinking 'schools' are groups of comrades who share a genuine brotherhood and are gathered together to drink. True, some men do drink regularly in groups, but few are the deep friendships which develop. 'Even those who drink together . . . are not friends, they only know each other' (Deutscher, 1955, p. 16).

We need to be meticulously careful indeed about making any assumptions about the quality of life on skid row. But it is particularly unwise to describe the life as if it is problem-free or desirable in any way. This point of view is as patronizing as the view which sees the men as in need of constant care and protection. Social workers are at times told that they meet their own needs in helping the clients. It is perhaps equally true that those who write so glowingly about the tramp ethic are also meeting their own needs. What evidence is there for O'Connor (1963, p. 177) to say vagrants are 'authentic outsiders'? What nonsense it is when Fletcher (1966, p. 10) says meths drinkers are 'the last great Victorian experience to be had in London'.

The positive qualities that do exist among skid row alcoholics are real enough but elusive too, and by no means always what we would like to believe. It is only when some of the cruder myths about skid row alcoholics are abandoned that we are likely to be able to feel less despairing about them as a group. 'Once you've seen one you've seen them all' seems a common attitude adopted towards the derelict alcoholic. A willingness to generalize shows itself in a way that is not the case with, for instance, sexual offenders. It may be the existence of an addiction which makes us less willing to look closer at the realities of what we describe; for drug addicts, too, seem to suffer from an excess of second-hand generalizations that handicap helper and addict alike.

The latent potential that the Project staff have seen emerge in a number of former skid row alcoholics is ample demonstration that the stereotypical down-trodden no-hoper is a waste-paper-basket category, like 'psychopath' and 'sociopath'. Our realization of this potential began in the residential settings of Rathcoole and Lynette Avenue: it continued in the shop fronts as soon as alcoholics were employed in those settings; it has taken new turns again with the establishment in 1973 of the Lambeth Friday Social Club, which is run by and for sober alcoholics in an attempt to break down some of the isolation and strangeness of sobriety. Clubs for alcoholics were referred to in the Report (Home Office, 1971, pp. 121–2) but there was no indication there that the initiative and strength of these might come from the men themselves. The origins of the Friday Social Club sprang from a meeting of men who had successfully come through the Kennington shop front which was held there. The history of the club is not for me to write. We comment on it here as yet another example of what can occur when a trusting and responsible response is given to the stimulus of the men themselves.

The problem of new approaches

From its inception, the Project has sought to test new ways of tackling age-old problems. We believe that some of the activities of the Project are an advance on earlier methods, though we are still far from being satisfied that we have done all we could. The hostels and the shop fronts are not in the old tradition of skid row helping agencies, though it has not always been easy to break clear of that tradition. The sense of options given to the men is crucial to our work and an element that has hitherto been lacking to a large extent in the skid row scene. Actual choice of accommodation, for example, may be limited, but discussion of even that limited choice with a client may involve him in his own life in a way that is too frequently denied to him. With the exercise of choice comes some acceptance of responsibility for the consequences of that choice. How is adequate social functioning manifested if the opportunities for being responsible first for yourself, and then for others, are never offered?

In breaking away from the tradition of the skid row man as the passive recipient of welfare we feel the Project has added something to the skid row scene. At the same time it would be difficult to claim that we are totally different from any other body already involved with the homeless alcoholic. The work – much criticized by more professionally trained workers at the time – of the Royal London Prisoners' Aid Society in the 1960s has had some lessons for us, as has the work of some of the officers of the Probation and After-Care Service. But in both these instances the better work has tended to be that of a few individuals, isolated even within their own organizations. That work certainly lacked support from a wider range of services. The Project has itself gained from its concentration on a single problem, with resources and support specifically designed to cope with the demands made upon it. A gradually increasing interest from some other services has also helped reduce the sense of isolation of the Project as a whole.

In considering the Project's total endeavours, it must be admitted that it seems at times to have become one further station on the 'rehab loop' – but we believe it is qualitatively different from previous activities of most other agencies. This is not the same as claiming that we have been enormously successful – that ultimately must be for others to determine. There are, however, a number of factors that have helped us to become a rather different agency: the combination of research and social work skills; the involvement of the men themselves; the setting-up of exploratory sub-projects within the main scheme; the early awareness that it was hard to do anything totally new; the avoidance of going for quantitative expansion as a way of 'solving' the problem – this last point particularly highlights some of the issues involved in what we have been doing.

Although, in absolute terms, the number of men on skid row at any one time is small, none the less, to the social worker who is engaged with one homeless alcoholic after another, the problem can seem enormous. In these circumstances it is naturally tempting to feel that 'if only we had more hostels or hospital beds' all would be well. Just around the corner is the money that will enable us to cover the land with the required provision. Yet we all know in our daily dealings with many complex individuals that even if offered one million pounds we would be uncertain as to how to spend it to best effect, as opposed to spending it with the greatest clamour. The sober millennium for all is far away. Many people fail to believe that: the message that is too often preached – that word is used advisedly – is that, for example, if only doctors knew how to recognize alcoholics, then we could make some real inroads into the problem. Doctors therefore demand more facilities for treatment: but the treatment agencies say 'we don't really know sufficient about what we do now'. Seeking to improve the lot of the alcoholic on humanitarian grounds is fine, but we must guard against claiming that we are certain we can make him sober.

When people talk about new approaches it is essential to examine whether they are old ideas that are simply being redefined under a new heading. There is a tendency to go from one diagnosis to the next before the implications of the first have been fully worked out. The lumber in the attic keeps piling up as the years go by, and no one dares insist on a spring-clean; it is always easier to acquire than to throw out. For example, the report found it very difficult on occasion to escape the clutches of the old concepts and tended to re-define skid row agencies rather than argue for their replacement and abolition. Lodging houses and shelters were thus re-described as 'a *necessary* element in the overall *treatment* system' (Home Office, 1971, p. 187, my italics).

Faced with the rather desperate re-definition, it is tempting just to try to cover the land with Rathcoole-type hostels and shop fronts, but it is highly unlikely that such a move would provide a solution. Each of the houses and each of the shop fronts has been quite different in practice, though often the intent behind them was the same. What are important are the general principles governing these houses and the fact that they have been considerably influenced by local needs and problems. It is surely for others to look into our experiences and to draw from them material relevant for their own particular areas' difficulties.

Further, the few facilities this Project has managed have not yet enabled us to answer questions about very long-term sobriety or about other ways of reaching out to the alcoholic. We have had to look as carefully as possible at what we have been doing, not merely to satisfy our own self-questioning needs but also to ensure that unwarranted claims are not made about a 'breakthrough' into the skid row alcoholic problem. It is rather sad, but new schemes that do appear can very quickly become jaded and 'just another agency' on the skid row scene. It is very difficult to sustain new approaches over a number of years. In a field as perplexing as the one we work in, there is therefore a readiness to acclaim a new scheme when little has truly been proven. Over-hasty and uncritical acclamation backfires in the end on the men involved, as once more they are regarded as 'hopeless': 'After all they didn't even stay sober at Rathcoole and that's a marvellous place.' Is it? Who said so?

Paucity of research

Comparatively speaking, American research workers have devoted a lot of attention to the phenomenon of skid row, whereas in this country there are few major studies of the problem. There seems recently to have been an upsurge of interest in vagrancy as a whole, but too much of this activity is still a kind of poor man's George Orwell. It would be unwise to advocate too rapid an expansion of research interest, since all the American research, with a few obvious exceptions, has really not yielded any new perspectives on the problem or ways of tackling it. It is all too easy to move from 'if only we had more hostels' to 'if only more research was done' – both equally desperate cries in the face of an undeniably difficult problem. To date, too much of the skid row research that has been attempted is trapped in the stockpiling of statistics which can be overwhelming in their intricacy, but in the end tell us surprisingly little about the skid row problem. It is perhaps too easy to ridicule statistics; but skid row study after skid row study seems to give us basically the same findings and makes basically the same recommendations. It is hard not to yearn for more understanding of the problem, as opposed to statements about it.

Clearly, there is a need for research to assist us to obtain the broad outlines of the problem, though by now I would have thought those outlines were clear enough. Doctors have told us that even methylated spirit drinkers are not 'bearded, schizophrenic tramps' but are 'more hopeful material than has been supposed for treatment and rehabilitation' (McDougall, 1956, p. 499). But how to move on from there has not yet been the dominant feature of research in this field. So far, research in the United Kingdom has been psychiatrically dominated, and few other disciplines have yet made major contributions to the area of study. Fortunately, however, sociologists, anthropologists and psychologists are now beginning to involve themselves more in this work and it is to be hoped that they will address themselves to the relevant questions.

Who is to say what is really a relevant field of study? I would like to suggest here a few questions that seem to me deserving of more attention than has hitherto been given to them. It would be foolish to hope that, if these areas were researched then all the answers would be known. However, some corrective is needed to the surveys that have too frequently been undertaken which finish by telling us that the homeless alcoholic is middle-aged, unskilled, working class, poorly educated, socially deprived – but nothing else. Much more than this needs to be known about the skid row alcoholic. One of the most perplexing questions is how and why some men and not others come for help. How do men come to define themselves as having a drinking problem? How are those seeking help viewed by the remainder? It seems evident to us that, at any one time, only a small minority of the homeless alcoholics are seeking help; even over a period of years the majority seem to steer clear of helping agencies. There may be many reasons for this but we should surely make some effort to discover what they are. The question then arises as to what happens to those who do come forward for help. We can ask again: whatever happened to last year's drunkenness offenders? There is some indication that men may enter the 'rehabilitation circuit' for a brief period and then leave it without apparently contacting any agencies again for several years. A minority seem to be permanently on circuit, well known to virtually all agencies; yet this minority may only serve to give social workers the impression that all homeless alcoholics constantly 'go the rounds'. At present, we only seem able to deal with individual men as they continually return to us; we have little idea about any wider movements within the sub-culture of which individuals are only a part.

We still need to learn much more about the ways in which men themselves define 'help' and whether this in any way coincides with the agencies' definition. The way in which men view the agencies is something we examined earlier: but that was only a tentative first step in exploring the client's view. At best this only served to pinpoint areas for a more detailed enquiry. Other questions that we should perhaps now ask might cover: why some and not other men beg. What do people who are begged from feel about it? Why are some men frequently arrested for drunkenness, while others in a seemingly similar situation, rarely ever are? Are there distinctive types of drinkers – for example 'loners' – and, if so, does this influence the nature of any rehabilitation programme that may be planned? Despite the research that has so far been done, too many possibly important questions remain neglected. Bahr (1973, pp. 292–5), in his study of skid row in the USA, listed twenty-two pressing questions that he felt represented 'the most fertile areas for future studies on homelessness and skid row'. We can be fairly certain, therefore, that research in this country has barely begun to tackle the most vital questions.

The organization of the Project

Through the methods it used to assist the homeless alcoholic and through the way in which the Project presented itself to the outside world, we had hoped to avoid simply being another addition to the skid row scene. In some respects, as indicated, that has been accomplished. Yet in other respects it is difficult to see how an outsider could distinguish this Project from similar exercises. Such an observer could well say: 'Fine, you have helped a number of individuals and you have tried out some new methods of working, but there still seems little evidence of co-ordination or of a planned comprehensive service.' It would be churlish not to agree in principle, though a few comments about the actual difficulties of the exercise might temper the severity of the criticism offered.

In order to achieve any sense of a jointly planned service for homeless alcoholics, an organization has to start from a base of authority from which to lead. If this base does not rest on finance, i.e. control of the purse strings, it needs to rest on the authority of respected experience. In order to acquire the latter takes time, however, and we feel that it was only after some years of the Project's activities that we have begun to be accorded that authority. It may now be possible to become more influential in bringing together agencies that remain wary of each other and, while accusations of 'empire building' float through the neurotic bloodstreams of hypersensitive voluntary bodies, statutory bodies may be sufficiently secure not to worry one way or the other. Only when the climate is right – which requires luck and hard work – will there be any chance of the stated ultimate goal of the Project being achieved.

Some hope may lie in the increased financial involvement of the DHSS. But too often, when government departments hand over public money to voluntary bodies, they are concerned mainly to see that it is honestly spent. More attention should in my opinion be given to seeing that it is also responsibly spent. More strings could legitimately be attached to the giving of grants than is currently the case and we are glad to see that in the 1973 circular on alcoholism services there is some slight suggestion of this. If the government department responsible for alcoholism services cannot be troubled to press for greater co-ordination and more rational treatment services, then who is it to be left to? For a funding department to make such statements as 'unless in this or that regard you can work something out together, no money will be forthcoming' does not seem unreasonable. The track record of almost all organizations to date hardly enables them to claim a prerogative of the knowledge and know-how in the area of co-operation.

This last statement can work both ways, for it also enables organizations to claim that, as no one has the best answer, then any method of helping will do. That may, however, be a recipe for failing to think about the implications of any work we do! As we have seen, there is no clear-cut model of response to the plight of the homeless alcoholic. The wide range and, indeed, the conflict of response, means that one is not seeking to work with similar organizations, who happen to disagree, but with vastly dissimilar organizations, who are almost unaware of each other's existence. There is little doubt that most agencies are ambivalent, contradictory and confused in their attitudes to the problem of the vagrant alcoholic who is everybody's problem but no one's responsibility; always calling but never welcome; diseased and degenerate at one and the same time.

Archard (1973) has said that society has a confused response and is asking the question, 'Sad, bad or mad?' I feel more and more that society and its agencies have always had a consistent response, in that in the same breath they are able to say the homeless alcoholic is 'sad, mad *and* bad'. Each agency seems to carry within it the seeds of these three elements. Courts punish but also remand for medical reports; hostels take in but also turn out a man when he is drunk; doctors heal but then lecture a man as to what will happen if he continues to drink; clergymen pray for him and then give him the price of a cup of tea. Missions and psychiatry co-exist painlessly and effortlessly. Further, the prevailing scene is never static: the rise of the medical model as a response to alcoholism is now being severely questioned; what hybrid, if any, will replace it remains to be seen. In the meantime, considerable uncertainty exists as to how large the medical role should be in, for example, detoxification centres. Even a few years ago, there would have been little doubt that the medical role should have been the major one.

It would not have been surprising if, faced with the difficulties of history, local pride and theoretical uncertainty, we had found ourselves drawn into more social work endeavour than we had originally envisaged, and had given up the unequal struggle to do much beyond that. While the balance is never totally right, I do not believe that this imbalance occurred. The social work that has been undertaken has had aims other than the constant rescuing of souls in torment! It has taken place in a context of continuous evaluation, and with an acknowledged desire to relate it to the work of other agencies and to other people's ideas. Partly through the social work element, it has been possible to establish the respected experience that gives us a recognized voice in more long-term endeavours. The work with individual alcoholics also serves to remind us continually that their disablement is very real. They are not in difficulties just because they have been 'labelled', 'stigmatized' or 'criminalized': some do have crippling disabilities, not always related directly to their alcoholism itself. The alcoholics' own disablement, while it should not be exaggerated, therefore needs always to be seen in conjunction with the agencies' limitations. Neither alone can be held responsible for our continuing failure to resolve the skid row alcoholic problem.

The social worker's position

I can imagine, without too much difficulty, some social workers who have read so far commenting to themselves, 'Well, this is all right, but I still don't know how best to deal with a drunken vagrant who calls first thing on Monday morning!' If some alcoholics do have disabilities, how do I help? The fact that in this book I have barely referred to treatment, casework, group therapy, nor indeed to the fact that some believe that skid row alcoholics have a 'negative ego image' (Rosenman, 1955), is deliberate. I have been involved on occasions in lengthy case conferences on skid row alcoholics. On one such occasion I was persuaded to see that an alcoholic who regularly gave away his watch when drunk was displaying some form of castration complex. In no way, though, did that information equip me to help him stay sober. That particular alcoholic stayed sober when he was put in charge of a small hostel for alcoholics. If pressed, I think I would say that it is more important to understand the sub-cultural phenomenon of skid row than it is to worry unduly about the case history of any one individual. That does not mean that an individual's history is ignored, but rather that we do not rely on an individual casework relationship to see us through.

Nor incidentally am I suggesting that we abandon the attempts to discover the causes of alcoholic vagrancy, though the multi-causal nature of it is evident. The fact, for example, that the majority of vagrant alcoholics in London are Irish and Scottish requires more examination than we have been able to give to it, though for me one man put the position neatly and graphically: 'One day I was on a farm in Ireland, and the next day I was on a building site in Birmingham. . . . I drank.' Social workers need constantly to take account of this broader canvas.

Even if we were to argue for a great increase in the availability of professional social work skills, we would surely have to admit that there would never be enough social workers to provide such a service. The vagrant alcoholic, no matter what the resources, is always likely to remain low on most agencies' list of priorities. In putting forward a view which tends not to see vagrant alcoholics as casework material, I am not saying they should be given a second-class service at a down-town dossers' dispensary. The history of the Project has been, we believe, to give the men a good service, but based more on how we organized it and presented it than predominantly relying on a series of one-to-one relationships. Such relationships have, of course, existed but have flourished because of the wider setting and our overall attention to skid row and its institutions. Without that wider attention being given, it is in my view too easy to see vagrant alcoholics as the weakest and most hopeless of all clients. Monger (1967, p. 141), for example, writes as if to suggest that alcoholics are in this weak category when he refers to 'offenders with the highest degree of dependency needs such as alcoholics, and extreme inadequates, perhaps with low intelligence or heavily institutionalized'. It is easy to see how some social workers have their minds made up before the 'client' even arrives.

I also think that when social workers or doctors ask for guidance on how to deal with the homeless alcoholic it is not so much a variation of casework technique that they seek, but rather encouragement in how actually to cope with the individual's drunkenness and their own fears and prejudice. Is he likely to get violent? How do you avoid being hit? What do you do if he drinks a bottle of wine in your office? How do you react if he threatens to cut his throat with a broken bottle if you won't help him? Worse still, how do you help the rest of your colleagues to be tolerant if your clients turn up drunk every day? Setting out what just we ourselves do in these circumstances is I think unhelpful: we may be doing the wrong thing. My own experience suggests that, even if advice were to be given, it is rarely fully accepted. There is too often a hidden resistance based, I sometimes feel, on the unspoken statement, 'It's all right for you, you actually like these people.'

The phenomenon of skid row

I have often considered that the time to write about the homeless alcoholic is after six months working with the problem, when it all seems so easy to solve! The longer I have worked in the field, however, the less certain my judgments have become and the more I realize how much I still need to understand. One certainly has the feeling – not substantiated by any objective data – that skid row has the capacity to absorb any amount of research and social work endeavour and to remain untouched by it. I use skid row in this context as something having an identity or will of its own which is greater than the sum of individuals on it. It is an identity of a will-o'-the-wisp character, and it is that which makes the problem so hard to resolve. There is in the skid row air, as it were, a notion of defiance and hopelessness, either part of which (or the combination of which) makes reaching out to and helping individuals, separately or as a group, extremely difficult. One of the men had this to say about his drinking friends:

Quite a few alcoholics are possessed of an iron will. This may seem odd to some who are devoted to helping or looking after alcoholics. If you were to see an alcoholic at his lowest ebb walking into a drinking school where there was an abundance of drink and if in that school there was someone he did not like, even though dying for a drink, he would turn on his heels and walk away; most alcoholics are capable of this show of will power.

This 'will power' is equally well demonstrated when the alcoholic is facing helping or 'correcting' agencies. This is the element in him that makes it useless appealing to him with arguments based on the premise 'surely you would be better off if . . .' Yet coupled with this outer defiance can be a resigned sense of hopeless despair. Harrington (1963, p. 96) wrote about his return to the New York Bowery six months after he had finished working there; he gives us the comment of an old Bowery friend: 'We wondered when you would wise up, Mike. Hanging around here helping us, that's nothing. Only nuts would do it. It's good you're wised up and going some place.' Harrington adds: 'They were happy that I had left. They couldn't understand why anyone would want to care for them.'

Vexliard (1957, p. 271, my translation) has probably an even more telling passage on these elements in the life of the 'clochard'. He wrote that the 'clochard' faced with crushing injustices and the excess of suffering

does not bother any more, he gives in to fate . . . some adopt an attitude of smiling 'philosophers', others an attitude of dark withdrawal. . . . Their pauperism is essentially solitary. . . . Their emotions fasten on to useless objects. The essential thing for them is not to get involved . . . they are at root timid, not able to project their personalities or affirm themselves socially as people. They are very ready to be self-accusatory. Some of them demonstrate feelings of culpability . . . they avoid, in particular, situations which entail criticism or competitive situations where they will fail. The state of permanent frustration creates a type of behaviour not reducible to concepts of learning and motivation . . . the future no longer plays any role . . . the reality does not consist of goals.

It may be that some of these feelings – portrayed by Harrington and Vexliard – incidentally in two quite different cultures – are only partly a reflection of the state of being a 'clochard'. They may also illustrate the wider sense of hopelessness that the powerless lower classes are said to feel faced with the local or national authorities. In writing of the community action programmes against poverty in the United States, Moynihan (1969, p. 107) states: 'The self-defeating attitudes of the lower class made them feel nothing could be accomplished.'

It seems to me that, underlying any particular situations at a court, in a lodging house, in a hospital or hostel or on the street, there are always the twin problems of defiance and despair. It is as if these two patterns mirror the ambivalence or 'motivation': alcoholics may be well motivated to stop drinking but equally well motivated to continue. They defy the helping agencies, yet are desperate to turn to them for help. They like and want the support of the hostel but walk out because there is one egg short at breakfast! Illustrations could be endless, but it is in these that I believe that an important part of the germ of the phenomenon of skid row lies, and this is the part that makes the problem so exasperating and perplexing for the agencies involved in it.

The future

In even attempting a few thoughts on the future, it is perhaps wiser to say what I would like to happen rather than what I think will happen. Predictions cannot take into account the chance elements that have already altered the course of the Project so often. An upsurge in really good job opportunities in northern England and in Scotland might for example radically alter the flow of migrant labour to the south, which could well have a long-term effect on London's skid row and on the lodging house population. New planning policies that made social demands on property speculators could have their effect. Increased interest in community psychiatry, radical penal policies, new housing laws, to name but a few remote possibilities, could play a part in altering the skid row scene in some way. But if we assume no great changes in the wider societal fabric, we must then at least try to answer the self-imposed question: what we would most like to see develop within or without the Alcoholics Recovery Project.

In attempting to list below some clear-cut recommendations, I have been made very conscious of just how much I am a prisoner of my own time and its particular attitudes. To read the recommendations from other periods (of not so many years ago) is to smile indulgently and to bemoan the authors' naivety. Higgs (1906, pp. 72–3) set down eight reforms for vagrancy which were nothing if not sweeping. She stated for example that 'There should be provision, ample and sanitary, for migration.' It is difficult not to relapse into such all-embracing generalities.

(1) There is an urgent need for the establishment of a body such as a standing conference on the subject of the vagrant alcoholic. Such a body may go some way to ensuring that any recommendations that are acceptable have a chance of implementation, as for example many of those in the report. It could also seek to plan future developments rather than continue a series of *ad hoc* responses.

(2) The basic housing needs of homeless single persons need greater recognition. The state of public lodging houses should be examined. At least two model lodging houses should be started immediately.

(3) More direction from central government should be given to the extent of its assuming greater financial responsibility and commissioning new approaches to the problem. Voluntary bodies could act as 'agents' for central government.

(4) Police districts with more than 2,000 annual arrests for drunkenness offences should be assisted to set up a minimum complex of facilities including residential and non-residential facilities. Day centres for homeless alcoholics have been developed hardly at all in any area.

(5) All schemes to assist the vagrant alcoholic should offer the opportunity for the men to become active participants, not passive recipients. The men themselves should also initiate new approaches to the problem.

(6) All social and medical agencies operating in areas with a high incidence of homeless alcoholics should ensure that staff are really

familiar with the skid row facilities. Such visits as are necessary should not be left to chance.

(7) There should be a continuing examination of the folk-lore so that we could recognize for example that 'motivation' is as much due to an agency's organizational response as to an individual's own attitudes. Similarly, we should not blandly state that we want to integrate homeless alcoholics 'back into the community' without spelling out just what that means and how it is to be done.

(8) Peripheral agencies such as the Churches should work out in more detail what their own role and philosophy is to be concerning provision of resources for the vagrant.

(9) The prison authorities have to accept that, for the foreseeable future, homeless alcoholics will continue to go to prison for petty offences. The Home Office should make a clear statement concerning the treatment of alcoholics in prison or say that nothing can be done.

(10) Alternatives to detoxification centres should be tried now rather than wait until 1980 for the long-term evaluation of the pilot centres.

(11) Evaluation of any scheme is necessary and should be an essential but non-mystifying part of the work. The findings of relevant research studies should be made available to and readable by the field workers, otherwise no folk-lore will be ever questioned.

(12) The issue of police involvement in any new procedure for dealing with drunks has to be taken much more seriously and looked at in more detail.

(13) There is a need to look closely at whether in future facilities for homeless alcoholics should be separate from facilities for other homeless people and also other groups of alcoholics. The hostels that at present assist the homeless alcoholic should make strenuous efforts to break down their isolation. Consortia of local voluntary projects covering a range of social problems is a key development that should be fostered.

(14) Front-line personnel in daily contact with the vagrant alcoholic should be given much more support and advice.

(15) Finally, work with vagrant alcoholics, though specialized in some ways, should still draw on wider experiences from other social workers, as well as be seen as having relevance for other areas of social work.

Whatever recommendations are put forward they will be of little value unless we continually seek to remove the feeling of the men that they are treated as second class. Asked why he was turned away from a hospital, one man said, 'I suppose they smelt the drink off me and I was an Irishman.' The limitations of all we do have also constantly to be recognized – 'It's not the end of the world when a man goes drinking' was one man's salutary rejoinder to a group of social workers who felt that they ought to have the key to sobriety. We have to avoid seductive solutions – 'If only social workers were better trained' – and live with the complexity of the task at hand. This also means that we do not oversell one idea after another: for example 'housing' can too easily be put forward as the latest panacea. Above all, I think we have to accept that the 'dosser', 'down-and-out' and 'vagrant' is not someone in whose life we can dabble at will. We need to be as professional and as sensitive in our work as with any other group of people who are temporarily or permanently at the receiving end of the helping agencies.

But when all the details have been thought out, I retain the feeling that what we still desperately need is a concerted and intelligent attack on the problem, which I believe can only come from the establishment of a commission or council as outlined earlier in this book. There is no guarantee that such a body could solve the problem. Yet such a move has not ever seriously been tried. I have a fantasy that our hopes and achievements will be higher when we know that somewhere, in the corridors of power, there is a handful of powerful well-informed people who come to work each morning worrying about the skid row problem. Such people should have no other professional commitments. Resolving any part of the skid row problem is – as I hope is evident – a very full-time job. It is not something that can be left to the tail end of a busy week. For someone or somebody it must be the sole item on the agenda.

BIBLIOGRAPHY

Anderson, N. (1923), *The Hobo: The Sociology of the Homeless Man,* University of Chicago Press.

Anstee, B. B. (1972), 'Psychiatry in the Casualty Department', *Br. J. Psychiatry* 120, pp. 625–9.

Apte, R. Z. (1968), *Halfway Houses,* Occasional Papers on Social Administration No. 27, Bell, London.

Archard, P. (1972), 'The Alcoholic Dosser: Some Problems of Research for the Participant Observer', paper delivered at the 10th National Deviancy Conference, York.

Archard, P. (1973), *Sad, Bad or Mad: Society's Confused Response to the Skid Row Alcoholic in Contemporary Social Problems in Britain,* ed. R. V. Bailey and J. Young, Saxon House, Farnborough, England, pp. 127–43.

Armstrong, G. (1972), 'Kenmore Hall: An Experiment in First Stage Rehabilitation for Alcoholics', *Journal of Alcoholism* (London) 6, pp. 55–60.

Arnold, D. O. (ed.) (1970), *Subcultures,* Glendessary Press, Berkeley.

Bahr, H. (1968), *Homelessness and Disaffiliation,* Bureau of Applied Social Research, Columbia University.

Bahr, H. (1973), *Skid Row: An Introduction to Disaffiliation,* Oxford University Press.

Bandt, A., Folland, G. and **Stephens, K.** (1970), 'A Supportive Programme for Alcoholics in a Halfway House', paper delivered at 29th International Congress on Alcoholism and Drug Dependence, Melbourne.

Barnes, M. (1972), Parliamentary Debates, House of Commons, *Hansard,* vol. 838, cols 229–31.

Bartholomew, A. A. (1968), 'Alcoholism and Crime', *Australia and New Zealand Journal of Criminology* 1, 2, pp. 70–99.

Bessell, R. (1971), *Interviewing and Counselling,* Batsford, London.

Bittner, E. (1967), 'The Police on Skid Row: A Study of Peace-keeping', *Am. Sociological Review* 32, 5, pp. 699–715.

Blumberg, L. W. and **Shipley, T. E.** (1971), 'The Skid Row Man and the Skid Row Status Community', *Quarterly Journal of Studies on Alcohol (QJSA)* 32, pp. 909–41.

Braithwaite, G. and **Harker, M.** (1972), *Consortium: A Review of the First Year,* Cambridge House, London.

Brandon, D. (1972a), article in *New Society,* 22 June.

Brandon, D. (1972b), *The Decline and Fall of the Common Lodging House,* Christian Action Publications, London.

Brickner, P. W., Greenbaum, D. and **Kaufman, A.** *et al.* (1972), 'A Clinic for Male Derelicts', *Annals of Internal Medicine* 77, 4, pp. 565–9.

Brunner-Orne, M., Iddings, F. T. and **Rodrigues, J.** (1951), 'A Court Clinic for Alcoholics', *QJSA* 12, pp. 592–600.

Buckley, M. (1972), 'Enter the Ex-Con', *Federal Probation* 36, 4, pp. 24–30.

Butler, J. (1969), Parliamentary Debates, House of Commons, *Hansard*, vol. 780, cols 1757–60.

Cahn, S. (1969), 'Alcoholism Halfway Houses: Relationships to other Programs and Facilities', *Social Work (USA)* 14, 2, pp. 50–60.

Cahn, S. (1970), *The Treatment of Alcoholics*, Oxford University Press.

Camberwell Council on Alcoholism (1972), *The Homeless Single Person in Southwark*, CCA, London.

Chafetz, M. E. (1961), 'Procedure for Establishing Therapeutic Contact with the Alcoholic', *QJSA* 22, pp. 325–8.

Chafetz, M. E., Bland, H. T. and Hill, M. J. (eds) (1970), *Frontiers of Alcoholism*, Science House, New York.

Channon, P. (1972), Parliamentary Debates, House of Commons, *Hansard*, vol. 833, cols 1955–62.

Clark, D. H. (1965), 'The Therapeutic Community – Concept, Practice and Future', *Br. J. Psychiatry* 111, pp. 949–54.

Coleman, J. V. (1968), 'Research in Walk-in Psychiatric Services in General Hospitals', *Am. J. of Psychiatry* 124, pp. 1668–73.

Cook, T., Morgan, H. G. and Pollak, B. (1968), 'The Rathcoole Experiment: First Year at a Hostel for Vagrant Alcoholics', *Br. Medical J.* 1, pp. 240–2.

Cook, T. and Hancock, D. (1971), 'Men released from Pentonville 10–21 November 1970 and a 3 month Follow-up', Alcoholics Recovery Project (mimeo).

Cross, J. R. (1967), 'Public Health Approach to Alcoholism Control', *Am. J. of Public Health* 57, pp. 955–64.

Crousaz, D. (1972), *Glasgow Homeless Single People*, Christian Action Publications, London.

Dean, P. (1972), Parliamentary Debates, House of Commons, *Hansard*, vol. 842, cols 639–92.

Demone, H. W. (1965), 'The Limits of Rationality in Planning', *Community Mental Health J.* 1, 4, pp. 375–81.

Department of the Environment (1973), *Consultation Paper: Grants for Hostels and Similar Accommodation for Single People*, HMSO, London.

Department of Health and Social Security (1968), *Report of the Committee on Local Authority and Allied Personal Social Services*, HMSO, London.

Department of Health and Social Security (1972a), *Local Authority Social Services Ten Year Development Plans 1973–1983*, Circular 35/72, HMSO, London.

Department of Health and Social Security (1972b), *Homeless Single Persons in need of Care and Support*, Circular 37/72, HMSO, London.

Department of Health and Social Security (1972c), *Report of a Joint Working Party on Homelessness in the Counties of Gloucestershire, Somerset and Bristol*, HMSO, London.

Department of Health and Social Security (1973), *Community Services for Alcoholics*, Circular 21/73, HMSO, London.

Deutscher, I. (1955), 'The Petty Offender – Society's Orphan', *Federal Probation* 19, pp. 12–18.

Edwards, G. (1972), 'A Community as Case Study. Alcoholism Treatment in Antiquity and Utopia', paper read at the 2nd Annual Alcohol Conference of the National Institute on Alcohol Abuse and Alcoholism, Washington.

Edwards, G., Hawker, A. and **Williamson, V.** *et al.* (1966a), 'London's Skid Row', *Lancet* I, pp. 249–52.

Edwards, G., Hawker, A. and **Hensman, C.** (1966b), 'Setting up a Therapeutic Community', *Lancet* II, pp. 1407–8.

Edwards, G., Williamson, V. and **Hawker, A.** *et al.* (1968), 'Census of a Reception Centre', *Br. J. Psychiatry* 114, pp. 1031–9.

Fletcher, G. (1966), *Down Among the Meths Men*, Hutchinson, London.

Freire, P. (1972), *Pedagogy of the Oppressed*, Penguin, Harmondsworth.

Garrett, G. R. and **Bahr, H. M.** (1973), 'Women on Skid Row', *QJSA* 34, pp. 1228–43.

Gartner, A. (1971), *Paraprofessionals and their Performance*, Praeger, New York.

Gath, D., Hensman, C. and **Hawker, A.** *et al.* (1968), 'The Drunk in Court', *Br. Medical J.* 28, 4, pp. 808–11.

Gibbons, J. S. (1905), 'Inebriety and Crime', paper delivered at International Congress on Prison Management, Hodges, Figgis, Dublin.

Gray, F. (1931), *The Tramp – His Meaning and Being*, Dent, London.

Greve, J. (1971), *Homelessness in London*, Scottish Academic Press, Edinburgh.

Grosz, H., Nordschow, C. D. and **Pratt, A. D.** (1972), 'A Court and Probation Centered Treatment Facility for the Jailed Alcoholic: History, Programme and Preliminary Findings', Paper delivered at the 30th International Congress on Alcoholism and Drug Dependence, Amsterdam.

Hammond, J. L. and **Hammond, B.** (1949), *The Town Labourer 1760–1832*, Guild Books.

Harrington, M. (1963), *The Other America*, Penguin, Harmondsworth.

Harrison, B. (1971), *Drink and the Victorians: The Temperance Question in England 1815–1872*, Faber & Faber, London.

Hasenfield, Y. (1972), 'People Processing Organizations: An Exchange Approach', *American Sociological Review* 37, 3, pp. 256–63.

Hensman, C. (1969), 'Problems of Drunkenness amongst Male Recidivists', in *The Drunkenness Offence*, ed. T. Cook, D. Gath and C. Hensman, Pergamon Press, Oxford, pp. 35–50.

Heraud, B. J. (1970), *Sociology and Social Work – Perspectives and Problems*, Pergamon Press, Oxford.

Hershon, H., Cook, T. and **Foldes, P.** (1974), 'What shall we do with the Drunkenness Offender?', *Br. J. Psychiatry* 124, pp. 327–35.

Higgs, M. (1906), *Glimpses into the Abyss*, P. S. King & Sons.

Hilton, W. S. (1967), Parliamentary Debates, House of Commons, *Hansard*, vol. 755, cols 1553–61.

Home Office (1966), *Residential Provision for Homeless Discharged Offenders*, HMSO, London.

Home Office (1970), 'The Use of Grant Aided After-care Hostels in 1969', unpublished.

Home Office (1971), *Habitual Drunken Offenders,* HMSO, London.

Home Office (1973), *Offences of Drunkenness,* HMSO, London.

Home Office Research Unit (1970), *Explorations in After-Care,* HMSO, London.

Janner, G. (1972a), Parliamentary Debates, House of Commons, *Hansard,* vol. 839, cols 705–6.

Janner, G. (1972b), Parliamentary Debates, House of Commons, *Hansard,* vol. 839, cols 1644–5.

Jansen, E. (1970), 'The Role of the Halfway House in Community Health Programmes in the United Kingdom and America', *Am. J. Psychiatry* 126, pp. 1498–504.

Jones, M. (1952), *Social Psychiatry,* Tavistock Publications, London.

Jones, M. (1968), *Social Psychiatry in Practice,* Penguin, Harmondsworth.

Kelly, M. (1966), 'The Medical Investigation of Short-term Alcoholics in the Open Prison at Springhill', unpublished.

Laidlaw, J. (1956), 'Glasgow Common Lodging Houses and the People Living in Them', Glasgow Corporation.

Lazare, A., Cohen, F. and **Jacobson, F.** *et al.* (1972), 'The Walk-In Patient as Customer', *Am. J. Orthopsychiatry* 42, 5, pp. 872–83.

Leigh, L. H. (1974), 'Powers of Arrest in Relation to Vagrancy and Related Offences', *Criminal Law Review,* March, pp. 157–65.

Lemere, F. (1953), 'What Happens to Alcoholics?', *Am. J. Psychiatry* 109, pp. 674–6.

McCourt, W. F., Schneider, L. and **Cobb, J.** (1972), 'The Rehabilitation and Resocialization of Chronic Skid Row Alcoholics; Report of a Two Year Research Project', paper read at Dublin International Conference on Alcoholism.

McDougall, A. A. and **Macaulay, K.** (1956), 'Addiction to Methylated Spirit', *Lancet* I, pp. 498–500.

Macleod, I (1967), Parliamentary Debates, House of Commons, *Hansard,* vol. 755, cols 1561–3.

Maddox, G. (1971), 'Muddling Through: Planning for Health Care in England', *Medical Care* 9, 5, pp. 439–48.

Manhattan Bowery Project (1969), First Annual Report.

Marris, P. and **Rein, M.** (1967), *Dilemmas of Social Reform,* Routledge & Kegan Paul, London.

Mayhew, H. (1967 edn), *London Labour and the London Poor,* Cass, London.

Ministry of Justice (1968), 'Detoxification Instead of Fines', *Sartryck vs Sov* 55, Stockholm.

Monger, M. (1967), *Casework in After-Care,* Butterworths, London.

Monger, M. (1969), 'The English Probation Hostel', Probation Papers no. 6, National Association of Probation Officers.

Moynihan, D. (1969), *Maximum Feasible Misunderstanding,* Free Press, New York.

Myerson, D. J. (1956), 'The Skid Row Problem', *New England J. Medicine* 254, pp. 1168–73.

National Assistance Board (1966), *Homeless Single Persons*, HMSO, London.

National Association of Mental Health (1972), 'Hospital, Prison or Pad?', *Mind* Report no. 7.

Nimmer, R. T. (1970), 'St Louis Diagnostic and Detoxification Center: An Experiment in Non-criminal Processing of Public Intoxicants', *Washington University Law Quarterly* 1, pp. 1–27.

Nimmer, R. T. (1971), *Two Million Unnecessary Arrests*, American Bar Foundation, Chicago.

O'Connor, P. (1963), *Britain in the Sixties: Vagrancy*, Penguin, Harmondsworth.

Olin, J. S. (1966), 'Skid Row Syndrome: A Medical Profile of the Chronic Drunkenness Offender', *Canadian Medical Association J.* 95, pp. 205–14.

Orwell, G. (1932), 'Common Lodging Houses', *New Statesman*, 3 September.

Osterberg, I. (1972), 'Alkoholistien Radikaali Hoitokoti' ('A Radical Treatment House for Homeless Alcoholics'), *QJSA* 33, p. 874.

Owen, D. (1965), *English Philanthropy 1660–1960*, Oxford University Press.

Pearl, A. and **Reissman, F.** (1965), *New Careers for the Poor*, Free Press, New York.

Phillimore, P. (1973), 'A Dosser's World: A Study of a Vagrant Population in London', MA Dissertation, University of Edinburgh.

Plaut, T. (1966), 'Fundamentals and Perspectives in Alcoholism. Programme Evaluation', *Am. J. Public Health* 56, 7, pp. 1142–52.

Pollak, B. (1970), 'The Role of the General Practitioner in support of an Alcoholic Rehabilitation Hostel', *Br. J. Addiction* 65, pp. 19–24.

Raush, H. L. and **Raush, C. L.** (1968), *The Halfway House Movement – A Search for Sanity*, Appleton-Century-Crofts, New York.

Redl, F. (1959), 'The Concept of a Therapeutic Milieu', *Am. J. of Orthopsychiatry* 29, pp. 721–35.

Ribton-Turner, C. J. (1887), *A History of Vagrants and Vagrancy and Beggars and Begging*, Chapman & Hall, London.

Richard, I. (1972), Parliamentary Debates, House of Commons, *Hansard*, vol. 833, cols 1951–5.

Robinson, D. (1972), 'The Alcohologist's Addiction: Some Implications of Having Lost Control over the Disease Concept of Alcoholism', *QJSA* 33, pp. 1028–42.

Rolph, C. H. (1971), *Homeless from Prison*, Special After-Care Trust.

Rooney, J. F. (1961), 'Group Processes amongst Skid Row Winos', *QJSA* 22, pp. 444–60.

Rosenman, S. (1955), 'The Skid Row Alcoholic and Negative Ego Image', *QJSA* 16, pp. 447–73.

Ross, T. W. (1970), 'A Descriptive Study of the Skid Row Alcoholic in Houston, Texas', *Criminal Justice Monograph* XI, 2, San Houston State University.

Rowan, J. (1973), 'Evaluation of Social Work Agencies', Consortium Seminar Discussion Paper, unpublished.

Royal Commission on the Poor Laws and Relief of Distress (1909), Cd 4499, HMSO, London.

Rubington, E. (1957), 'Alcoholic Control in Skid Row', *Crime and Delinquency* 13, 4, pp. 531–7.

Rubington, E. (1958), 'The Chronic Drunkenness Offender', *Annals of American Academy of Political and Social Science* 315, pp. 65–72.

Rubington, E. (1958), 'The Skid Row Subculture', 3rd Annual Institute on the Homeless and Institutional Alcoholic, National Council on Alcoholism, New York, pp. 50–60.

Rubington, E. (1965), 'Organizational Strains and Key Roles', *Administration Science Quarterly* 9, 4, pp. 350–69.

Rubington, E. (1967), 'The Halfway House for the Alcoholic', *Mental Hygiene* 51, 4, pp. 552–60.

Ryan, W. (1969), *Distress in the City*, Case Western Reserve.

Schmidt, W. and **De Lint, J. J.** (1972), 'Mortality of Alcoholics', Paper delivered at 30th International Congress on Alcoholism and Drug Dependence, Amsterdam.

Shandler, I. W. (1967), 'Alternatives to Arrest', Philadelphia Diagnostic and Rehabilitation Center.

Shandler, I. W. (1969), 'Alcoholics of Special Community Concern', Williamsburg Papers, Comprehensive Community Services for Alcoholics, National Institute of Mental Health, USA.

Shandler, I. W. (1972), 'The Housing and Treatment of the Public Inebriate', paper delivered at Conference on Alcohol Abuse and Alcoholism, Maryland, USA.

Snow, J. (1967), Parliamentary Debates, House of Commons, *Hansard*, vol. 755, cols 1564–9.

Spradley, J. F. (1970), *You Owe Yourself a Drunk*, Little, Brown, Boston.

Tatham, R. J. (1969), 'Detoxification Center: A Public Health Alternative for the "Drunk Tank"', *Federal Probation* 33, 4, pp. 46–8.

Trotter, T. (1804), *An Essay, Medical, Philosophical and Chemical on Drunkenness and Its Effects on the Human Body*, London.

Tuominen, E. (1968), 'The Halfway House as a Social System', paper delivered at the 28th International Congress on Alcohol and Alcoholism, Washington, USA.

Turner, M. L. (1960), *Forgotten Men*, London Council of Social Service.

Turner, M. L. (1971), *Who Cares?*, Annual Lecture of BBC Wales, BBC, London.

United States Senate, Special Sub-Committee on Alcoholism and Narcotics of the Committee on Labor and Public Welfare (1969), *The Impact of Alcoholism*, US Government Printing Office, Washington.

United States Task Force Report on Drunkenness (1967), US Government Printing Office, Washington.

Ventner, R. A. (1963), 'Analysis of Treatment Organizations', *Social Work* 8, 8, pp. 3–15.

Vexliard, A. (1956), *Introduction à la Sociologie de Vagabondage*, M. Rivière, Paris.

Vexliard, A. (1957), *Le Clochard*, Desclée de Brouvier, Paris.

Wallace, S. E. (1965), *Skid Row as a Way of Life,* Harper & Row, New York.

Walley, J. (1972), 'Problem of the Skid Row Alcoholic – A Look at Detoxification Centres', Alcoholics Recovery Project (mimeo).

Walmsley, R. (1972), *Steps from Prison,* Inner London Probation and After-Care Service.

Warren, R. L. (1973), 'Comprehensive Planning and Co-ordination: Some Functional Aspects', *Social Problems* 20, 3, pp. 355–64.

Watson, J. P. (1969), 'Alcohol and the Accident Department', *Br. J. Addiction* 64, pp. 223–30.

Wiseman, J. P. (1970), *Stations of the Lost. The Treatment of Skid Row Alcoholics,* Prentice-Hall, Englewood Cliffs, NJ.

Wiseman, J. P. (1972), 'Sober Time: The Neglected Variable in the Recidivism of Alcoholic Persons', Paper presented at Second Annual Alcoholism Conference of National Institute on Alcohol Abuse and Alcoholism, Washington, USA.

Wolins, M. (1960), 'Measuring the Effect of Social Work Intervention' in *Social Work Research,* ed. N. A. Polansky, University of Chicago Press, pp. 247–72.

INDEX